D0821998

PLAYING
WITH FIRE

PLAYING WITH FIRE

THEO FLEURY
WITH KIRSTIE McLELLAN DAY

TRIUMPH
BOOKS

Playing With Fire
Copyright © 2009 by Theoren Fleury and Kirstie McLellan Day

No part of this publication may be reproduced, stored in a retrieval system, or transmitted in any form by any means, electronic, mechanical, photocopying, or otherwise, without the prior written permission of the publisher, Triumph Books, 542 South Dearborn Street, Suite 750, Chicago, Illinois 60605.

This book is available in quantity at special discounts for your group or organization. For further information, contact:

TRIUMPH BOOKS
542 South Dearborn Street
Suite 750
Chicago, Illinois 60605
(312) 939-3330
Fax (312) 663-3557
www.triumphbooks.com

Printed in the United States of America
ISBN: 978-1-60078-637-2

Published simultaneously in Canada by HarperCollins Publishers Ltd.

For Jenn, Josh, Beaux, Tatym and Skylah.
Thanks for your unconditional love, understanding and forgiveness.

CONTENTS

ACKNOWLEDGEMENTS

KIRSTIE AND I WANT to thank our agent, Ian Kleinert, and the good folks at HarperCollins, with a special shout-out to Jim Gifford for stepping up and helping us make this book what we always hoped it would be.

We'd also like to thank Kirstie's husband, Larry Day, for his input, and Kirstie's kids; Geordie—who came up with the book title—Paul, Charlie, Lundy and Buddy; and Kirstie's sister, Julie Sinclair, for their love and support.

And thank you to the following people for their expertise, stories and memories: Jenn Fleury, Travis Fleury, Teddy Fleury, Wally Fleury, Donna Fleury, Shannon Griffin-White, Veronica Haugaard, Chuck Matson, Pete Montana, Bearcat Murray, Sheldon Kennedy, Ian McKenzie, Ede Peltz, Murray Falloon, Dr. Robin Reesal, Mark McKay, Barry Trapp, Cam Ftoma and Steve Parsons.

FOREWORD

I REMEMBER the first time I noticed Theo. He was 19 years old, and he had just jumped on the back of one of my L.A. team-mates, Ken Baumgartner, to keep him away from Tim Hunter, one of Calgary's enforcers. I couldn't believe it. Theo was almost a foot shorter than Ken, and he seemed oblivious to the fact that he was about to be murdered. I skated out and grabbed Theo by his jersey and threw him back on the bench. The kid had no fear. We played together for Team Canada several times over the years and I was always amazed at how he was a force at crucial times. He truly was a big-game player.

When it came time to choose a team for the 2002 Olympics in Salt Lake, I wanted Theo there. Nobody came through in a big game like he did. I played against him when he led the Flames in the mid-'90s. At five foot six and 150 pounds, he played at twice that size.

In 2002, the world saw our Canadian team as having too much of an advantage. We had too much talent; they thought it wasn't fair. I knew that Theo represented who we really were, a team that deserved to win, not because we were lucky, but because we worked harder than anyone else. When Roman Hamrlík cross-checked Theo in front of the Czech goal and it wasn't called, it really woke us up—and the rest is history.

Today, Theo and I are still friends. We catch up every once in a while and talk about our battles and triumphs with both Team Canada and the NHL.

I want to wish him luck with this book, and I know that I, for one, will be reading it.

—Wayne Gretzky

PROLOGUE

LUCKY. Everyone but me thought I was lucky. I had built a fifteen-year career on speed, skill and fearlessness. From a World Cup in junior, to an NHL Stanley Cup, through Team Canada and an Olympic gold medal to a guy way overweight, speed gone and full of rage.

When I was younger, playing with the Flames, if you hit me I was a rubber ball—I'd come back harder and faster—but now I was danger-ous. Touch me and I would kill you.

What took me down was rage. Rage fuelled by drugs, alcohol and relationships. I had two exes and three great kids back home in Can-ada, and I lived in this fantastic mansion on two acres in the middle of the desert, yet I wanted to die. I went on a three-month bender. Just me and mounds of cocaine. I would run out into the desert at night and scream at the trees. At the end of the three months, I was just fuckin' crazy. Could not stop doing drugs, could not stop drinkin,' could not stop partyin.'

I blamed God. I was so pissed off with Him. All my life, I had bought into what Father Paul had told me when I was an altar boy: "Don't worry. God will give you only what you can handle, no more." *Nobody* could handle all the guilt, self-hate and dark secrets I had.

It was a beautiful dawn, and I ran out into the middle of the scrub, screaming at the universe, "Fuck you, fuckin' asshole-son-of-a-bitch.

I've had enough. I can't take it anymore. Don't give me any more shit!"
I was delirious. I had been up for weeks.

I ran back to the house and jumped into my pearl-coloured Cadillac Escalade and booted it to town. I stopped at the first pawnshop I came to, pulled out everything I had in my pockets and slapped it on the counter. About five grand in cash. The owner handed me a gun and one bullet.

I drove home, laid the gun and the bullet on the glass coffee table in front of the couch. Then I grabbed one of about ten bottles of lemon Stoli from the freezer and sat there swigging. I was trying to build enough courage to load the fucker. Night came.

I hated night because of everything I had been through in the dark. I remembered the weird, eerie feelings. Night was the reason I stayed out and partied until the sun came up. Then I could pass out and not have to relive one moment of my miserable fucking existence.

At 2 a.m., I reached over, picked up the gun, loaded it, flipped the safety off and put the barrel in my mouth with my finger shaky on the trigger. I sat there forever, shivering so hard the barrel was bouncing off my teeth. How did it taste? It tasted lonely. Cold, lonely and black.

A small, sane part of me said, "Don't do it, don't do it, don't do it, it'll get better." But I fought that voice off. "Fuck this shit, it's not going to get any better." The battle in my head went on and on.

In one quick movement, I threw the gun down on the floor. I did a couple of lines, took another shot of Stoli, and that mellowed me out a little. I remembered being at an AA meeting in Malibu on a Sunday morning just a few months earlier. A guy with sixteen years of sobriety got up and said eight words—"You are only as sick as your secrets"—and then left the podium.

I had to make some changes in that direction in order to survive. I picked up the gun, ran outside and chucked it into the desert.

I think that people need to understand why. What it was that made me do what I did. I knew I was crazy, and so did everyone else.

"Theo's in chaos all the time. He's outta control, outta control." A fifty-million-dollar career gone up my nose, down my throat and into the hands of the casino owners across the country.

When I was with the New York Rangers in 2001, I had thirteen dirty tests in a row, but I was leading the NHL in scoring. So what were they going to do? I was putting Gatorade in the tests. And although he didn't know it, my baby Beaux was peeing for me too. The NHL doctors kept warning me, "Another dirty test and we're taking you out." So what did I do? C'mon, I've never followed a rule in my life.

At the time, the Rangers were writing me yearly cheques for eight million bucks, so I'd be surprised if they weren't having me followed. I could feel these guys in the shadows, and once in a while, out of the corner of my eye, I'd catch someone zipping across the street when I turned my head.

I didn't hang out on the surface with your average Joe. I would go five, six, seven, eight levels below the streets of New York City and party with freaks, transvestites, strippers and all kinds of shady people. On a typical game night, I'd walk home dressed in my custom-made suit from Giovanni's in Montreal with three or four bottles of wine. Then I'd head for the Chelsea Piers, where 23rd Street meets the Hudson River, and hang out with homeless guys around a burn barrel for the rest of the night. I would ask them how they got there—I've always been interested in that kind of stuff.

The Rangers must have been shitting bricks. I don't blame the team for coercing me into the NHL Substance Abuse Program in 2002. I'm sure they could see the headlines: "NHL Superstar Found Dead in Alley." Twenty-eight days after entering treatment, I was sober and stayed that way for about ten or eleven months. But I was completely insane, totally out of my mind, a dry drunk. White-knuckling it. I was told if I drank again I would be out on my ass. Did I believe them? I don't know. I know I switched addictions. I started going to the casino every day. That year, I kissed three million bucks—and my marriage—goodbye.

Just before I signed with the Chicago Blackhawks, I started hanging out in strip joints. Strippers were like me—damaged. It was one-stop shopping—sex, drugs and booze, all under one roof. Grease the bouncer at the front door, next thing you know, you've got an ounce of fucking blow. Party's on.

A year later, I was in the gym, doing cardio on the bike at the end of my workout. About halfway through, I looked up in the mirror. My right cheekbone was still shattered from a puck, and it hurt like hell. I stopped pedalling and said, "This sucks. I hate working out. I hate my life. I hate the game. I can't do this anymore." I walked out, and I didn't even phone the Blackhawks to tell them that I wasn't coming back.

1

THE END OF THE WORLD

AS FAR BACK as I can remember, every hockey rink that I walked into, people would whisper, "That's him . . . that's him. That's that kid." They'd say I was the best damn player they ever saw and that I could skate and handle the puck like nothing they had ever seen. They'd use words like "shifty" and "crafty." These were big compliments in Russell, Manitoba. I'd hear how people would drive in all the way from the cities—Brandon, Manitoba, or Yorkton, Saskatchewan—to see "the kid from Russell." I was always trying to get attention from my parents, and failing, so I loved hearing this stuff. I absolutely loved it, but it was never enough.

You see, my dad was a bitter man. He was an alcoholic—selfish, angry and unavailable. He went to a job that he hated every day. He would get up at 6 a.m. in the freezing cold and sit in a loader that didn't have a heater. A dozen brews and three packs of smokes helped him get through the day because he was always thinking about what he could have been.

Five years before I was born, his dreams were shattered. Wally Fleury was an outstanding hockey player, a crack shot who always hit the net. He was scheduled to go to the New York Rangers training camp in September 1963, but three months before camp, he broke his leg playing baseball. He was catching. There was a pop fly between home plate and first base, he caught it and the guy at third base tagged and sprinted for home. My dad headed back as fast as he could and they collided at the plate. My dad ended up on the ground with his nose an inch from his big toe. The doctors said he would never walk again. He rehabbed his leg at home. Every day, my grandma filled up a rain barrel with boiling-hot water, and he stuck his leg in it and moved it around. He ended up playing nine games of senior hockey after that, but the leg was never the same.

My grandma, Mary Fleury, was the toughest lady ever. She was Cree. I watched her clean the clocks of three guys in a parking lot one night. They were lipping off, so she beat the shit out of them. She was really proud and didn't take crap from anybody. Her nickname was Bulldozer. It wasn't like she was extremely mean, it was just that you didn't want to get on the wrong side of her. Grandma was a champion jigger. She always carried a piece of plywood in the trunk of her car so she would have a hard surface to dance on. My grandpa played the fiddle, and his kids played guitars and she would jig. An unbelievable jigger.

We used to go to my uncle Robert's on Sundays for big jam sessions. Everybody would be dancing in the dirt outside and having a great time. My uncle had twelve kids and they all slept in one room. Wall-to-wall bunk beds in a place called Chinatown, overlooking the Assiniboine Valley. A beautiful place.

My folks were night and day. Dad was this partying athlete, while my mom was a quiet, conservative, churchy type. She was a complete emotional wreck. She was prescribed Valium when she was 16 and became hooked. When I was young, she spent time in the hospital getting shock treatment. I remember her being so nervous about everything. Her biggest worry was that she would run out of pills, so she hid them—in the teapot, behind the radiator, on top of the fridge, between the cushions. She had them stashed everywhere.

My two younger brothers, Ted and Travis, had to put up with all this bullshit too. None of us trusted our parents enough to go to them with any sort of problem, so we learned how to deal with things on our own. We were acting out in school because that is what kids do when they don't have great home lives. We got into fights and caused all kinds of trouble. My dad was always drinking and screaming at my mom, and she was always angry with him. Chaos, chaos, chaos, always chaos. Somebody mad at somebody. Not physical violence, just arguing. Swearing, yelling. When I think about my mom and dad, I realize their behaviour was unacceptable for kids to see.

Being the oldest, I took on the role of protecting my mother. The first time I stepped up I was ten. I remember Dad was hassling her. We had no money for groceries because he'd spent his entire paycheque in the bar. She was crying and begging him to stop doing that. He started calling her all sorts of awful names, telling her she was a fuckin' bitch and always on his back. He started moving closer and closer to her, really threatening. To us he was a big guy, five foot ten or so, and he weighed about 190. She was only five-two and maybe 120 pounds. I was a lot smaller than both of them—four foot nine and 80 pounds, tops. Seeing him looming over her so unsteadily and feeling how scared she was, something snapped in me. You know those stories about a mother lifting a car because her kid is trapped beneath? Well, I ran at him. I was violent, screaming and forcing him all the way down the lawn and into his car, telling him to get the hell out and never come back. I remember he looked confused, but he understood. My anger made me dangerous. When you're raging and you have absolutely no fear, you can do a lot of damage. That quality would really become a part of who I was on the ice. Because when you act crazy, people back away.

I became a bully at school. I was small, always about half a foot shorter than all the other guys, and I needed to take up space in the world. How do you do that? You have to be tougher than everybody else.

7

Every day, I intimidated people. I was always picking on somebody I shouldn't have picked on. I was aggressive, putting schoolmates down, calling them out, trying to make myself feel better. I could pick out a weakness within five seconds. Teachers hated me—oh, they hated me. In Grade 4, I started the year at the back of the room. Within a week I was sitting beside the teacher, facing the class, because I was so mouthy and kept interrupting the class, trying to get attention. I was the king of comments.

In Grade 6, we were playing charades in class and the subject was television shows. This girl went up. She was a little ahead of the game in terms of physical development, but didn't wear a bra yet, so she had the brights going. The teacher gave her a TV show title, and when she turned to face the class I yelled, "*Knight Rider!*"

We used to have winter games at school in Russell. One of the activities was kicking—a co-ed game where you kicked at a rubber puck like a soccer ball. Well, I absolutely levelled another one of the girls in my class. Knocked her right on her ass. My teacher came over, and—*wham!*—reached back and whacked me a good one across the face. I still remember it to this day. Mrs. Kleemack. She couldn't help herself—I pushed teachers to the point of no return. That is how much I can piss somebody off. It's funny, the last couple years, now that I've really got some solid sobriety behind me, I sit down and think, "Holy shit, I've got some amends to make to people, you know?"

Being subjected to so much dysfunction at home, I needed an outlet. Sports were my salvation and escape. Right from day one, I was special. I had this gift. I was good at anything and everything that had to do with sports, and I knew it. I mean, what 5-year-old puts on an old, dull pair of men's skates for the first time and just glides across the ice?

We were living in Binscarth, Manitoba, when one of my buddies, Greg Slywchuck, and I were walking home from kindergarten and he said, "We are startin' hockey tonight. Would you like to come play?" And I was like, "Sure, why not?" So I went home and asked my mom, "Do we have any hockey equipment or anything?" She found a rusty pair of my dad's skates and a broken hockey stick and shoved them into a pillowcase. I walked down to the rink by myself. It was an old barn with two sheets of curling ice on the sides and a tiny skating surface in the middle. And you know what? I don't recall falling down. I just laced 'em up, stepped out onto the ice and *zoom*. It was like I belonged somewhere for the first time. Three hours later, when the game was long over, they had to force me to go home.

Once I started playing hockey, my goal was to play in the NHL. From the time I was 6 until January 1, 1989, when I got called up, that was exactly what I was going to do, and there was nobody who was going to stop me. My dad did all the maintenance at the rink in Russell for a few years, so I had unlimited ice time. I spent six hours a day, every day from October to March, skating and stickhandling through a phantom defence, then shooting from every angle you can imagine. He would pull me around behind the Zamboni and I would practise waving to the crowds. For me, it wasn't a fantasy. It's not like I *dreamed* of getting in the NHL, I was *getting ready* to go into the NHL. And as shitty as my childhood was, my parents treated it as a reality too.

I was probably the luckiest kid to have the group of guys I played with growing up. We were together from the time I was 6 until I left for the Moose Jaw Warriors at 14. And our coaches were three super, focused, caring parents who loved each and every one of us. Doug Fowler, Jim Petz and Walter Werschler each treated me like I was his own son. Walter, the team trainer, was deaf, so we all learned sign language. These men taught me all the things my dad didn't—respect your elders, mind your manners and nobody, no matter how talented, is bigger than the team. They taught me that every member has to care about the others. We were like one big,

9

huge family. We travelled all over Manitoba and Saskatchewan and we killed everybody. The Russell Rams. The coaches' kids were Kent Fowler, he's a geologist now; Ted Petz, he's got a karate studio in Winnipeg; and Bobby Werschler, who is happily married with two girls. Bobby still plays recreational hockey. I don't know what my life would have looked like if it weren't for those people who fell in love with this little shit hockey player.

I think that 90 per cent of that team ended up playing junior. These three coaches, their wives and the parents of the other kids on the team were the main reason I made it in hockey. They always made sure I was fed, watered and encouraged. I never left the house with any money at all, but when I came home after a game, my tummy was full and I wasn't thirsty. And after stepping off the ice, there was always a hug or a pat on the head and a "Great game!"

My mom refused to watch me play. She was paranoid, always terrified I'd get hurt. And my dad was an embarrassment. He'd come to games half cut and he'd be weaving around, bragging about me and taking credit. "Look how good my kid is. I told him to go out there and score. You are goddamned lucky to have my kid on your team."

Unfortunately, the Central Hotel was about five steps from the rink. My dad would wander around the boards, watch a period, go have some beers and then return to watch the next one. After showers, I'd be the last guy out of the dressing room. I always took my time because I didn't want to go home. But it really didn't matter how long I took. Even when it was forty below, my dad never showed up to drive me. He'd be back at the Central, bending his elbow for the rest of the night. Funny how I always had hope. I'd stand at the door and wait for him. The first half-hour, I'd lean my head against the window, breathing on the glass and writing my name in the fog. For the next half-hour I would walk the lines between the tiles on the floor, pretending I was on a tightrope fifty storeys high. Whenever I got bored, I'd pull out my stick and balance a puck on the end of it, tossing it around and trying not to let it hit the floor. Most times, I just gave up waiting and walked home. Winters in Russell can get so cold that your eyelids freeze shut the minute you step outside. But the worst thing was that I would have to walk past the Catholic church—St. Joseph's. That scared the hell out of me.

As I said, my dad is part Cree—his great-grandmother's last name was Blackbird—and the Catholic missionaries were active in the area when his Native ancestors were being moved onto reservations. My dad grew up a Catholic but stopped going to Mass. I went every Sunday, beginning when I was 6. My hockey buddies were Catholic, so I tagged along, and we all became altar boys together. I received my First Communion, First Confession and Confirmation at St. Joseph's. The church was a nice place to hang out. I felt comfortable there. I was wanted and needed. The atmosphere at the church was calming. From the smells of burning candles, incense and waxed pews to the quiet chords on the organ. I liked the way my shoes moved over the carpets without making a sound. Most of my clothes were old and patched and grubby, so I loved putting on the altar boy's black cassock and the smell of the clean, white starched vestment over top. No matter how badly I felt when I arrived, by the time I left I'd be relaxed and centred.

There was a priest there named Father Paul. I liked him because he was solid. He was something I didn't have in my life—a constant. At the time, I thought he was really old, but it turns out he was in his 40s. He was from Poland, kind of short and bald. He looked a bit like Pope John Paul II at the time. I used to go help him serve Mass on Wednesday nights. Generally, he liked to have a nip after supper, so I'd help steady his hand while he served Communion to the three or four old people in the audience. He smelled comfortable, like Old Spice, whisky and Listerine.

And whenever I wanted to talk, he would listen—I mean, really pay attention. I'd tell him about hockey and baseball and school. If something was wrong at home or I was feeling sad, I'd talk. I told him about how I wished my dad would stop drinking and get more involved in my life, and how it sucked that my mom was always sleeping or sick. Father Paul would reassure me. He'd tell me to pray and to have a strong faith. He'd say that God was watching over me and not to worry because He had a plan for me. I'd go away thinking, "Okay, things are rough now, but that is just God throwing a few problems my way to make me stronger. He won't give me anything I can't handle."

I arrived for church early one Sunday to serve Mass, and there was an ambulance there. Father Paul had had a heart attack and dropped dead while shovelling snow. I was so hurt and pissed off, I didn't even go to his funeral. The one person I could count on was gone. I paced outside the building while the service was going on, thinking, "Oh man, what am I gonna do now? Where am I gonna go? Who's gonna be there? Just be there?" I never went back after that. I was 12. It was a devastating loss.

When I was growing up, Thursday nights were the worst nights. My mother was a Jehovah's Witness, and each week there was a small Jehovah's Witness Bible study at a farm about five or six miles from town. My brothers and I were forced to tag along because she couldn't leave us alone and my dad would be out drinking. Going to that Bible study gave me all these crazy, wild, mixed messages because I was a Catholic. JWs believe the doctrine of the Holy Trinity is inspired by Satan—yet here I was, praying to the Father, Son and Holy Ghost every day. I was in league with the Devil.

My mom's religion says that everything is all bad all the time. The world is going to come to an end any minute, and Satan is everywhere. This scared the crap out of me. I was so worried about Armageddon that I tried to stay awake every night because I figured if I went to sleep, that was it. I usually made it to 3 or 4 a.m., then the bad dreams would come. I still remember running through burning

buildings, ducking the hail and trying to hide as big, scary, screaming angels with black wings shot across the night sky looking for me.
Or I'd turn a corner and a weird, freaky face would come at me from
behind a wall. And Satan, fuckin' Satan, he would open his mouth
and swallow houses and churches and people. Oh, those meetings
were a lovely thing to take an 8-year-old to.

Every morning, I would wake up thinking, "Okay, I made it
through last night, but what about today?" You know how, when
you're a kid, you latch on to one thing? You don't hear the whole
story, you just hear one thing. Well, that's what I heard—the world
is ending. Don't know when, but soon. When I left for school in the
morning I was convinced it was the last time I would ever see my
home or my brothers or my parents. I became extremely anxious,
unbelievably worried.

And nothing made sense. Birthdays and Christmas were not
allowed in our home, yet I celebrated Christmas Mass. I didn't
understand why we didn't have a Christmas tree or stockings hung
by the chimney with care like all my friends did. Whenever there was
a little money, my dad would try to do something. Not on Christmas
Day, of course, or my mom would've had a fit. But during Christmas
season he'd buy us hockey gloves or a game like Monopoly and bring
it home out of the blue.

When it was my friends' birthdays, they would hand out invita-
tions and have parties and stuff, but I was rarely invited. People knew
my mom was a Jehovah's Witness and probably wouldn't let me go
anyway. To this day, I hate my birthday. Hate it. I hate getting things
and I hate people giving me stuff. I love giving, but I hate to get stuff.
It's weird. It feels wrong.

2

THE CUT

OUR TEAM, the Russell Rams, had just obliterated the number one team, Portage La Prairie, in the final at a tournament in Minnedosa, Manitoba. Portage could not believe it—how did this shitty little team of 12- and 13-year-olds from Russell beat them? After all, Portage was a town of 13,000, while Russell was only a tenth the size. They were convinced it was a fluke. So they invited us to a two-day, two-game tournament a couple of weeks later. The first game was held on March 21, 1982. There were eleven seconds left in the second period, and we were coming out of our zone when our defenceman Greg Slywchuk, the same buddy I had been playing with since the first day I laced up, went around the net to break out the puck. I skated up the ice too fast, landing at the blue line far ahead of the play. Because I was not in a good position, I had to turn back to pick up the puck, and when I did, their defender, who had been rushing my way, suddenly tripped and rocketed down the ice toward me on his butt. His skate came straight up and caught me under the right arm.

There was a collective gasp from the crowd, but I had no idea what was going on. I could feel something warm spreading under my bicep, so I dropped my left glove and cupped the top of my arm in my hand to have a look. There was a huge cut. I could see muscle—it looked like raw meat. Suddenly, it was like somebody had turned a sprayer nozzle on. Blood spurted out a good foot across the ice. My feet pushed through quicksand as I made my way over to the bench, and Coach Fowler ripped my jersey off me. His wife, Buella, appeared from nowhere, balled up her scarf and stuffed it into my arm. Coach wound a tourniquet tight below by bicep, and one of the mom's friends, Mrs. Petz, squeezed my arm tight.

Coach lifted me up in his arms like a baby and ran out to his car. He and Mrs. Petz and her son, my teammate Ted, loaded me into a car and, pedal to the metal, raced all the way to Portage District General. The tourniquet and pressure had stopped the bleeding, so the emergency room staff took care of a baby who had been badly burned first.

How do you grasp a situation like that when you're 12 years old? All I was thinking was, "Okay, I'll get stitched up and hopefully I won't miss the third period."

Finally, after about twenty minutes, the doctor came out and the first thing he did was place two fingers on my wrist to take my pulse. This weird look came over his face, and I heard him make a little choking sound. He said, "You need to go to Winnipeg to the Children's Hospital. *Now.*" There was no pulse. My brachial artery had been severed. I was bleeding to death.

Coach went back to the rink, while Mrs. Petz stayed with me on the trip to Winnipeg. I told Mrs. Petz I knew I wouldn't make it back to the rink in time for the end of the first game, but hoped that if we hurried I could be there for the second. Portage La Prairie is located near the junction of Highways 1 and 16 (the Yellowhead) in south central Manitoba, about fifty miles west of Winnipeg. Cars and roads were not as good as they are now, and there was a lot of snow and ice so we slipped around a bit, but she made it in two hours.

Thankfully, a lot of farm kids go to the Children's Hospital in Winnipeg. Farm kids mean farm accidents. Twenty per cent of these accidents are related to farm machinery—tractor rollovers, or hands, hair and clothing caught in moving machinery. It was rare to shake hands with a farmer who had all ten fingers.

Dr. Robertson had reattached his share of limbs and digits, so although they didn't have much time to figure out what to do, they came up with a brilliant plan. They extended the original cut from two to nine inches, folded back the skin and did what is called a venous graft. Along with the artery, the radial nerve had been cut. The path of that nerve moves down from the upper arm to the thumb, the index finger and the side of the middle finger. The ulnar nerve has a couple of pathways into the fingers. So they cut a portion of the ulnar in my wrist and attached that section of nerve to the severed part of the radial nerve. They wanted the nerve to grow back down my arm so that I would get back the feeling in my lower arm and index and middle fingers. It was six hours of surgery under a microscope. I was left-handed, but before the accident, I played sports with my right hand. After the operation, I became ambidextrous when playing sports. To this day I can flip the Ping Pong paddle back and forth between my right and left hand during a game.

Once a month for an entire year, I would visit Dr. Robertson in Winnipeg. He'd come into the room and shove a two-and-a-half-inch needle into the soft pad on the palm of my hand, in between my index finger and thumb. This was done without any anesthetic. Every time Dr. Robertson went to jab me, I would squeeze my eyes shut and pray to God to make it not hurt. The needle was attached to an electromyogram, or EMG machine. It produced a graph of the electrical activity in the muscle and measured nerve growth. The needle was like an antenna to detect the electrical voltage changes occurring on the surface of individual muscle cells. Next, Dr. Robertson would pick and prod at my arm with a pin, asking, "Can you feel that? Can you feel this?" As much as I hated that needle, the real pain came each time I'd ask, "So is it okay to play hockey now?" Dr. Robertson would shake his head sadly and say simply, "No."

There is a line in a John Cleese movie where he says, "It's not the despair. I can handle the despair. It's the hope!" That totally sums up my feelings at the time. I would be so excited on the way to Winnipeg Children's Hospital that I'd be bouncing up and down in the seat. Each time, I figured I'd get the go-ahead to play hockey again. The adults kept me out of the loop. They knew it was going to take a year at least, but they wouldn't tell me. Was I any better? How was it progressing? They were trying to protect me from disappointment, but it had the opposite effect. At the end of each visit, I'd hold off crying until I got into the car. Then I'd crack the window, letting the freezing wind bite into my face as I quietly sobbed for the next five hours all the way home.

I missed a whole year of hockey. My lifeline, my sanctuary was gone. I couldn't play baseball or any contact sports at all. The nerve had to regrow all the way back down to my wrist. Progress was slow—a millimetre a day—and delicate. Any sort of trauma and I could lose function in my hand permanently. My arm was taped up to my chest in a bent position for six weeks. A local physiotherapist helped me rehab it. No matter how hard she reefed on it, it wouldn't go straight.

As I said earlier, my mom was terrified that exactly this kind of thing would happen, so she never came to any of my games. But there is a school of thought that if you put that energy out there, it is going to happen. To this day, I wonder about that.

3

THE TRADE-OFF

IN JULY 1981, five months after the accident, I had just turned 13. To pick up my spirits, my teammates' parents pitched in and paid for me to go to a three-week camp, the Andy Murray Hockey School in Brandon, Manitoba. Before I left, they made me promise that I would not play any contact hockey, and they made sure the instructors knew about it too.

Today, Andy Murray is head coach for the St. Louis Blues, but back then he was famous in Manitoba as the coach of the Brandon Travellers of the Manitoba Junior A Hockey League. In 1981, he had taken the Brandon University Bobcats to a league championship and the number one ranking in Canadian university hockey. The chance to play in front of Murray was exactly what I had been waiting for. I figured if I could get his attention, he would be my ticket to the NHL. I know that sounds kind of silly, typical of what an unsophisticated, small-town 13-year-old would think, but as it turns out, I was right.

I was a keener—first one on the ice, first in line for every drill. I put my heart into everything the coaches asked of me. I skated, shot and passed as if a championship was on the line.

One of the instructors that Andy had recruited for his hockey school was a scout for the Winnipeg Warriors, a junior team in the Western Hockey League. His name was Graham James. You've probably heard of him. He wanted my whole story, and I gave it to him. We started with my hockey background—right winger for the

Russell Rams. He wanted my stats before the accident and details on my rehab. By the second week, he was questioning me about my parents. What did they do? Where did I live? I was a fairly open kid, used to the entire adult community of Russell taking care of me. Telling an adult about myself was perfectly natural. By the third week, I felt very comfortable and a little in awe of James. Mostly, I was flattered that he was interested in me. He told me I definitely had the raw talent to play in the NHL and said he was going to draft me even though I was still not cleared to play. He asked me what my dad and mom would think of me living away from home, and I told him the truth—it wouldn't bother them at all.

I went home and shared all the promises James had made to me. Everyone was thrilled but worried about my arm. I was determined to play in the fall. Dr. Robertson told me that golfing would be good for mobility, so I golfed all that summer. My Grandpa Fleury gave me some old clubs and the Peltzes, a couple of honest-to-God angels who'd been watching over me for years, paid my fees at the Russell Golf and Country Club. Len Peltz was a teacher, and his wife, Ede, was a casual acquaintance of my mother's. They owned the Jolly Lodge Motel on Highway 16 in Russell. Len and Ede are good people. They, like the rest of Russell, watched my brother Ted and me run around half-wild. But unlike most who just shook their heads and tsked at the lack of parenting, Len and Ede stepped in. And they did it without condemning my parents.

They bought us clothes when ours got a little too ragged. They fed us when we were hungry, and it was Mrs. Peltz who drove me to Winnipeg every month to see Dr. Robertson. She also worked on our table manners. Len often supplied my hockey gear, and both of them made sure our homework was done. Ted and I grew to love Len and Ede and to this day I think of them as a second mom and dad.

That fall, Coach Fowler put me back on the team. The only problem was that I was not allowed to play. I could skate and handle the puck in practice, but there was to be absolutely no contact. I'd watch the guys from the bench and cheer them on, but inside I was dying.

One really cool thing was that, even though I was always the highest scorer and often selected as MVP, the team was doing well without me. We had great coaches and a lot of good athletes. They seemed to come together as a group and realize that it would take tremendous effort from each person to win. It goes to show what kind of character those guys had. They could have packed it in because they had a good, built-in excuse, but instead they found a way.

A year after the accident, a team from Roblin, a small town forty minutes north of Russell, came down to play us for the Manitoba Provincial B Championship. I called Dr. Robertson and begged him to clear me to play. I knew that the transplanted ulnar nerve had not completely regenerated, because I had no feeling in my index and middle fingers. I could bend them and move them around, but they were dead. To impress my friends, I would hold them over a lit flame. Would the nerve ever make it all the way? Or was I as healthy as I would ever be? Dr. Robertson said he'd consult with some colleagues and get back to me.

The night before the game, I could not sleep. My friends had told me about how they would lie awake Christmas Eve, wondering whether Santa Claus had left them the gifts they had asked for. Now I knew what they meant.

The morning of the tournament, the phone rang and I tore across the linoleum in my bare feet and grabbed it. I knew it was Dr. Robertson because nobody ever called us. "Theoren," he said, "I know it's been a tough, difficult year for you, and I know you've had a lot of disappointments coming to Winnipeg each month." He cleared his throat. "I think your arm has progressed enough that you can play." The only other time in my life I felt so much excitement was at the end of the third period of game six in Montreal in 1989, but we'll get to that later.

I had two younger brothers, Teddy and Travis. Hockey was as important to them as it was to me. Teddy was standing beside me, watching my face while I talked with Dr. Robertson. When I let out a "Yeah!" he started jumping up and down, shouting, "He can play! He can play! Theoren can play hockey again!"

That day at the rink as I got dressed, I started a routine that continued all the way through my career: left shin pad, right shin pad, left skate, then right skate. I put everything on left to right and made sure I was the first player after the goalie to step on the ice. As soon as I did, I'd genuflect and scoop up some ice shavings, then cross myself. Protection from ever getting hurt again.

We lined up and the ref dropped the puck. I took it from the draw, and eight seconds later I scored. That goal sealed my fate forever. Tommy Thompson was in the crowd. Today, he is assistant general manager/player personnel for the Minnesota Wild, but at that time he was the general manager of the Winnipeg Warriors. Graham James was his buddy.

Graham started phoning me—"How's it going? What are you up to? A bunch of us are planning a trip down to the States this summer to watch some baseball. Ask your parents if it would be okay if you come along." It was like a dream come true—the WHL wanted me, and not only that, they *liked* me.

My parents loved the idea of me going on a vacation to the States with a scout. It was like, "Where do we sign?" Graham picked me up in Russell and we drove to North Dakota. We picked up two other bantam hockey players from Winnipeg on the way. He had reserved a room at the Super 8 Motel, which had an indoor pool and a hot tub. I had never seen such luxury. The room had two double beds. James told the boys to take the one on the left near the door, and he and I would share the one on the right by the window. Around two in the morning, I woke up. There was a hand on me, rubbing my ass. "What the hell is going on?" I thought. I was facing the wall, away from Graham. I froze, trying to figure it out. Was he sleeping? He must be. I sweated it out, trying to figure a way to move out of his reach without waking him up. I worried he'd be mad. It is almost painful to think about how innocent I was.

That is all that happened that night. Nothing was said the next day. But the next night, I wrapped the top sheet tightly around my body, like a mummy. That way, if he had another dream and accidentally touched me, he would have no access to any part of me.

I returned to Russell tired and anxious. James had tried it a few more times, but the sheet trick worked, so he wasn't able to get anywhere. Trouble was, after the second or third time, I stopped sleeping. I'd lie awake, staring at the pinpoints of street light that made their way through gaps between the curtain and windowsill while the silence in the room thundered in my ears.

By the next summer, I'd convinced myself it had all been one big mistake. James had continued calling me through the year and promising that I would be drafted by the Warriors, but first, he wanted me to play a season with a Tier I midget team in Winnipeg, the St. James Minor Midget Canadians. I would get to practise with the Warriors at the same time. He did not want me facing off in games against players who had eighty pounds and a foot in height on me. I was five foot two, 115 pounds.

The next year, in Grade 9, I was drafted in the second round by the Warriors. Graham was the coach. It was a trade-off. I would take it back today if I could, because it cost me my soul.

4

A VERY BAD THING

ON THE RIDE from Russell to Winnipeg, I sat in the back seat. My dad was driving and my mom was beside him. They were almost giddy. My dad always had a nice voice and was singing to the radio, and she was humming along. I had rarely seen them like this—happy. Their boy had made it. My dad was no longer a worthless drunk and my mom drugged out and helpless. They were Wally and Donna Fleury, and they had parented a winner.

I was so conflicted. On one hand, I was fuckin' terrified knowing what Graham wanted. On the other, my parents were finally happy because of me. I had to make a choice. I chose to protect them and my secret.

At 14, I figured I could get through it myself. I remember that, when my parents left that day, I stood on the driveway watching them drive off and I thought, "What the fuck did I just do?" I planned to wrap myself up in a blanket at bedtime again. I still had some fight left in me.

I was billeted with a woman named Mrs. Bennett, but Graham insisted I sleep over at his house at least twice a week. The physical stuff was one thing, but the mental manipulation, that was the worst. The days I had go over to Graham's filled me with dread. From the moment I woke up I would start making up excuses, which never worked. I could say, "My dad died." "So what? You're comin' over and you're not getting a paycheque if you don't." I couldn't rub two nickels together, for fuck sakes. And I couldn't ask my parents for money, because they had none. I relied on Graham for everything. And that's the way he wanted it. I could not shake him with a sledgehammer. Then he would pull the "poor me" stuff. "You don't like me. You think I haven't done anything for you." Whatever. I fought him off for a long, long time. I continued with the blanket trick so he would have no access. I would get absolutely no sleep. *None.* I was on guard. I'm a pretty determined guy—I can hang on for a long time.

He'd wait until the middle of the night, and then he'd crawl around the room in the dark on his hands and knees. He had the blinds ducttaped to the windows so no light could get in. It was the same every time. He would start massaging my feet and I wouldn't move, pretending to be asleep. He would try to come up higher, but with that blanket wrapped so tight, he couldn't get at me. The whole charade was taking a toll. I would drag myself to school the next day and fall asleep in class.

Graham convinced me that, if not for him and his help, I would not be going to the NHL. As far as I was concerned, the reason for my whole existence was to make it to The Show. It was all I had. My only worth to anyone was my ability to play hockey. What was the point of living if I had no value? He was in my ear that whole year. He told me I had to listen to him, do as he said because he was my only chance to make it. No one else had been beating the door down to draft me. I hadn't grown much, and although I ate nonstop I put on maybe fifteen pounds, tops. A guy my size in the WHL was unheard of.

It took a full year, but finally, in the spring of 1983, on the night we heard that Winnipeg had sold the team to Moose Jaw and we would be moving there, he just broke me down. I was exhausted. He had put himself in a position of full power and control. In 2005, I read an article in *The New York Times* that described how military doctors at Guantánamo Bay in Cuba advised interrogators on how to break prisoners down by increasing their stress levels and exploiting their fears. Boy, did I relate to that.

At least twice a week that first year, Graham would bother me and I'd fend him off. But that night in 1983, I left the blanket on the bed. I was 14. Kids are funny. Each time I stayed over, I hoped that maybe he would leave me alone. I mean, he would act perfectly normal all evening. We'd watch a movie and he would make popcorn. We'd talk hockey and strategy. He would give no indication about what he was planning to do. No sidelong looks, no touching, nothing.

The first few times he got at me weren't so bad because I was gone. I would open my eyes and he would be standing over me, cleaning himself up. I knew something had happened, but I was not sure what. The mind can do some amazing things. Even years later in therapy, when telling the counsellor about it, I would check out—leave my body. She'd have to literally shake me to bring me back. But I wasn't always able to do that. He started a routine whenever I was over— masturbate on my feet, then give a blowjob, then let me sleep.

I thought about telling, but who could I turn to? Who would believe me over him? And what would happen if I did tell? I turned it over in my mind, trying to find a way out, but every option had major consequences. Would the consequences go against me or him? I didn't know. I wasn't stupid, I could see how it would play. I would have been stigmatized forever as the kid who was molested by his coach. The Victim. Would minor hockey have said, "Wow, we better watch out for Theoren and protect him because he told the truth"? No. It would have been, James was a pervert and Fleury "let him" molest him. Or I would be the equally pervy kid who had a "rela-tionship" with his coach. Would I have been invited to the Hockey Canada camp that led to Piestany, which led to the NHL? Get real.

If I could go back in time, knowing I would never make it in hockey because I told, would I? Fuckin' A, I would. But at my age, with my background, in my position, driving to the NHL, I didn't say anything and it was a very big price to pay. And every person I ever loved, they paid too. It fucked up my sexual identity big time. I thought maybe I was fuckin' gay, I didn't know. I mean, I know now how it works with boys. It doesn't matter if it's an elephant, if something touches your penis, you will get aroused. When I found that out, I felt relieved and the world started to make a little more sense. To this day, I still have a real tough time with blowjobs, and women have to have nice feet. I dated a beautiful girl once, but she had the nastiest feet ever. I had to break up with her 'cause I couldn't fuckin' deal with it.

Graham was always working me. He used professional language and methods to get me to co-operate. He knew I was shit-scared of him, that I couldn't understand why he was doing what he was doing to me. Lots of times after molesting me, he would call me up and say, "Let's go get a milkshake." We would sit in his car and he would talk for hours about why he was the way he was and how what he was doing was not sexual. I was helping him by donating my sperm because he couldn't manufacture enough. He said that when I ejaculated, it stimulated his glands and helped him become fertile. All kinds of weird fuckin' stuff. "It is a purely medical need," he would say. "This has nothing to do with sex." And I would be so confused. It's not like I believed him, but I thought maybe *he* believed it. You know that picture *The Scream,* by Edvard Munch? It is a picture of me. I would leave those conversations with Graham just beside myself. Fuck! It doesn't make sense. It doesn't add up. Why is he telling me this? What does he really mean? It was torture, absolute torture. I was tied up, maybe not with rope, but it was the same thing. He was my coach. He was helping me. He knew so much about hockey. He controlled my fuckin' destiny.

In truth, he was holding me back. I was having a hard time concentrating on playing hockey while having to deal with that dirtbag. I let him do what he needed to do to get it over with so I could get some fuckin' sleep. I needed to function the next day. A few times he tried to go further, but I said no. He must have had an insatiable drive. Think about it: I wasn't the only guy he was doing this to. He had no conscience. The direct result of my being abused was that I became a fucking raging, alcoholic lunatic. He destroyed my belief system. I didn't trust what I was thinking or feeling. My parents had not instilled a strong sense of right and wrong in me, but I had developed one thanks to my Russell coaches and the Peltz family. Graham stole that from me. The most influential adult in my life at the time was telling me that what I thought was wrong was right. I no longer had faith in myself or my own judgment. And when you come down to it, that's all a person has. Once it's gone, how do you get it back?

I'm writing about this for one reason: I want any kid that has been—or is being—abused to tell. Bring what someone is doing to you into the light, because it happens every single day.

Graham was on me once or twice a week for the next two years. An absolute nightmare, every single day of my life. It made the dreams I had in elementary school about the world ending seem like a cakewalk. I worried constantly. What should I do? How the fuck do I get out of this situation? What if somebody finds out? Will I go to hell for this?

So when I was 16 years old and I took that first sip of alcohol, it was like—*snap!*—medicine. I was like, "Oh this is *goood* stuff."

It is not like I had a slow descent into alcoholism. I was an alcoholic as soon as I tried it, just like some people try crack for the first time and they are instantly addicted. I had been weighed down by all the shit that was happening to me, and suddenly none of it mattered. I was able to have fun. From that day on, drinking became something I could not live without, like oxygen or hockey.

5

THE TRIP TO DISNEYLAND

BARRY TRAPP made Graham James quit the Moose Jaw Warriors.

The Warriors' executive board offered Barry the general manager's position in the spring of 1985, and Graham was totally pissed off about it. He wrote a letter to the board saying he didn't want anyone to tell him what to do. He did not want to lose the control he had—and he had everybody eating out of his hand. At our hockey banquet in April, Graham was the master of ceremonies, Graham was the guest speaker, Graham told all the jokes and Graham gave out the awards. But Barry is a super hard ass. He was there to do a job, no matter what.

The team had gone 21–50–1 and finished thirteenth in a fourteen-team league. Barry told Graham he wanted to get together over the May long weekend to look at the direction the team was heading in, discuss what they wanted to do with the players and get things ready for training camp. But Graham refused to co-operate. He said he was going to be in Minneapolis to watch a ball game. So Trapp offered to go with him. Graham said that wouldn't work because he was going with some friends from Winnipeg. Barry decided to phone some of the players himself. He placed a call to one of the 16-year-old rookies, and the parents told him the kid was in Minneapolis with Graham. This set off alarm bells in Barry's head.

There had been whispers going around the Regina Pats, where Barry was the assistant GM before joining us. And he had heard a couple of former Warriors talking amongst themselves, saying things like "James is a fag," which had planted a couple of seeds of doubt in Barry's mind. But being gay was a long way from being a pedophile.

Barry went to the board in Moose Jaw and said Graham lied to him and he didn't like the situation. He said he'd had an offer to work in the NHL as a scout and he would leave if the board didn't let him get rid of Graham. The board told him to do what he thought was right.

Barry decided he would coach the team himself and offer Graham the assistant's job. That way, Graham would quit for sure. But the community of Moose Jaw was totally invested in our team, so before he could do anything he had to go to a public meeting. That stirred up a shit storm. People were outraged. *How could you do this to this guy? Graham James is the nicest person who has ever been around here. Look how he treats everybody.* Graham had just about everybody fooled. But he didn't fool Barry. Barry knew there was something going on, he just couldn't prove it. Practically no one in Moose Jaw believed him. Later, when the Swift Current Broncos turned around and hired Graham, no one called Barry for a reference.

So Graham quit, and when he called me on the phone and told me he was leaving, I was literally jumping up and down, raising my fist in the air, I was so happy. It was a freeing experience. He tried as hard as he could to get me to go with him to his next stop, a Tier II Junior A team in Winnipeg. He worked on me night and day, just grinding me. "You need to come with me on this route now. I won't be in Moose Jaw to give you the ice time you need." And I was thinking, "Fuck you, man. I can make it on my own. I am a good hockey player. I'm doing good here." Graham even typed up a letter to Trapp saying that I was quitting. I signed it, but Trapp gave me call and said, "You know what? If you're not coming to Moose Jaw, you won't be getting a release from me. So I guess you'll be a hell of a high school player in Russell, Manitoba."

So who was the first guy at camp in Moose Jaw that fall? Me.

Of course, this was unfortunate for Sheldon Kennedy, who went with Graham to the Tier II team in Winnipeg. (I spoke with Sheldon while I was writing this book, and he told me to go ahead and talk about this. It was very important to me to respect his privacy, as he respected mine when he wrote his own book.)

Sheldon and I first met when he was seven and I was eight. I was a friend of his older brother Troy—we called him TK. In the summer of 1980, I had just turned 12. My family didn't have two nickels to rub together, and the Kennedys didn't have much more, but TK had a cool new toy called the Rubik's Cube. He handed it to me and I solved it right away. Sheldon says he remembers being amazed.

Sheldon and TK were both very talented on the ice. Sheldon was the best skater I have ever seen. Anyway, we grew up playing tons of minor hockey against each other. They lived on a farm in Elkhorn, about sixty miles south of Russell. Their dad was violent and left the family when Sheldon was young. Sheldon's mom, Shirley, was looking for a father figure for the boys. Enter Graham.

Graham first spotted Sheldon at that same Andy Murray hockey camp he and Tommy Thompson scouted me at in 1981, the summer after my injury. Graham cultivated a relationship with Sheldon and me by isolating us from our families and from the other players. Graham was a very personable, smart guy. He wasn't a guy who sat on the corner of your sleeping bag, drooling. In Sheldon's case, he gained the trust of everybody around him, including his mom and his brother. He hinted that Sheldon was headed for trouble and claimed that Sheldon was a drinker. Graham set himself up to look like he was Sheldon's saviour. In truth, Sheldon didn't start drinking until Graham got hold of him.

Anyway, the first time Sheldon was assaulted by Graham was when he was 14 years old. He came to Winnipeg for the Lions tournament. I was playing for the St. James Warriors and Sheldon was playing for Elkhorn. Sheldon arrived to stay at Graham's, and the fat fuck went after him. I feel badly about it now, but I was too involved in my own shit to worry about what was happening with anyone else. I was just trying to survive. I didn't know what the fuck was going on and I didn't understand it. I couldn't go to Sheldon for support, and he couldn't turn to me, because it was too hard.

The first time I ever got drunk in my life I was at Sheldon's. I was 16 and staying with his family for a four-team tournament. By this time, Sheldon had been in Graham's clutches for a year—and it had been two years for me. Sheldon had started some serious drinking in order to cope. I hadn't got into it yet because my dad drank enough for three families. That Saturday night, when I first tasted beer and kind of instantly became an alcoholic, I got into the O'Keefe's Extra Old Stock around a bush fire and passed out after trying to tippy-toe into the campfire. Sheldon and his buddy scooped me up and threw me into the back of a van and tore up fields on the way home. Sheldon says he can still remember hearing the sound of me retching and the bumping of my body bouncing off the metal walls of the van. The next morning, each of us was extremely worried that Graham might find out. Although we never talked about it, I think that was when Sheldon knew about me and I knew about him.

Anyway, Graham was desperate for me to quit Moose Jaw and to go back to Winnipeg with him. He tried crying and begging, and when that didn't work, he decided to try to bribe me and Sheldon by driving us to Disneyland. It was insane. A twilight zone trip. It was so bizarre. The shame, the guilt, the self-hate. I hated myself. Sheldon hated himself. Sheldon is actually quite shy, but he is one of the funniest fuckers I have ever met. He says he didn't want people to look at what was really happening, so he went overboard to make sure he came across as really funny and happy. That kept people at arm's length. Anyway, Sheldon kept me laughing and relatively sane on that trip to Disneyland.

As we set out on the trip, Sheldon and I started to wind each other up. Sheldon would make some comment or other toward Graham, razzing him, which would make me laugh, and that would get Sheldon going again. Before long we were both calling Graham names and laughing like crazy. At first, Graham pretended he thought it was funny, but then he started getting mad. It was the strangest dynamic. At night, Graham was creeping around the room accosting us, and during the day we did our best to punish him. At the hotels along the way, he would book one room with two beds and each night he'd switch back and forth. Think about how sick that is. The room would be still, no sound or light, and then all of a sudden he would grab you. The most horrible part was the wait. I just wanted it over with so I could check out.

When it was Sheldon's night, I was so exhausted from dealing with Graham all day I would pass out like a dead person. But when it was my turn, Sheldon says he would lie awake, and no matter how he tried, he could not block out what was going on. Poor buddy.

Day by day, Sheldon got bolder, which I thought was hilarious. I had been so intimidated by this monster, and here was Sheldon putting him in his place. Sheldon was relentless in hounding him for booze. "Go get me some beers, you fat bastard. Move that fat fuckin' walrus butt of yours!" Graham would grumble at him to keep his mouth shut and show some respect, and Sheldon would look at me and we would laugh like maniacs. When we got to San Francisco, Graham finally went out and got a six-pack, which Sheldon downed in about half an hour. All the while, Graham was pouting and acting like he was a victim of Sheldon's meanness. In Graham's mind, the bad guy was the 15-year-old kid who was begging for beers so he could deal with the sexual abuse Graham was subjecting him to. It was like when you have a girlfriend and you go to a party, and you and a bud get to talking about a camping trip you went on before you knew her, and she gets pissed off. Being pissed off was part of the way Graham controlled us. He was an angry man. We would pick on him because we hated him, and he got so sick of it that by the time we got to Disneyland he was barely speaking to us, which was great. We checked into our hotel and he told us to go to the Magic Kingdom by ourselves. Yeah!

We got on the Mad Tea Party ride and said, "Let's see how fast we can get goin.'" We spun the wheel of our teacup as hard as we could, and it was flying around. We were having a gas and could not stop laughing. I stepped off and fell flat on my face, and Sheldon got off and fell right on top of me. This started us up again, and everybody around us was laughing too. We just went crazy—it was so much fun.

On the way back to Manitoba, Sheldon and I did all the driving. Neither of us had a licence. After Sheldon's book came out, there was a story in the paper about me sleeping in the back seat while Sheldon was being abused in the front seat. It is true. Sheldon says that while he drove, Graham would reach over and start doing his shit, but I don't remember any of that. I was asleep. Fuckin' deep asleep. As I said, when you were with Graham, any time you could get some quality sleep you took full advantage of it, 'cause you knew you were going to be up all fuckin' night.

When he dropped me off at my parents' place after that trip, that was it. It was over. I was out, home free. We still maintained contact. I would go to Swift Current to golf with him, but I never once let him near me again. He would try to get me to stay over, but I'd always say something like, "Nope I'm headin' 'er back to Moose Jaw."

By that time, I had a girlfriend, Shannon Griffin. She was one of the prettiest girls at high school in Moose Jaw. She was a typical small-town girl, a sweet, innocent cheerleader. The local guys hated us hockey players because we got all the women. I went to Peacock Collegiate, and she was a cheerleader at Vanier. We were both 16. She was the first girl I slept with. We did it in the back of my dad's car back in Russell when I took her home for a visit. It was a huge relief for me because, thanks to Graham, I was worried I might be gay, even though I felt absolutely no attraction to men. It was a hard situation. She'd ask, "Why do you have to go to your coach's house all the time? Why are you always over there?" And I would make up excuses. She never suspected the truth, and I never said anything. I was very, very conflicted and really pissed off.

Shannon would fight with her dad and I would mediate and calm her down. I laughed at her jokes and cared about her feelings. We would have had the perfect high school romance if she hadn't become pregnant. What did we expect? We didn't use contraception. We were young, ignorant and horny.

I still considered myself Roman Catholic, and she was one too. Abortion was definitely a thought, but we both felt it would be killing our baby. Her parents were willing to raise it, but we did not want that either, and so the next option for two young people who are not prepared to have a child was adoption. We thought the right thing might be to give him to a family that wanted, and was waiting for, a baby. Because we were in the process of making the decision, we knew that if we had anything prepared, like clothes or a crib, we would just take the baby home, so we did not purchase any baby items at all. Zero.

The night before Josh was born, I didn't have a clue what to do. I switched into survival mode. The Moose Jaw Warriors had finally won after a long, dry streak, so I did what we players always did: I went out and got absolutely shit-faced drunk. Of course, I slept in, and Shannon had to call me from the hospital the next morning to get me up.

I was bagged but wanted to do the right thing, so with each contraction I hopped up and held her hand, enduring it with her, then I would plop back down on the chair and sleep until the next one came. Josh was born at 7:45 p.m. on November 18, 1987.

Once he was laid in my arms, that was it. In my mind, there was no question we were going to keep him and do what we needed to do. That meant we were going to make our relationship work.

34

Shannon's grandmother was 91 years old. She took a taxi to the Sears store and bought every last thing you could possibly think of. She was not a wealthy woman—she was living on a fixed income—but she showed up at the hospital and behind her was the taxi driver carrying a car seat and bags full of washcloths and bath towels and sleepers and a few outfits—everything needed to get started.

I was 18 and still living at a billet home. I was getting paid by the Warriors, maybe a couple of hundred a month, but not enough to support a family. Shannon and Josh moved back with her folks. We did eventually move in together when Josh was a year old, and I proposed to Shannon, but a few months before the wedding, I called it off. She was really loyal and took care of me. The laundry was always done, food on the table, that kind of thing. But we still had these issues with her family and I acted like a single guy. As soon as I left the house, look out—it was on. I had no business committing to her.

My drinking was escalating. I liked rum and Coke, but whisky made the feathers come out. I knew I had to stay away from it because of something that happened during my last year in Moose Jaw. I was at a social, downing Crown Royal, and I picked the biggest guy in the crowd and decided to beat the shit out of him. I went over and said, "Hey, man, that your girlfriend?" He said, "Yeah." I said, "I saw her go down on one of the guys after the game the other night." He told me to piss off, so I said, "Yeah, you're right. It couldn't have been her—she's too fat and ugly." That was over the line. He took a swing at me and I said, "Let's go outside."

I had to get the first couple of shots in or get killed. We stumbled out through the front door and started squaring off, doing the old bare-knuckle shuffle. I was unsteady thanks to the two-six. We each threw a few; he landed a few puffballs on my head and I got him in the nose a couple of times. Finally, we both fell to the ground and my teammates came and broke it up.

When I was drunk, I wouldn't feel the fight until the next day, but after a few of these incidents, I woke up one morning with a black eye, my nose swollen to about three times its normal size and a broken rib or two, and I looked in the mirror and said, "Okay, I better stop drinking whisky. I could get seriously hurt." That last year in Moose Jaw, a lot of the players spent their spare time getting wasted.

I remember smoking a lot of hash because it was always available. We'd put it on the end of a cigarette, hot-knife it or rig up some kind of tinfoil pipe or whatever. I never had to buy it because somebody would always bust it out. How could our coaches or management not know what was going on with that team? They saw us every fuckin' day.

In January 1997, after Sheldon made his revelation about the abuse, *Maclean's* magazine said that when Graham coached the Moose Jaw Warriors, team officials had become suspicious. Dev Dley, who was the commissioner of the Western Hockey League, is quoted as saying that no one filed an official complaint, so the league didn't investigate. Uh-huh. If the league indeed really knew of the suspicions about Moose Jaw, I find it incredible that without an official complaint it would simply turn a blind eye.

Moose Jaw was a great place to play junior hockey. Still is, to this day. Great community, great people there. But I will always ask myself, Did our trainer Stan Szumiak know? Or the assistant coach, Cam Ftoma? He says he was shocked when he found out. How about the director of marketing, Bill Harris—did he suspect anything? I dunno. One thing I do know is that I was a naive 16-year-old kid living away from home, and they were all grown men, and not one of them came to me and said, "Kid, is there anything you would like to tell me?"

And I know the Moose Jaw Warriors are ashamed now. Just go to their website. In our 1984 team picture there are nine guys sitting in the front row, and only eight of them are named.

6

PIESTANY

I WASN'T SELECTED in 1986, my first year of eligibility for the NHL Entry Draft, so it was super important for me to make the team that represented Canada at the 1987 World Junior Championships in Piestany, Czechoslovakia. Most of the teams had seen me and written me off because of my size. But if I performed well at the World Juniors, I knew they would have to take a second look. I was invited to a five-day training camp in Orleans, Ontario, just outside Ottawa. It was an opportunity to step out. I was always able to capitalize on those moments. The more pressure, the better I played.

I had an unbelievable performance at that camp. I flew across the ice as if I were hydroplaning. And when somebody passed, it was as if the game slowed down. Everything I shot went in the net. To me, it looked like a soccer net, not a hockey net. I was just super, super focused. There are times when you can't do anything wrong. Every elite athlete has experienced this. Everything is perfect, no matter what you do—you are in the zone.

I made the team. It was my first major international tournament. I was glad my good buddy and fellow Warrior Mike Keane was there too. Moose Jaw has retired his number 25 sweater alongside my number 9. Keaner is the most competitive person I have ever met. If I were going to war, he would be the first guy on my list. He had no talent at all—*none.* But no matter what we were doing, he had to win. Didn't matter what. First in line to fucking get McDonald's—that kind of guy, you know? He was funny, really funny, and had red hair, an Irishman. Boy, he was tough! He wasn't very big—five foot eleven, 180 pounds— but he was voted the toughest guy in the Western Hockey League two years in a row. Keaner was an interesting guy, for sure. I felt ten feet tall when I was playing on the ice with him. Nobody messed with Keaner, which meant nobody messed with me. He was killing guys. I saw him knock out twenty guys in the three years I played for Moose Jaw. Literally one-punch them flat on their asses. Mike and his dad and brother Billy lived hockey the same way my brothers and I did. His dad was a prison warden, but he also coached his sons. Mike was the youngest, so he had to keep up, and Billy showed him no mercy. Keaner won three Stanley Cups and wasn't even drafted. He became captain of the Montreal Canadiens—an English-speaking, Irish kid. Think about it. I see him every once in a while, but he's not on my speed dial or anything. He's 41 and he's still in the game, playing for the Manitoba Moose.

Nitra, our home base, was an absolute shit hole. But I was the kind of guy who always made the best of every situation. Through the whole tournament, everybody would complain about how shitty the food was and everything. For me, it was an adventure. True enough, the food was absolutely horrendous. I didn't eat caviar, so that eliminated half my choices. I mean, what 18-year-old Canadian kid wants to scarf down fish eggs? I think they thought they were doing us a big favour by serving it. We were so hungry we would try it again and again, then end up spitting it out. We ate fries three times a day because none of us were interested in eating German shepherd or whatever the hell that lardy mystery meat was that they stuffed into the sausages. Hockey Canada finally flew over a whole bunch of Kraft Dinner, but the cooks in Nitra managed to fuck that up too. They served it all soft and mushy.

Each apartment had two single beds in two bedrooms. Keaner and I dragged ours into the room with Yvon Corriveau and Greg Hawgood so we could stay up and talk all night. The four of us hit it off instantly, like we were held together by Velcro. I was a little awestruck by Yvon because his sweater was already hanging in the Washington Caps' dressing room. He'd talk about what it was like. "You don't have to carry your hockey bag, and they sharpen your skates without you telling them to. The hotels are great, the food is great and the girls are better-looking." Unbelievable! He was a good guy. A big guy. He was ripped and had a full beard. I don't think I even had hair on my nuts.

Greg Hawgood was a special player too. He was not much bigger than me, five-nine or so, but he played defence. He was a tough little guy. Greg ended up playing in the Stanley Cup finals, for Boston against the Oilers in 1988.

Steve Chiasson was our captain. Another defenceman. He played hard and had some skill. Steve had been drafted by the Detroit Red Wings in 1985 and had already played half a season with them. We ended up as teammates in Calgary from 1994 to '97. We were buds because he liked to party. Thanks to Steve, I started smoking. We were in Engelberg, Switzerland, at a practice camp and had the night off. Engelberg is a little ski village below Titlis Mountain—swear to God. Anyway, he had some Marlboro Reds and I said, "Hey, lemme try one of those." He gave me one and it was love at first puff. I haven't stopped since.

Our goalie, Jimmy Waite, was this quiet French kid. He played for the Chicoutimi Saguenéens. We had no clue who this kid was. Then, the first day, Jimmy came out and stoned everyone. And he stood on his head for the rest of the tournament. He was on another planet. The next year, when we went to Moscow, he was even more insane, even better. I thought, "Man, this guy is going to be a great goalie," but he never really got there. He was picked up by the Chicago Blackhawks, but it would be tough to see ice with Ed Belfour and Dominik Hašek sitting in the row in front of you. I heard he is still playing in Germany, with Ingolstadt. The guy loves hockey.

In our first six games at the 1987 WJCs, I had five points (two goals and three assists). It was what I would consider a successful tournament for me. The team was also doing well; we'd won four times, with one loss and one tie, and were assured of a medal. We had to play the Russians in the last game of the tournament. If we lost, we went home with the bronze. If we won, we were guaranteed a silver, and if we could beat them by five goals, we would win the gold medal. The Russians had had an awful tournament—they were out of the running for a medal, and the coach and players were really pissed. Nobody on that team was happy with how they played. And the Russian media really slammed the coach, Vladimir Vasiliev. The way they were playing, it looked like we were at least a lock for the silver.

I scored twice in the first period. For goal number one, the puck was dumped into the corner and bounced out to Keaner. He shot it on net, and I followed up on his rebound and buried it—top shelf: 1–0. The second goal was a turnover that happened because, if Europeans don't see a play developing, they always circle back and try to regroup. So when the Russian D-man came out from behind the net to regroup, he drop-passed it to the second D—basically serving up a pizza to me. I saw the slice sitting there, raced in, picked it up, deked and scored. For our third goal, they served up another pizza and Dave Lada put it in. The fourth one was Steve Nemeth. He went in and took a slapshot and just roofed it.

The game was chippy as anything, lots of penalties. The Russians had nothing to gain by beating us. They were done, regardless of the outcome, so they were spearing and flying at us with elbows and dirty shots. We weren't choirboys, either. Hockey Canada had put together a team of fighters and instigators. You came at us with a knife, we'd come back at you with a bayonet.

I felt for Everett Sanipass, a first-round draft pick of the Chicago Blackhawks in 1986. He and I were the only Aboriginals on the team. He was a Mi'kmaq from the Big Cove Reserve in New Brunswick.

He was so unsophisticated that he made *me* look smooth. Anyway, he was supposed to be interviewed during the intermission, but thanks to my two goals, the CBC called on me instead. I believe it was the worst interview in the history of hockey. It was my first time on national television, and I was so wired from the game, it was as if I had done several 8-balls of cocaine. I was talking 300 miles an hour. I remember seeing it when I got home and all I could do was bury my head in my hands and say, "Oh God." I saw a dopey kid from a very small town trying to say hi to everyone he ever met. It was fun, though, and it foreshadowed the years to come. I have never met a microphone I didn't like. The media always liked to talk to me because I was colourful and I was totally honest all the time.

Back on the ice in the second period, there were more and more altercations after the whistle. Then, near the fourteen-minute mark of the second period, Sanipass and a big Russian started throwing punches with their gloves on. It started when I skated toward Pavel Kostichkin, who had just been checked by Sanipass. He got up and— *bam!*—took a shot and knocked me down. This all happened directly in front of the ref, Hans Rønning, who just stood there thinking about what he was going to have for dinner that night.

When you are 17 years old your testosterone is at a high, high level. Our players at the WJCs in 1987 were born in the late '60s and early '70s. What was happening in the world at that time? The Cold War. What were we fed by teachers, parents, the government and the media for breakfast, lunch and supper? That the Russkies are your enemy. And what do you think the Russian students were taught? The same thing about us. The evil Westerners want to take over the world. By the time we met in Piestany, North America and the Soviet Union were starting to make nice, but that did not erase years of suspicion and tension.

And as far as hockey goes, back home we had been brawling almost every game. Everybody was. There was always a big brouhaha. It put butts in the seats. We were taught to react to situations, not to think. The coaches really planted that one in us. Hockey Canada knew the situation very well. We'd already had two brawls against Switzerland in an exhibition game, and then on New Year's Day we played the Americans and had a big shindig at centre ice during the warmup. Chiasson was suspended even though he wasn't involved. Did anyone from Hockey Canada sit us down and say, "Look, boys, this is a sensitive situation. We are concerned. You stand to lose if you fight"? No.

So what happened? Valeri Zelepukin, number 10, was after me the whole game because I'd been bugging the hell out of him. "Hey, Natasha, you fucking Commie Russki!" He didn't speak English, but he got the gist. Anyway, once the fight got going he came at me. We circled each other, throwing a couple of punches, and then both of us went down punching and rolling around. We found our feet again and continued just hammering each other. I was vaguely aware that next to us Chiasson was trying to hold back another Russian from joining us.

Zelepukin had me in a bear hug. I managed to break free and look up, and both benches were coming at us. It was like, "Holy cow, here we go." I have since heard that Evgeny Davydov, who eventually played for the Winnipeg Jets, led the charge. Anyway, Keaner got hold of Zelepukin, and that was it for him. Then Keaner took care of two more Russians, including Vladimir Malakhov. Greg Hawgood was chasing a guy while swinging his helmet at him. And Sanipass, who was tough as hell, was a wrecking machine.

The refs went from fight to fight trying to break each one up, but these guys were completely ineffective. The problem was they chose the ref, Rønning, for political reasons. He was a Norwegian, and the International Hockey Federation figured he was neutral. The ref is the policeman. If the policeman lets everybody run red lights, well, everybody's going to run red lights, right? And these refs were not cops—they were more like mall security. They didn't skate off the ice, they *ran* off. I watched them go.

The whole thing lasted for a good forty-five minutes. They tried turning the lights out, but that didn't solve anything. It was still dark when we all eventually got tired, picked up our shit and skated to the dressing rooms, waiting to be called for the next period. We were sitting there trying to recover when Dennis MacDonald, who was the head of Hockey Canada, came in and told us we'd been disqualified from the tournament and what a black mark on hockey it was and how ashamed we should be. He was doing his Hockey Canada thing and we were just amazed. This kind of stuff happened every night in the WHL! This was normal! And the Russians had been in bench-clearing brawls at the World Juniors before, with the Czechs in 1978 and the Americans in 1985. Don Wittman of the CBC blamed us for coming off the bench first, when it turns out it was the Russians who were first over the boards.

Some have accused Steve Nemeth and Pierre Turgeon of being cowards because they didn't step up and fight with the rest of us, and I can see where that level of frustration comes from, but you know what? Some people just aren't made that way. They're really not. Turge was one of the most skilled guys who ever played in the NHL. He wasn't your typical in-your-face, brash guy. He was just a nice guy who played hockey. Nemeth was the same way. Everything happened so fast. We were in the brawl and the next thing you know we were on the bus going, "What the fuck happened?" Obviously, we were disappointed that we weren't able to finish the job.

I think it was such a bizarre incident that everybody reacted poorly, but I have one good memory. When I got home I received a medal in the mail from Harold Ballard. He'd had them made up because he agreed with what we'd done. Brian Williams (with CBC then, and now a commentator with TSN) kept beaking off, calling it an ugly, disgraceful incident. The guy probably never even laced up in his life. The most adversity he ever faced on ice was making it to his car in the winter. Don Cherry was behind us because he played the game, so he understands the game. I don't think it gives him the right to be as critical as he is sometimes, because he was never a big success story in the game, but he knows what goes on in the heat of the moment. It gets out of hand at times. That is the nature of hockey.

7

NO JOKE

IN 1987, the Calgary Flames went into the draft determined to be very selective. They had a very good team. They had been to the Stanley Cup finals in '86 and finished third overall in 1986–87, so there were not many job openings. They had had bad luck with their draft the previous year. The Flames' first-round pick in 1986 was George Pelawa from Bemidji, Minnesota. They had a lot of confidence in him and considered him a great big surefire NHLer. He looked a bit like Philadelphia Flyer Paul Holmgren. But Pelawa was killed in an automobile accident right after he was drafted. They say that Tom Cochrane's song "Big League" is about him. Calgary's third pick, Tom Quinlan, quit hockey to play baseball for the Toronto Blue Jays.

I was ranked 197th out of 200 in the rankings compiled by the NHL's Central Scouting Bureau. But thanks to Piestany, people at least knew who I was. And in 66 games with Moose Jaw in '86–87, I'd led the team with 61 goals and 68 assists for 129 points, fifth-best in the Western Hockey League. I was also gaining notoriety around the WHL. In Regina, they nicknamed me "The Weasel," and it spread. Whenever I skated on the ice, the organist played "Pop Goes the Weasel." They just fuckin' hated me there, which was perfect. That hatred fed me. It was attention, right? They went nuts when I scored, booing and screaming. One time during a division final, I skated down the middle of the ice, dropped the puck back between my legs and shot it at the goalie from behind my knee, roofing it and

45

making him look like Bambi in the headlights. Then I rode my stick all the way to our bench. It was a real hard goal on Regina. We were already up 8–2. When I opened the gate, Barry Trapp, our head coach, grabbed the back of my jersey and threw me onto the bench for hot-dogging. Later, he said it was one of the most amazing goals he'd ever seen, but he hated that I just rubbed it in like that. Barry was popular with me for getting rid of Graham, but behind his back we all complained that he still had one shoe back behind the bench with his former team in Regina. The crowd lined up against the boards when we left the ice at the end of the game, and they were chirping me and actually waving fists at me like a mob out of a Frankenstein movie. I just chirped back.

I was on the Flames' radar. One of their scouts, Ian McKenzie, was a former RCMP officer, and he was always in the stands. He used to get a real kick out of it when Regina razzed me. I knew Ian was concerned about my size. Later, he said that if I had been three inches taller and fifteen pounds heavier, I would have been everybody's number one, but I wasn't, so no other team was looking at me. At that time, the NHL was dominated by huge bodies. The Philadelphia Flyers had some humongous players in 1987–88. They had a guy from Sweden, Kjell Samuelsson, who was six foot six and 235 pounds. Dave Brown, a good old boy from Saskatoon, and Willie Huber, from Germany, were both six-five and weighed 210 and 225 respectively. Greg Smyth, who I played with in 1992 on the Flames, was six-four and 235, while Tim Kerr was six-three and 225 pounds. The Flyers had two other players who stood six foot four: Jeff Chychrun and Mike Stothers. Craig Berube, at six-one and 205, was one of their smaller players. Even their fuckin' goalie, Ron Hextall, was a tank at six foot three and 200 pounds.

Still, Ian kept coming to Moose Jaw to watch players, and each and every game he would put it in his notes that I was the best on the ice. Ian says he's responsible for drafting more than a hundred players who played in the NHL, and every one was different. He took big chances on three players who weren't supposed to make it: Brett Hull, Gary Suter and me.

People had written Brett Hull off. He wasn't in good shape. He was playing in Tier II, not even major junior. People accused Ian of taking Brett because his dad was Bobby Hull. But Ian said, "No, I'm taking Brett Hull because he scored 125 goals in one year in Penticton." And Suter turned out to be rookie of the year, after everybody thought he was too small to be a defenceman in the NHL.

Ian used to tell us, "You can divorce your wife, but you are always stuck with your draft pick." Good or bad, that pick is yours forever. He said he always looked for a unique quality in a player, some special thing about them. A player can look good and have talent, but if he doesn't have that special quality, he is not going to make it in the NHL. I was fearless. I did not let myself be intimidated, no matter what an opposing player did. Spear me or cross-check me or whatever, I kept coming. And the one thing I could do that made up for my size was accelerate off a dime. I had great speed and could beat a player off both sides. Defencemen were always backtracking instead of trying to take me out. That cheating was to my advantage. In my first training camp with the Flames, Ian would say to me, "Don't forget the biggest weapon you have is speed. Don't let down on your speed."

Cliff Fletcher was the general manager of the Flames, and Ian had an office next to Cliff's in the Saddledome in Calgary. Ian kept bugging Cliff about me, and of course the size factor kept coming up. Ian had to convince him to buck the trend—to go against the wisdom of Central Scouting. I was putting butts in the seats in Moose Jaw, so Ian suggested the Flames could capitalize on my showmanship. He said, "Look, if we take a chance, he'll fill the building for our farm team in Salt Lake. I promise you that."

Of course, I was totally oblivious to all this. All I knew was I belonged in The Show.

Draft day was June 13, 1987, in Detroit. In the first round, with the nineteenth pick, Calgary chose left winger Bryan Deasley. The Flames' scouts liked him. He was a college player, he had size and he could skate. Turned out he was at his pinnacle and never developed after that. When you're drafting an 18-year-old, you don't know whether he is going to level off or progress, and there are intangibles you can't count on. That's why mistakes are made. At the time, Deasley was a prospect. He played a few years in the minors but never played an NHL game. He did go on to find a good career as a player agent.

Stephane Matteau, taken twenty-fifth overall, was next. He had a thirteen-year career in the NHL and won a Cup with the New York Rangers. In 1994, in the conference finals against New Jersey, he scored at 4:24 of the second overtime period in game seven. That got the Rangers into the finals against the Canucks. Fortieth overall, the Flames took Kevin Grant, a big defenceman from Kitchener who had a long career in the minors and in Europe.

Teams draft by committee, and each of the scouts have their special picks that they make a case for. Scott Mahoney, taken in the third round, is now a police officer in Oshawa, but the Flames had a scout who lived there at the time who liked him, so they drafted him next. Tim Harris, taken seventieth, never made it out of the minors. The same went for Tim Corkery, taken in the fifth round from Ferris State in Michigan. In the sixth round they got Joe Aloi, who ended up playing one more junior year in Quebec before quitting.

Keep in mind that, just because someone is drafted ahead of you, it doesn't mean the team thinks he is a better player, it means the team is worried that someone else might pick him up first. In my case, the Flames were confident nobody else was willing to take a chance on me, so they had the luxury of choosing what round they would take me in. Why waste a pick by taking me in the first or second round when they knew they could get me late, probably after the fifth round? Even so, Ian was getting jumpy. He worried the Flames might lose me. "Cliff," he said, "we can't wait any longer or we're not going to get this guy." And Cliff asked, "Can we ride him one more round?" Cliff wanted Peter Ciavaglia, a really good player who wound up at Harvard and led the Eastern Collegiate Athletic Conference in scoring in both his sophomore and senior years. But he just had a cup of coffee in the NHL, ending up in five games for the Buffalo Sabres.

Finally, in the eighth round, Cliff gave Ian the nod and whispered, "Okay, go ahead and take him." Then he said to the room, "Gentlemen, this next pick is mine and Ian's." And, in the eighth round, with the 166th pick, they called me up. The room erupted. Al MacNeil, who would become one of my biggest supporters, had never seen me play, and he threw his new Cross pen across the room. At the next table, the Flyers were laughing and their assistant general manager, Gary Darling, snorted, "Ian, where's this guy going to play?" Ian leaned right across Bobby Clarke, the Flyers' general manager, held his fist up under Darling's nose and said, "A little short-ass bastard like you shouldn't be talking." Underneath all this was Al MacNeil, on all fours, trying to to pick up his Cross pen.

When I got the call, my family was excited and I was pumped, but you know what? I honestly expected it.

My first training camp, I came in cocky. *Very* cocky. But I had nothing to lose and everything to gain. The Flames were an awesome team, but they were complacent. Some of the veterans were just rounding themselves into shape. I wanted to make an impression, so I figured if the coaches saw a guy right out of junior, an eighth-round pick half their size, making monkeys out of the defence, that would do it.

In the first half-hour I managed to get big Joel Otto (six foot four, 220 pounds) really pissed at me. I was driving him nuts. I'd scoot around him on the left side one time and the right the next. Every time I went past him, I'd hear, "You short little shit." Otts didn't think it was very funny at the time. He and three of our defencemen,

Al MacInnis, Ric Nattress and Dana Murzyn, wanted to splatter me against the boards.

Up till now, the coaches and management had been skeptical—they'd figured I had been drafted solely for the farm team in Salt Lake. Now, to their amazement, they felt I might be able to step right onto the club, but they didn't need me yet. I went back to Moose Jaw, where I had 68 goals and 92 assists for 160 points in 65 games. I tied Joe Sakic for the league scoring title and racked up 235 penalty minutes. I ended junior with 201 goals and 271 assists in 274 games. My total of 472 points is tenth all-time in WHL history.

Midway through the season, I was off to Moscow for the World Juniors. They named me captain of Team Canada. We were still pissed about Piestany and I think that helped us win gold. We went through the tournament unbeaten, winning six games and tying one, and finished one point ahead of the Soviets, a lot of the same guys we had played the year before, including Alexander Mogilny and Sergei Fedorov. Even though they had the home-ice advantage, on New Year's Day we managed to pull off a 3–2 win. I honestly have to give the credit for that series to our goalie Jimmy Waite. I scored six goals, and so did Rob Brown. Adam Graves came up with five and Joe Sakic added three, but that fuckin' Jimmy Waite put on a clinic. I am not sure I have seen goaltending like that since. Waite, with a 2.29 goals-against average, was named top goalie of the tournament. He was named to the All-Star team, and so was I, along with Teppo Numminen, Greg Hawgood, Alexander Mogilny and Petr Hrbek. Pretty good company.

I signed my pro contract for more money than I had ever seen in my life—$350,000, plus a $65,000 signing bonus and a bonus for games played. I was sent to Salt Lake in time for the team's last two regular-season games (three goals and four assists) and the IHL playoffs. I was soaring, and put up 11 goals in eight playoff games. We came home with the Turner Cup.

When I went back to Moose Jaw for the summer, after being in the dressing room with the pros and seeing how ripped they were, I dumped all cardio exercise and started lifting weights like crazy. I came to the 1988 camp twenty-five pounds heavier, at 175, and it cost me. I didn't have the same speed. The team was really disappointed. They called Paul Baxter, my coach in Salt Lake, and told him to whip me back into shape.

I remember getting sent down. It was the only time in my life I didn't make a hockey team. I unpacked in Salt Lake and sulked for a while.

In my very first game, I scored a hat trick and two assists—five points. I thought, "This is kind of strange," because honestly, I thought it was going to be harder. But because I was pissed, I started not to deliver and I was taking stupid penalties—81 minutes in 40 games. Baxy was always on me. He constantly preached at me to play in my own zone. It was something I'd never worried about. I grew up controlling the puck, so I never had to play defence. Baxy wanted to play me all the time so I could shave off the weight, but first he had to change my head.

We were on the road playing the Denver Rangers when Baxy called me up to his hotel room. I slumped in a chair and stared out the window. Baxy had just come off a very successful eight-year NHL career as a defenceman with the Pittsburgh Penguins, Quebec Nordiques and the Flames. My penalty minutes didn't bother him so much—he retired with 1,560 of his own—but he could see that I was losing my temper and not putting out.

"What is wrong with you?" he asked me. I said, "I should be in Calgary. I never should have been cut. It fuckin' sucks." I could feel him looking at me, but I refused to look back. We both just sat quietly. I am sure he thought I had some nerve. Not quite five foot six and back down to 150 pounds, most guys in my position would consider themselves lucky to have made it to Salt Lake. Finally he said, "Okay, listen. I know I have been hard on you and I know you can take it, but I need you to work with me. I'll make you a deal. From the blue line in, you have to play my system. Stick to your own zone. Once you get the puck over the blue line, you can do whatever you want."

It was a really smart move on Baxy's part. He wasn't just making a deal with me so that I would step up on defence, he was validating my talent by showing me that kind of respect. Up to that point, I'd been told, "You are paid to play hockey, not to think." But Baxy knew my confidence was shot to hell from being sent back down to the minors. By offering me this deal, he was telling me he believed in me enough to let me follow my instincts. It worked. I went on a tear like you would not believe. I had 74 points (37 goals, 37 assists) in 40 games and I led the International Hockey League in scoring.

Salt Lake was a strange team. Half was made up of grizzled old veterans who had played anywhere from five to ten years in the minors—their whole careers. And then you had a bunch of us young guys who were prospects and recent draft picks. It was a weird combination. I was the last piece of the puzzle to go down there, but it worked. I lived with Brian Tataffie, the trainer, in his basement. He had a nice family, but I was never there.

If you know anything about grizzled old guys who have spent a lot of time in the minors, they still love to play hockey while they make money and party. They are usually 26 to 34 years old. Still living the dream. I liked hanging out with them because they were fun and they partied, which was right up my alley, right? I was 19 years old and walking right into the bars because the people there were fans of the team.

When I first played for Salt Lake, late in the '87–88 season, there was a pretty skilled guy on the team; he was in his mid-twenties and still single. He'd played in Manitoba, and his mom lived in Moose Jaw, so he and I kind of clicked right off the bat.

I was pretty naive about drugs at that time. This guy came and picked me up for my first day of practice. He had a convertible that he called "Big Daddy Love" with a white leather interior. It was a beautiful day, sunny and warm, and he pulled up with his sunglasses on, looking cool. He used to call me Billy—"Hey, Billy, what're you doin,' Billy?"

It's about a twenty-minute drive to the rink, and we were going fast. He pulled out a joint and said, "Hey, man, do you want to try some of this?" And I said, "No, man, you're nuts." He got blasted right before practice. I learned to enjoy that lifestyle pretty quickly. After practices we'd head for the golf course. There was still snow on the ground in Moose Jaw, and here I was in Utah, teeing off. We'd go to the golf course, get into the beer, smoke a couple of doobies, and I'd get home and Tataffie would say, "Baxy called. He's looking for you. He wants to know where you are." So I think the Flames knew I was a bad-ass from day one, but they didn't say anything because I was playing so well.

My alcoholism was, let's say, developing at the time. Every single night after a game, we'd all go out and get wasted. Almost everybody on the whole team. We were always together, drinking and partying. There was a bar called the Green Parrot across from the rink. We used to go there all the time. Mainly what we tried to do was pick up girls. I looked like I was 12, but most of the guys were pretty successful. We had a really good-looking team.

Rich Chernomaz was the captain. He was a buddy. He played a few games here and there in the NHL. He was originally drafted by the Colorado Rockies. Jeff Wenaas liked to enjoy himself. He was an old-school kind of guy who'd played junior in Medicine Hat. I had played against him quite a bit. He was the Flames' number two draft pick, thirty-eighth overall, in 1985, but he never ended up making it. Dougie Clarke was part of the group. Same kind of fellow, right out of college, liked to have fun. Steve MacSwain was a good guy. He was small too, a lot of skill. Played for the University of Minnesota, never made it to The Show.

Kevan Guy, Martin Simard, Marc Bureau and Dave Reierson were all team players and tight with their families. Randy Bucyk was a straitlaced guy, and Stu Grimson was pretty religious at that time.

Bobby Bodak, now there was a grizzled old veteran. He'd been around forever, played three games with the Flames, spent ten years in the minors. Bodak was a beauty. Jim Johannson, who had played for the USA team in Piestany, works for USA Hockey now. I saw him in Ottawa when I was there recently for the reunion with the World Junior team that played in Piestany. Rick Hayward was fun and had the kind of looks the ladies liked. He had to beat them off with a stick. All these guys were ripped. The team was part of the Flames organization so everybody was in good shape. The Flames were the first team in the NHL to put a lot of emphasis on conditioning in the off-season.

Peter Lappin was, like me, a late-season addition to the team in 1987–88. He was an All-American at St. Lawrence University, and in 17 playoff games he had 16 goals and 12 assists. He had great hands and could score. He ended up making an appearance in six games with the Minnesota North Stars and one with the San Jose Sharks—that's it. Marc D'Amour, our goalie, was funny. I'd have to light his cigarettes between periods because he was so fuckin' unsteady from alcohol chill. His nickname was "Shaky." But he was unreal in goal. I heard he owns a bar in Salt Lake now.

After we won our first playoff round in '88, we had four days off before we played the next round. One of the guys had a party at his place. I was on my way to the bathroom when one of the guys followed me in, pulled this little stash of white stuff in a baggie from under the lid of the toilet tank, cut up a couple of lines on the counter and said, "Hey, do you want to try some of this stuff?" I was like, "Sure."

You know how I talked about being at Sheldon's and taking that first drink? Well this was a hundred times better than that. I was

54

euphoric. I had never felt anything like it. It gave me goose bumps, I was so happy. Suddenly, I wasn't this awkward, snot-nosed rookie. I was going up to these beautiful older girls, talking to them, confident—it was just an amazing state to be in. It was like I was Superman or something. Not human.

The next season, it was New Year's Eve and we'd just played Denver. I was getting ready for one of the biggest parties of the year. There was going to be coke and girls and I was pumped. I had just come out of the shower and was towelling off when Baxy came up to me and he said, "Can you be on the plane tomorrow?" I laughed. "What are you talking about?" He said, "I just got off the phone with Cliff Fletcher and the Flames want you in Calgary tomorrow." I said, "You're kidding." He looked at me and shook his head. "This is no joke."

I went back to the locker room to tell the guys. I remember thinking that it was about time the Flames woke up and smelled the coffee.

8

A FULL-BODY ORGASM

ON JANUARY 1, 1989, the Flames were going through a bit of a midseason slump. They were struggling with complacency. And after the in-your-face attitude I'd shown in training camp, I guess they thought this snotty-nosed little bastard from Russell might stir things up.

I remember being extremely nervous because I knew that I was only going to get two, or at most, three, games to show that I belonged. Was I afraid? Absolutely. For the first time in a long time, I felt some doubt. "Don't fuck up. You've got to play better than you have ever played in your life."

The team booked me a room at the nicest hotel in the city, the Palliser. I dumped my stuff and immediately headed for practice. The next day, we were scheduled to play Quebec. My dad's sister, Auntie Rose, and her husband, Uncle Don Odgers, drove in from Oxbow, Saskatchewan, and took me out to dinner at the Calgary Tower. It was the tallest structure in the city at that time and had a revolving restaurant on the top. They told me to have anything I wanted on the menu, so I ordered lobster. A few hours later, I woke up puking all over the place. I couldn't believe it—of all the times to get sick, but I managed to get back to sleep. The next night, I remember stepping onto the ice and looking at the team. The Calgary Flames were the biggest and deepest team in the NHL. Except for the goalies, Rick Wamsley and Mike Vernon, and three players—Dougie

Gilmour, Joey Mullen and Håkan Loob—everyone else was over six feet and weighed more than 200 pounds. Cliff Fletcher had been building the Flames since they started in Atlanta in 1972, and they were always known for size. I read that after a game with the original Atlanta Flames, Stan Mikita—who, at five-nine and 169, was a star centre with the Chicago Blackhawks—said, "It was like skating in a forest of giant redwoods."

When I showed up in the dressing room, I remember Al MacInnis sitting with his back against a wall and his arms crossed, saying, "What the fuck are you doing here?" I didn't say much, just kind of quietly answered, "They called me up."

I'm sure they all knew that I was just fuckin' lighting it up in Salt Lake. Vets watch the farm teams. They want to know who is coming up on their asses. Back then, you'd ask the scouts—"How's this guy doing? How's that guy doing?" We didn't have the Internet like we do now. I don't think players feel enough of that fear that pushes them to play hard now. Under the collective bargaining agreement, teams aren't allowed to bring a player in halfway through the season and start fucking around with the chemistry of the team unless there are injuries. The rules are different, and this is why you have so much complacency.

The coaches were behind me. Obviously, my call-up was their decision, so I knew I had their support. Al MacNeil was always great to me, always talking to me and giving me pointers. "Do exactly what you have been doing down in Salt Lake. Play that way. That's why you are here, that's why we called you up. Don't change a thing, and don't worry about what the guys are thinking. You are here because you deserve to be here. You have earned your chance, make the most of it."

But most of the guys had the deep-freeze thing going on. I didn't like it, but I could live with it. I didn't blame the guys. They didn't want their group messed with. They were all pretty comfortable. For the most part, they were kind of mellow and cool, and in comes this dorky kid who is full of energy. They didn't like the dynamic. I sat between Colin Patterson and Rick Wamsley, and those two guys treated me well from day one. They knew that I was fuckin' shit-scared sittin' there, but if Lanny McDonald sat out and I played instead, you could feel that shit. My linemates were Brian MacLellan and Timmy Hunter. Timmy was another one who was great to me, 'cause he got more scoring chances playing with me than he ever did before.

I played my first game that night. It was pretty awesome—twenty thousand people at the Saddledome. I came out and hit everything in sight. I was going after guys left, right and centre. Joe Sakic moving toward the puck? *Boom!* Into the boards. Peter Stastny? *Wham!* A mid-ice collision. Big Walt Poddubny? No problem. Hit after hit. I didn't see size and I didn't care about the name. I hit every guy that came my way. I had two secret weapons: anger and a high tolerance for pain. I played with swollen eyes, missing teeth and bruised cheekbones. It did not bother me. Our coach, Terry Crisp, said I was like an India-rubber ball. "You throw it against the wall and it comes back at you twice as hard." I don't think this made me any more popular in the dressing room. Because I was so aggressive, bigger guys had to start hitting too. They didn't want to get embarrassed by this jerk-off little rookie.

I didn't score any goals in that first game, but I was part of the power play and took a regular shift. In my second game, against L.A., we were down 5-2 after two periods when they put me on a line with Gilmour and Mullen. I ended up getting three assists, we won 8-6 and people started to think, "Okay, this guy can contribute." In the very next game, against Edmonton, I scored my first two NHL goals. So in three games, given a limited amount of ice time, I had five points. After that, there was no doubt in the minds of the management and coaching staff that I belonged, but I still had to win over my teammates.

Then one night against L.A., I had to fight Ken Baumgartner. When I first arrived with the Flames they'd also called up Kenny Sabourin, another rookie from Salt Lake. Kenny was six foot three, 205 pounds. His first time on the ice he took a run at Wayne Gretzky—just smoked him, flattened him in the corner. This was not easy to do, because Gretz had tremendous peripheral vision. He could see guys coming from behind. Unfortunately, when it happened, Jay Miller and Ken Baumgartner were on the ice with him. I was on too, with Timmy Hunter and Jiří Hrdina. So this five-on-five brawl broke out. When their tough guys, Baumgartner and Miller, went two-on-one with Timmy Hunter, I thought, "Oh fuck, I gotta go help my teammate."

So I skated in and jumped on Baumgartner's back. He's huge and I was maybe 145 pounds. He reached behind his neck and plucked me off like I was a spider crawling up his sweater. Then he held me out in front of him at arm's length, with my skates dangling in the air, and—*wham!*—a fist to my forehead. He split it open about eight inches, from above my right eyebrow to the corner of the left, and dropped me to the ice like a dirty Kleenex. Blood gushed out, streaming down my face. I was a little disoriented for a minute. "Where am I?" I wondered as I looked around at the crowd.

I got up and put up my fists ready to go at it again, but I felt this hand on the back of my jersey pulling me out of there. It was Gretz. "C'mon, kid," he said, "let's get you to the bench." Gretz was always good to me. I dunno why. We skated a little ways, him keeping me steady on my feet and me feeling conflicted. I wasn't too sure of my obligation to the team—"Should I sucker Wayne? Should I pop him one?" It took me a minute, but I realized that would be stupid.

Why did so few go after Gretz? Well, would *you* want to fight Dave Semenko and Marty McSorley? These guys could split hockey helmets with their fists. Marty suckered me one night in L.A., out of the blue. I was standing near the blue line, then *pow!* Now, I have a hard head, but I felt that one. It knocked me over, but it didn't knock me out. So I got up and shook it off, sticking my chin out. "Is that all you got?" Geez, that pissed him off. "You little fucker!" he growled.

Anyway, Wayne dropped me off at our bench and I went in to get stitched up, came back and scored two goals. What was really weird is that my skin is extra thick, like rhinoceros hide, so they broke three needles closing the wound.

That altercation turned out to be the statement I had to make to be accepted by my team. I could see it in their eyes—"This guy is here to help us win and he will do anything to make it happen." Suddenly, I was not just a phenom or a five-foot-fuck-all circus act.

DOUG GILMOUR joined the Flames in a trade just before the 1988–89 season. He was called Killer. He got the nickname because when he played with Brian Sutter in St. Louis, Sutter thought he looked like Charles Manson. He called him Charlie for a while, then it became just Killer. Doug looked and dressed like a movie star, with his perfect smile and tailor-made double-breasted suits. He was kind of the last piece of the Flames puzzle—not huge, but a highly competitive player. He had leadership qualities, and at the same time he was fun to be around.

Playing in the west means life on the road—fifteen road trips to twenty cities, more than sixty thousand miles in a season. In order to keep everyone loose, Killer was always dreaming up practical jokes. We all used blow-dryers to get that swept-back look. It was a cool late-'80s hairstyle. Sometimes Killer would shake half a can of baby powder into one of the blow-dryers at the sink so that when you turned it on you would get it full in the face and you'd have to head back to the showers. He'd put shaving cream in the towels and fold them back up on the rack, so when you pulled a towel you'd be covered in it. Saran wrap on the toilet seats was another one of his favourites. Everyone was a target. You would never know.

Joe Mullen, Killer and Lanny McDonald were the best of friends.

Joe had a million nicknames, the most common were Mullie, Pecka or Schmoe. He answered to all of them. He was really well liked. Joe came from Hell's Kitchen in New York, yet he was one of the mellowest guys you'd ever meet.

There were jokers, and there were victims. Joel Otto was a victim. Colin Patterson and Rob Ramage were always cutting the toes out of his socks. They got off on foot jokes. I cannot tell you how many times I came out after a game and saw good Italian loafers screwed onto the bench. And if you were late for practice, you would find your skate laces sliced down the middle.

Jim Peplinski—we called him Pep—was sometimes a victim and sometimes a joker. Lanny roomed with him on the road and scared the shit out of him at every opportunity. One time, Lanny lay under Pep's hotel room bed for what must have been three hours, waiting for Pep to come in and crawl into bed just so he could grab Pep's leg.

An interesting fellow, Mr. Peplinski. He treated me like a little brother and dragged me around everywhere. After a practice in Washington he said, "Wanna do something this afternoon?" I was like, "Sure, I got nothing planned." So we went to the Vietnam Veterans Memorial, that long stone wall engraved with all the names of the servicemen and -women killed over there. There are nearly sixty thousand names so it makes an impression. And there are flowers and letters lying at the base of it. I had a lump in my throat and I could tell Pep did too.

For about three months, every time Mark Hunter got into the shower after practice, Pep would steal his ignition key from his locker bag, take it to the skate sharpener and shave it off a little. Each day it got harder for Hunter to turn the key in the ignition. And he was constantly complaining about his cheap fuckin' car. We would all be falling over laughing every time he said anything about it. Hunter thought it was because his stories were so enjoyable. I roomed with Mark. He was a grizzled veteran, tough and strong—a middleweight who was sent to fight the heavyweights. He never backed down. But off the ice, real quiet. He was a gullible, big teddy bear.

Another good gag was the shoe check. At dinner, someone would crawl around under the table and dump a dab of butter or mayo or some sort of food on a guy's shoe and try not to get caught. When the perpetrator took his seat, he would use a spoon and ding-ding-ding his glass to get everyone's attention. And you'd check to see if it was you with the shit on your shoe. Nick Fotiu, a tough, tough left winger who was gone by the time I got there, was the king of the shoe check. One night, he got every player at one meal hiding under the buffet table.

It was a solid group of guys. But there were occasions when some-one went too far. I was not all that big on anything that destroyed property. It's not that I put all that much importance on material goods, but I'd had so little while growing up. I didn't have a new pair of skates until I was in junior. Once, someone cut my new tie while I was sleeping on the plane. I found out it was a rookie named Todd Harkins. Some vet had put him up to it. I retaliated by chopping the sleeves of his $1,500 leather jacket. After that, most guys left me alone. I think they felt I was not quite into the spirit.

Drinking was a favourite pastime for lots of us. I rarely drank with the boys because I was 20 and I thought most of them were grandpas. A lot of get-togethers were family events—what was I going to do, sit and gossip with the wives? Even though I had my fiancée, Shannon, and our baby, Josh, living in a hotel with me for the first three months, I would take off to the bars by myself. I was a full-blown alcoholic, hooked from the first time I took a sip at age 16. How much did I drink? As much as I could, as often as I could.

As I said before, drinking in the NHL happened. It was like any group of college kids or twenty-somethings. Getting pissed was a great way to bond. Most of the coaches left you alone as long as you produced. I showed up many times in the morning completely annihilated. I hadn't even gone home yet. How did I perform? Awesome. Sometimes, I would come in a little slow, hung over from the night before, but I dealt with it by drinking a coffee and smoking three or four cigarettes. I was having a full-body orgasm. Money, fame and chicks. I made the most of it. What was I going to do? Slow down, stay home every night and watch TV? Forget it.

Of course, if I had, things would have turned out very differently.

9

THE CUP

IN 1988–89, the Calgary Flames won 54 of 80 regular-season games, a team record. We never lost more than two in a row. Lanny McDonald scored his 500th career goal and his 1,000th point. Joel Otto emerged as one of the NHL's top power forwards, a premier faceoff man. Al MacInnis was nominated for the Norris Trophy as the league's best defenceman. Sergei Pryakhin made headlines around the world as only the second Soviet to play in the NHL. Mike Vernon was nominated for the Vezina Trophy as the league's most outstanding goalie. Colin Patterson turned checking and penalty killing into an art form. Joe Nieuwendyk had his second 50-goal season in a row. Joe Mullen scored 50 goals and set a new single-season points record for an American-born player. Doug Gilmour scored 85 points and was the best two-way centreman in the NHL. On right wing, Håkan Loob had another great season. A year earlier, he'd been the first Swedish player to score 50 goals in the NHL. He's still the only Swede to do it. He's also one of the few players in the world to win a Stanley Cup, an IIHF world championship and an Olympic gold medal. And I was credited with adding some offensive punch, having scored 14 goals and added 20 assists in 36 games. For me, it was a heck of a rookie season.

With 32 wins at home and only four losses, we were ready for the playoffs. I scored the last goal of the regular season in a 4–2 win over the Oilers. The *Calgary Herald* said the game had the "intensity level of a Sunday afternoon snooze on the couch." The only big moment occurred when Dave Brown broke his stick over Pep's ankle and they both got ten minutes. You can end a guy's career with that kind of thing, and our assistant coach Doug Risebrough went absolutely haywire. He put his mouth up against the partition glass and started calling down the entire Oilers bench. They, of course, were telling him to fuck off and eat ass, which only made him madder. Meanwhile, Timmy Hunter mixed it up with Craig Simpson and forcibly took Simpson's stick from him, carrying it to our bench.

Timmy demanded respect and got it. He really trained for fights. The key was balance and strength. What most people don't realize is that it is really hard to fight on skates. Timmy had a technique of grabbing a guy and holding on to his sweater while bracing himself on his skates and then just hammering away. A lot of guys copied him. I got into it with Esa Tikkanen, who would hang on like a humping dog. He got in my face and followed me around the ice, jabbering nonstop in what we called "Tikkanese." I would hold my hand behind my ear and come back at him with something like "Take the marbles outta your mouth" or "What? I can't understand you." This bugged the ever-living shit out of him.

We were unusually subdued as we came off the ice from that game. There was no question we were happy we had won, but now it was time to get on with business. In the dressing room, there was a low buzz. As usual, Crispy's white shirt was too tight. He had unbuttoned the collar and kept yanking at the knot in his tie. Pep was moving around the room, carrying his 2-year-old baby. Nothing fazed him. He was grinning from ear to ear, and every guy he came up to tickled her tummy and called her cute. She was too.

With his big red mane and bushy mustache, Lanny was the Lion King, Mufasa. He commanded so much respect. He moved from man to man, gripping every hand, and even tough guys like Killer had to look down so he wouldn't see them tear up.

Bearcat Murray was our trainer. He started with the Flames in 1980, when they moved to Calgary from Atlanta. He was inducted into the Hockey Hall of Fame in the spring of 2009. You gotta love the guy, everyone did. He was an awesome trainer and the most humble person ever. He was totally self-taught.

Bearcat played hockey with and against my dad in intermediate and senior leagues in Saskatchewan and Manitoba in the 1960s. He was small—five foot seven, 124 pounds—but wiry and hardy. In fact, he started out as a jockey.

We liked Bear because he was always ready to go to war with us. He had even been injured behind the bench. In the 1976 World Hockey Association playoffs, the Quebec Nordiques played the Calgary Cowboys in the first round. Bearcat was the Cowboys' trainer. In a game in Quebec City, there was this big bench-clearing brawl that also involved fans and the police. Bear was helping the guys when one of the fans, who had been straddling the cement wall with his foot over the edge toward the bench, kicked him in the face. Bear ended up with seventeen stitches, but the guy ended up in worse trouble because Bear grabbed his leg and pulled him down hard. And then another guy took a swat at Bear and he karate-chopped his attacker in the throat. Another crazy Nordiques fan took a run at Bear's son, who was only 16. Bear tackled him and smashed him in the face. Bear says it was awful, and I've heard that the Cowboys goalie, Don "Smokey" McLeod, said it was the only time in his career he was ever scared on the ice.

The other day I watched a game and I could not believe how long it took the trainer to get to a player who was down. Bearcat was known for how quickly he got out to a player. He tried a few different types of shoes so he could handle himself on the ice. First was a pair of broomball shoes, but he says they came apart "like a two-dollar watch." So he designed his own shoes with indoor track spikes that caught the ice but barely stuck out of the soles. He could walk around on a regular floor without too much trouble, and anytime they got dull he changed them, like golf spikes. Those shoes really helped him in injury situations. I remember how fast he got to Al MacInnis in a game we played in Hartford in 1993. Patrick Poulin had hooked Al, and he went into the boards wonky—feet first, doing the splits. Bearcat ran out and felt around and told Al he had dislocated his hip. Al was in serious pain, but Bear called an ambulance because he didn't want to pop it back in—he was afraid he might sever an artery. Before I played for the Flames, Gary Roberts was in a fight and lying on the ice, hurt, underneath two guys who were still going at it. Bear ran out, grabbed Gary by the shoulders and pulled him to safety so he wouldn't get cut to pieces by their skates.

Bearcat worked in public relations for the Flames after he quit training. He was a great ambassador for the game. Eventually, the Flames took him off the payroll, but he still does hundreds of school and charity events for the team, and he visits the suites at every game, signing autographs and stuff. The only thing he is retired from is getting paid. The guy is 76, but he runs around the Saddledome shaking hands like a 30-year-old.

Before each game, Bearcat used to make up a mixture called "magic tea"—apple cider vinegar mixed with honey and hot water. He said it made your system more alkaline so you could handle stress, and it was full of potassium, which he felt was essential to fitness and making muscles working properly. We'd also pop a cayenne-pepper capsule for energy.

The tea was good, and it usually worked. But in our first game of the 1988 playoffs, against the Vancouver Canucks, we were playing tentatively. The Canucks had finished 43 points behind us in the standings, and most experts were predicting we'd have an easy time eliminating them. They were underrated. After three periods, we were tied 1–1 and the game went into overtime. We lost and it was my fault. Paul Reinhart, who had just been traded to Vancouver for a third-round draft pick after eight years with the Flames, snuck in behind me and scored. Basically, we lost game one of the playoffs because a grizzled old veteran schooled a rookie. I thought, "That's it, I have just fuckin' blown it. I'm not gonna play again." When I got off the ice, Crispy didn't say anything, but I felt like any guy would feel—horrible. I had let my team down. I had made a mistake and it had cost us the game. I went right home, lay in bed and stared at the ceiling, replaying the goal over and over. If only. If only I had followed him into the corner. If only I had moved my feet a little faster, stuck out my stick, picked him up sooner. I was such a stupid fuckin' beginner. It hurt. A lot.

As I got older, I learned that this kind of thing is going to happen. Every goal is scored because somebody makes a mistake. But you're talking about a 20-year-old who doesn't really feel he belongs yet and thinks he has let the guys down. I beat myself up all night. The next day, I was called into the coach's office. Crispy, Tom Watt and Doug Risebrough knew what kind of competitor I was and knew that I would be pissed off at myself. Crispy had already had a few one-on-ones with me earlier in the season. Some were inspirational. Other times, "Get your fuckin' head outta your ass. Tone it down. Quit taking so many bonehead penalties. You're a target, easy to disrupt, and the vets have got your number, you fuckhead." But the session I remember most is the one after that Vancouver goal. His eyes were full of compassion, and he said, "Keep 'er goin, li'l guy"—Flower, Fuckface, Numbnuts or whatever name it was he called me that day. "We'll let you have this one mistake."

Before game two, I taped up my socks, moving very slowly so my hands wouldn't shake. I dressed carefully, because everything I did was designed to bring me luck. Wind the tape three times over my left sock just below the knee. Rip it top to bottom, keep the tape tight to the roll, pat it into place. Pat it again. And then my right knee, same thing. Next, I'd tape the left sock just above my ankle. Wind, wind,

wind, rip, pat twice. And now the right side. This left-to-right ritual had become more important to me after the Graham James thing. My world had been rocked and I needed something solid, something I could count on. So I became very superstitious about taping my socks. I knew if I fucked it up, we would lose the game that night.

True to his word, Crispy let me play. And I did well. I was hitting, making plays and then got one in, so I was able to let go of my anxiety. As soon as you get an opportunity to do something about your mistake, it goes away. But if you are sitting in the stands, there is not a whole lot you can do to redeem yourself.

We put early pressure on the Canucks goalie, Kirk McLean. Otts opened the scoring. Patterson added another just before the buzzer at the end of the second. We dominated, 5–2, and the series moved to Vancouver tied at one game each.

Our snipers tried to take control of the series in game three. Håkan Loob had such great hands. He shot one off McLean's pads and into the net. Then I got hold of the puck and took it into the boards. I had two Canucks on me and passed across to Newie (Joe Nieuwendyk), who was standing by the net in the open, and he scored. Then Loob put one in on a wraparound. When you are offensively talented, you expect to make good plays every night. If you get an opportunity to score, it's in the net. That's just the way guys who have that ability have to think. Any time I could contribute offensively I felt really good.

After those two convincing victories, everyone thought the Canucks were finished. Everyone except Trevor Linden and the Canucks. We were dragging, so Crispy sent Gary Roberts out to pummel Brian Bradley to change the momentum, but it backfired. Bradley was a former Flame who felt he had been traded for a bag of hockey pucks. Crispy didn't think much of Bradley. He felt the guy was in way over his head. Bradley thought he had something to prove, so he slammed Roberts to the ice. Then he scored a few minutes later.

The Canucks jumped out to a 4–0 lead and held on to win. We were now tied 2–2 with a team we should have put away by now. They had no business winning, but that's playoff hockey.

On April 11, fans in the Saddledome turned out in a sea of red, expecting us to regain the series lead. During the national anthems, I was so focused nothing around me existed. In those types of situations, when you are an elite athlete, 95 per cent of your performance is mental and 5 per cent is ability. I was thinking about all the things I did well—skating, shooting, hitting, passing. Positive affirmations. I'd started this ritual when I was a kid, and the Flames had psychologists who told me to keep it up. It's the power of positive thinking: whatever you put out there, you are going to get back. I look back on my life, and from the time I was five years old, all I said was, "I'm gonna make the NHL, I'm gonna make the NHL, I'm gonna make the NHL, I'm gonna make the NHL, I'm gonna make the NHL." And sure enough, *bang,* it all fell into place. Why? Because I put it out there.

We got started early. Loob centred the puck and Pep picked it up in front of the net and put it in just under the crossbar on the goalie's glove side. Incredibly, he buried another one. Then I scored. Tight checking and a lightning-quick transition game gave us another 4–0 victory. It was a tough, physical game. One of our defencemen, Gary Suter, was toast thanks to a Mel Bridgman elbow. Gary's defence partner, Brad McCrimmon, was totally pissed about it, especially because the Canucks had launched this big publicity campaign talking about what a bunch of fuckin' goons we were. Yet in this game alone, Vancouver took a five-minute high-sticking major and broke Suter's jaw with a dirty hit. McCrimmon told the press it was time to get serious and play hockey and fuck the PR campaigns.

We struck first in game six. Because of Suter's injury, we had been forced to change our power-play lineup, so there I was, suddenly paired with Al MacInnis on the point for the rest of the playoffs. One man's misfortune is another man's opportunity. I felt bad for Gary, but for me it was incredibly exciting. My job was to feed the puck to MacInnis, who had a howitzer. I had never seen anybody shoot a puck that hard, ever. He wasn't the greatest skater, but he was built like a brick shithouse and such a smart, smart player. Because I was taking the place of Suter, a left-hand shot, I was playing on my off side. When I took the puck off the boards I was on my backhand. My job was to get it to my forehand and over to Al, not an easy task, especially since I'd gone from occasionally playing on the point to playing it on the number one power-play unit in the NHL.

Anyway, Trevor Linden replied and we were in a seesaw battle. Then Vancouver's Brian Bradley broke away for a shortie that turned out to be the difference. The series headed to a seventh-game showdown.

Our power play scored first again in game seven. Loob picked up the rebound from Al's point shot and Newie funnelled it in. What a lineup we had—it was insane: Al MacInnis, inducted into the Hall of Fame in 2007; Joe Nieuwendyk, who will be there soon; Håkan Loob, who should be there; me on the point; Gilmour will be there; Mullen, the highest-scoring American during his career, inducted in 2000; and Otto. But the Canucks kept fighting back in what would turn into a playoff classic. They tied it up with two in a row and the series went to sudden-death overtime.

The team was nervous, and we were playing nervous. I was sitting on the bench in overtime, my head swivelling back and forth. Every shot, every pass sent a jolt of electricity directly into my nutsack. The puck would go this way—"Yeah! It's going in their end, we're going to score!"—then that way, "Oh no!" Then Vernie made an unbelievable save on Stan Smyl, who somehow got past everybody and was heading in alone. That save, that single save in a split second, gave us the chance we needed. It saved our season and it bought Vernie a year's worth of beer.

Overtime continued, with more back and forth. Then finally Loob shot it into the corner, Otto won it off the boards and centred it, and somehow Pep stuck it in the net. I'm not even sure if he got a stick on it. He might have scored with his skate—or his shin pad or butt crack, for all I know—but he was tough enough to fight his way to the net and in that crash of bodies, somehow the puck got in. The Saddledome exploded. I thought Crispy was going to pass out. This time, we came off the ice bear hugging and high-fiving. I remember entering the dressing room and just letting loose a big whoooo-hoo-whoo!

Everyone went out and celebrated. I did my own thing. I'd drop in at the bars, usually the louder, seedier places. And despite Shannon and our baby at home, I would end up in bed with some blonde puck bunny. I hadn't been promiscuous until my move to Calgary. But after what I had experienced with Graham I was out to prove my manhood and women became sex trophies. During that period, I was young, famous and out for a good time.

The Smythe Division final matched us with an old Alberta rival— Wayne Gretzky, who was now wearing the black and silver of the L.A. Kings. I was pumped. We had a tough team—a smart, tough team. Our guys knew where, when and how to pick their fights. Timmy Hunter was probably the smartest fighter I ever played with. Never saw him get hit once. We were still on the same line.

I opened the scoring against the Kings, banking a fifteen-footer off their goalie, Kelly Hrudey. I almost got another with five minutes left, but Hrudey grabbed my shot labelled for the corner with his glove. Gary Roberts saved the day for us, grabbing a wild bounce off the boards and sending it into overtime. A few minutes in, Gilmour sped in on McSorley and checked him from behind, which made him serve up a pizza to Colin Patterson, and Patter passed it back to Killer, who ended the game with a beauty. Final score 4–3, and we were ahead in the series. But Hrudey stood on his head making 43 saves that night.

We started game two in a hurry with the first goal, and then one of the strangest things I've ever seen happened. It started when Bernie Nicholls turned and decked Vernie in the crease, and the ref put his arm up to signal a delayed penalty. While the play carried on, Bearcat came flying out on the ice to tend to Vernie. Meanwhile, we scored. Gretz was just beating the shit out of the boards with his stick, screaming at the refs that you couldn't score with your trainer on the ice. Gretz would become quite animated when calls didn't go his way. In Calgary, the fans really rode him for it. They would chant, "Whiner . . . whiner . . ." It was about the only rink in the world where people didn't think Gretz was some kind of god.

In order to take the spotlight off Bearcat, Pep went after Dave Taylor. Pep could be a great instigator, and Taylor was one of the Kings' most competitive veterans. He had played on their Triple Crown line with Marcel Dionne and Charlie Simmer, scored a ton of goals and assists and was captain for a few years before moving upstairs to management. Watching Pep and Taylor was like being at the zoo and seeing two big apes tangle.

When the game got going again, we were served another pizza. This padded our lead, and the game got really chippy. McSorley, who had been trying to get something going, went after Pep but was held back by Gretzky. McSorley got loose and just started beating on Pep, pounding on the back of his neck, inflicting real damage. A five-on-five broke out near the players' bench. With all the fighting going on, the linesmen were split up. Lanny got pissed, dropped the gloves with Jim Wiemer, and they went dancing. Lanny was so tough, even in this, his last year. He was pummelling Wiemer. Lanny had guts, but he wasn't a goon, and he was getting old. Not many 36-year-olds want to take on a 28-year-old, six-foot, 210-pound defenceman in one of his last games in the NHL. This was huge. The Kings had tried to bully us around, but Lanny was letting them know that would not fly. I mean, that is worth appreciating.

I used to call the Saddledome the Saddlemorgue, because every-body sat on their hands. It was one of the quietest rinks in the league. We had the best team in hockey, but too many suits in the crowd. I jumped up on the players' bench and turned around, gesturing with my arms asking them to make some noise, to get involved. Then I wheeled and encouraged the other side of the rink to help out. The crowd went nuts. It was absolutely deafening for about five minutes. We piled on a few more goals en route to an 8–3 blowout and headed for Hollywood.

In Los Angeles, Sly Stallone pulled up in a stretch limo and told the cameras the Kings were going to turn it all around that night. Rocky was my hero. One of the highlights of my teens was being 13 with a two-hour dose of Rocky under my belt, and jogging in the dark, hunching my shoulders and punching at the blackness around me. Giving 'er and humming that *Rocky* theme. If you look at my story and the Rocky stories, they are not much different. The guy comes from nothing, works his bag off, gets a break, fights Apollo Creed, deserves to win but doesn't. Comes back and wins in *Rocky II*. In *Rocky III*, he loses somebody really important in his life, his trainer—and for me, that was my innocence—but he's able to overcome and forge ahead.

I met Stallone after the game and was surprised he was about the same size as me—way shorter than I expected. He talked just like he does in the movies, low and slow with his mouth kind of pulled down to one side. "Hey, feisty li'l guy, I been watching you, man," he said. "It's cool." I didn't know what to say. On the inside, I was freaking out. I put out my hand and mumbled, "Oh, thank you, sir."

John Candy was there too. Uncle Buck! Standing right in front of me. This was L.A. This was the shiznit, the place to be.

Once again, we opened the scoring, with Lanny's line. Then Otts made it 2–0 by fooling Hrudey into going down, then putting it upstairs. The Kings decided to take aim at our top guns. Baumgartner flattened

Mullen and the Kings cut the lead. But there was no stopping Mullen and Gilmour. Killer was getting really beat up in the playoffs. He was so determined that he got more than his fair share of pucks, sticks and elbows in the face. Bearcat tried to put Steri-Strips on his cuts, but he'd shake him off. Most guys would say, "I can't go on. Get me stitched up." But not Killer. He would say, "Leave me alone, I'm fine. I'm playing hockey." All he would let Bearcat do during a game was stop the bleeding. Geez he was tough. We took the third game 5–2.

With the Kings facing elimination, Gretzky scored first in game four. But a rebound out to Mullen tied things up. I found the puck, took it behind the net, passed it out in front, and Roberts muscled his way in and scored to take the lead. But Gretz showed great patience in front of our net and tied the game. "We'll get it back," I thought. "No big deal." And we did. Thankfully, Rob Ramage played goaltender and stopped the puck with his glove when it slipped past Vernie, who was too far out of the net. Rammer had so much heart, he gave us spirit and extra edge. Then a second effort from Newie gave us the lead and the series, four games straight.

Gretz was a real sportsman. He credited Mullen and Gilmour and said we were one of the most disciplined, methodical teams he had ever played. I loved the guy. Gretz was the kind of guy you could tell your kids you wanted them to be like. During the series, he scored the 86th playoff goal of his career, passing Mike Bossy as the NHL's all-time leading playoff scorer. Right after that last game, he was asked about it. He said he would trade all his goals for a Stanley Cup any year.

Two series down, two to go. There was so much pressure on our team from the fans and media in Calgary. They wanted to win a Stanley Cup so badly because Edmonton had been kicking our asses every year—in football too. Our city needed something to take pride in, and having Vancouver take us to seven games showed everyone how fragile we could be. We had lacked confidence, but Lanny's fight and the sweep of the Kings brought it back.

In the Campbell Conference final we went up against the Chicago Blackhawks. They were a chippy team, and if you wonder why, well, look at who was coaching, Mike Keenan. Here's a guy who has never played in the NHL, yet he thinks he's the big cheese. I don't know how far he made it in his hockey career, maybe tyke? And you've heard all the stories about Keenan and his mind games. He'll pick on a third- or fourth- line player and ride him, just grind him down.

One of his standard tactics is to intentionally bump into his victim coming out of the showers and call him a fag. "You fag, I saw you looking at the guys in the shower. You fag." After weeks of this shit, the player snaps and Keenan will be like, "Who are you to talk to me like that? I'm your coach, show some respect." But I heard it backfired when he was hard on Dave Manson, who played for him in Chicago. Apparently, Manson had had enough mental abuse and went into Keenan's office, grabbed him by the shoulders and hung him right on the hook on the back of the door. I thought that was great. It's funny how some coaches have a whipping boy that they use as an example. The problem with that is that word gets around about the asshole things this coach does. And after a while, nobody listens.

Chicago had talent. At centre they had Denis Savard, Troy Murray, Adam Creighton and Jeremy Roenick, but we had Newie, Otto, Killer and me. At left wing they had Steve Larmer, Dirk Graham, Wayne Presley and Duane Sutter up against Colin Patterson, Pep, Gary Roberts and Brian MacLellan. And we had Mullie and Håkan Loob on the right wing, backed up by Lanny and Tim Hunter. On defence, Gary Suter was out with a broken jaw, but we had veterans Brad McCrimmon, Rob Ramage, Al MacInnis, Jamie Macoun and Ric Nattress, as well as rookie Dana Murzyn. They had depth too: Keith Brown, Bob Murray, Steve Konroyd, Bob McGill and Dave Manson. We had Vernie in goal and they had Alain Chevrier. It was Chevrier's first playoff.

In the first game, Chicago targeted Newie, who was bloodied several times. Newie was tremendously hardy. A lot of guys who took the beating he took in front of the net would have moved out of there. He was just getting chopped to pieces. Bearcat turned for help to the Calgary Stampeders' trainer and learned to make special padding to protect Newie's ribs and spine. Newie was great in front. He and Roberts had played lacrosse together before they made the pros, and he had unbelievable hand-eye co-ordination. He had swift feet, was a good stickhandler and had a really quick, accurate shot. That's how he scored 50 goals in his first two seasons.

Macoun opened the scoring with a rocket through Chevrier. Then Newie broke into the clear on a Chicago line change and—*bang!*—it was in. Finally, Brian MacLellan was in the right place at the right time, finding himself in front of a wide-open net, and we took the game 3–0.

The Blackhawks bounced back with three quick goals in the first period of game two. They hung on to win 4–2, sending the series to the unfriendly and noisy confines of Chicago Stadium.

The Gilmour line jumped on the Hawks early in game three, with Mullie finding the target. I was doing my thing, chirping at them and getting under their skin, drawing some penalties. Steve Konroyd knocked me down and Keith Brown pitchforked me behind the net. Loob was cross-checked by Brown, Mullen was slashed by Troy Murray—with no penalty called—and Newie was flipped upside down by the blue line, but he got his revenge on the power play. As the clock wound down, Mullen iced a 5–2 win. We led the series 2–1 and the Hawks expressed their frustration. A battle broke out between Pep and Manson. Savard and Otts were sizing each other up when goalie Alain Chevrier shoved Otts, pinning him against the bench. Otts got loose and put Savard in a bear hug, then Chevrier jumped on his back from behind. All three came down and wrestled on the ice. Hunter, McCrimmon, Graham, Larmer and Konroyd joined in, and it was an all-out square dance.

No doubt these fights were part of Keenan's fuckin' tactics, but they didn't work this time. We were so much better than they were talent-wise. Like I said, you are not going to see a lot of teams like ours, with so many future Hall of Famers.

In the fourth game, Newie took six stitches on the bottom of his tongue thanks to a high stick from Konroyd, but we were dominant. We outshot the Hawks 12–3 in the first period. Late in that period, Chicago's Jeremy Roenick hit Colin Patterson from behind, crushing him into the glass, and got five minutes for boarding. Then Dave Manson slashed Otts on the leg. The hack was so vicious that Otts went down and had trouble getting up. Remember, Otts was a tough, tough guy. The last thing he wanted was to lie around on the ice. The ref, Andy Van Hellemond, ignored the infraction, which made Otts even madder. So when he was finally able to get to his feet, Otts skated over to the Hawks' bench and went after Manson, jabbing at him with his stick like a Masai warrior, and he was sent to the box.

A minute later, Rob Ramage slashed Steve Larmer and we were two men down. Larmer passed to Trent Yawney at the left point, and he gave it to Savard, who was standing next to Vernie. Vernie got a piece of it, but the puck made it past him. Savard was dangerous. It was his 46th career playoff goal.

Next, Gary Roberts was off for tripping Bob Bassen and we were down a man again. But MacInnis passed to Gilmour and it was in. We went on to overtime. Roberts drop-passed to me and I moved it across, point to point, to Al, who took a couple of long strides, put his head down and just gave 'er. From Alain Chevrier's point of view the puck must have looked like a cruise missile coming right at him. It went off the outside of his left pad and just under his glove and we were ahead in the series 3–1. Chevrier saved the Hawks from a major thrashing, but he said it didn't really matter how he played because he didn't stop the puck enough to win. Crispy, who had been riding the glass with excitement, leaned over and kissed the first pretty face in the crowd. In his excitement he didn't realize it was Al MacNeil's wife, Norma.

I was the fifth one out of the gate for game five. We were looking to wrap up the series. As I skated past Keenan, he started lipping me and I beaked, "What are you gonna do? Hit me with your man purse?" I heard him say, "Oh you little shit, we're gonna get you," so I looked him in the eye and said, "Bring it on, man. If you wanna come out here, I'm ready. Me and you, right here, right now. Let's go. You think you're tough? You're not tough." I always hated it when opposing coaches yelled at players. For what? I used to just laugh at 'em.

Loob blocked a clearing pass and set up Newie in the slot. Mike Hudson tied up the game late in the second on a centring pass off Vernie's stick. Ric Nattress set up the game-winner as Brian MacLellan tipped it through Chevrier's legs. Newie got the insurance goal by skating through their entire team. We were on our way to the Stanley Cup final. It was a proud day, but no one was jumping up and down in the dressing room because we knew we had a lot of work to do. Lanny reminded us all, "It's not party time yet."

The final series featured the two best teams in the league—us and the Montreal Canadiens, who had finished second overall. We opened the series in Calgary because we'd finished first overall in the regular season. Man, were we ready to put on a show. After Stéphane Richer picked the corner on a power play to give the Habs a 1-0 lead, my line got it to MacInnis, who evened the score. Patrick Roy was an amazing goalie, maybe the best of all time, but in this series, MacInnis got his number early and his big slapper had Roy shit-scared all the way to the Cup.

I had two of the biggest Flames as my wingers, Timmy Hunter and Brian MacLellan. Not only were they the biggest, they were two of the strongest guys you'll ever meet. When I first saw MacLellan take off his shirt in the dressing room, his arms were so ripped that his biceps looked like cantaloupes. I thought, "What am I getting myself into? I'm gonna get killed." Crispy called those two guys snowplows 'cause they cleared the way for me.

I was on left point with Al and we broke in on a three-on-one and scored again. Then Larry Robinson came back and banked a centring pass off Jamie Macoun and the score was even. After that, the most amazing thing happened. Out of the blue, Jamie Macoun made an unbelievable little feather pass. I broke in on the left wing, and as soon as it was on my stick, I snapped it and caught Patrick Roy off guard. It went right between his legs. I will never forget that feeling. It was like watching a girl take her clothes off in front of you for the first time. Unbelievable. Hunter grabbed me and Macoun grabbed *him*. Even though it was early in the second period, we could taste victory. After that, we protected our lead, playing defence like we could. When the game ended, I was pumped. "I scored a game-winning goal in the Stanley Cup finals. Wow." I wonder how many times that goal was re-enacted on the streets of Russell, Manitoba.

Growing up, I liked the Canadiens. My heroes were Guy Lafleur, Guy Lapointe and Yvan Cournoyer. *Hockey Night in Canada* would often switch over to the Montreal game because the Leafs played so terribly. My Grampa Fleury was a huge Montreal fan. My whole family was. In fact when we won the Cup in 1989, my cousin Dave was so pissed off he ripped his phone off the wall.

After that first game, we were focused and in a good place as a team. When you win because your fourth-line guys like me are chipping in with big goals here and there, it makes life even sweeter.

In a playoff series, you really want to win your first two home games before heading to your opponent's rink. It gives you a stranglehold, and even if they win their two home games, you're still tied. Unfortunately, we fucked that up.

Game two was close. Two awesome teams playing each other. The whole series came down to a break here and a break there. Personally, I could not get one. We had a power-play opportunity in the first period. I moved in from the point, picked up a pass and saw an opening just above Roy's shoulder, but my shot hit the post. Then Larry Robinson blasted a screen shot through Vernie: 1–0, Canadiens. Chris Chelios set up Mike Keane, and Vernie came out to cut him off, but Smith scored on the vacated net to make it 2–0. We stormed back, but Chelios made a miraculous skate save. Then Newie put one in. Next, Otto's tough play in front tied the game. The Canadiens pulled ahead with a nifty back pass from Brian Skrudland that set up a slapshot from Chelios. They held on, tying the series at one game apiece.

Chelios and I had a good rivalry, but we used to go out and have beers together after regular-season games. I made him better and he made me better. If you are an elite athlete, you want to play against the best guys the other team has every night. You want to stick it up their asses. Games where you play highly competitive guys, like the Montreal series, made me a better player. If you play against Joe Blow, where's the challenge in that? You know you're going to beat him. Still, it was another sleepless night as I agonized over everything that had gone wrong in game two—a backhand that I couldn't get up, shots that had gone wide, and that first shot that hit the post. It really bothered me. I kept thinking, "Son of a bitch, a goal right then could have made the difference."

Game three was played in front of a sellout, shirtsleeve crowd of 17,909 at the Forum. Montreal scored first, then we got a break with a five-on-three. I was set up in front and made a great shot, but Roy read me and came up with the puck. I had never played a goaltender like this. Finally, Mullie tipped in a pass from McCrimmon and tied it up 1–1. The Canadiens scored, but the net was off the magnets and referee Kerry Fraser waved it off. The crowd took him to the mat over that one. On another power play, I took a pass and deked with it at the blue line, then passed it over to MacInnis. He sent it to Mullen by the net and we scored. Calgary 2, Montreal 1. But immediately after that, Bobby Smith evened it up for them. Gilmour regained our lead with a phenomenal effort, fighting through both defencemen and just pounding it in. We hung on until there were forty-one seconds on the clock in the third period, then Mats Naslund scored on a desperation slapshot.

This sent us to OT and thirty-five minutes of the best hockey a guy could ask for—until Kerry Fraser made an unbelievable call. I never liked that guy. I always thought he was jealous of me because, although he had an inch on me, he was a small guy who was only reffing, not playing, in the NHL. Every time he was in charge and I stepped on the ice, I might as well have stayed in the dressing room. He'd throw me in the penalty box all night. I once yelled at him that he was such a hot dog there wasn't enough ketchup, mustard and relish in the world to cover him.

The veterans would take him in stride, but I didn't have my anger under control, so I would toss a spark on the gas. This was always to my own detriment, but I couldn't help it. Look at the ref's role. He's an authority figure, right? And I was already a little upset by authority figures in my life. I looked at Fraser as my dad, Graham James and the school principal I never liked. Each time he made (yet another) ridiculous call on me, I would skate past him and make a comment like, "Next time, kiss me before you fuck me." He'd lift his head and scratch his chin and drawl, "That will be ten." All those penalty minutes I got were not because I was scrapping.

Anyway, I think Fraser was still embarrassed from the bruising he took in calling off the Montreal goal, so he made a tripping call against Mark Hunter. At that time, it was unheard of to call a penalty in OT, let alone a marginal tripping call—thirty-five minutes in. Fraser did the same thing to the Flames in 2004 in game four of the final against the Tampa Bay Lightning, giving Tampa a five-on-three advantage and basically handing them the Cup. Some say that call in 2004 cost him some status and the officiating job in game six. But back in 1989, I doubt Fraser was called on the carpet. John Ziegler was the president of the NHL at the time, but he didn't seem to me to do much except collect a paycheque. The other guy calling the shots was Alan Eagleson, and what was he going to do? Tell Fraser he's out of line? Especially when he is busy stealing hundreds of thousands of dollars from the player pension fund at the time? The Canadiens took advantage and beat us in a heartbreaker, 4–3.

We needed the next game to stay alive. And Crispy had to come up with something unexpected, something to throw the Habs for a loop. We had the number one power play, so he instructed me to draw as many penalties as I could. "You're small and fast, you little fucker, so keep your feet moving and stir up some shit." My first chance came when Petr Svoboda high-sticked me. We scored on the power play. Later, Svoboda told the *Calgary Herald,* "I hate to play against small guys. When they're small, tough and fast it's hard to catch them. It's frustrating. Every time you touch him, [Fleury] goes down and it's just ridiculous. The referees have to take a closer look at him. You don't want to let stuff like that go to your head, but it's too bad we get the penalties and end up having to work twice as hard to kill a power play." Hey, I was a competitor, what did he expect? If you hook me and I can draw a penalty, I am going down.

Next, Larry Robinson cross-checked me. I fell and Robinson was pissed when Joe Mullen scored. He told the *Herald,* "I can see if I went behind and rammed him, but I didn't. I just came from behind and gave him a little nudge. There are more than a few dives going on out there. Maybe we have to play a non-contact game or something because I don't know what's going on."

I was really becoming a pain in the ass for the Habs. Guy Carbonneau was next—he got called for hooking. The game was all about clutch and grab—it was like skating through a jungle. Eventually the NHL would change the rules to open the game up more, but by moving fast to the net I was forcing the Canadiens to spend time in the box, and they were sore. In the same article in the *Herald,* Carbonneau said, "I just had my stick on him and he dove. That's the kind of game that's happening. You can't say it's Fleury's fault because for his team it's a good thing. The refs have to get to know him better. It's only his first year and I'm sure he's going to be watched more. It's almost like it is for Claude Lemieux now. He used to draw a lot of penalties, but they watch him closer now and don't call penalties as much."

For me it was all about the W. We beat them 4–2. Crispy got a real kick out of goading Montreal. "Theo is fast and he's quick. They've got to do something to slow him down and they're taking penalties. But that's what speed does. It demands you stop him anyway you can."

Game four was the biggest game of my career to that point. It was also the most violent. Don Cherry had been beaking off on *Hockey Night in Canada* about how I was too small to make it through the series and was going to get killed. This did not please my dad. So when my dad was being interviewed by Chris Cuthbert, he spotted Cherry along the glass, called him over and said, "Well, my kid has been fighting six-foot players his whole life. And I've seen him beat up a lot of big guys in his day, so I would appreciate it if you wouldn't say that he is too small anymore." And Cherry said, "I have to admit I would never have believed he could make it in the league and do what he is doing." I thought it was cool that my dad stepped in to defend me.

Everybody in my family drove up to Calgary from Manitoba for game five on May 23. I had twenty or so people sleeping on the living room carpet, couches, chairs—even the kitchen floor in my little two-bedroom apartment. I was desperate for tickets. I would go up to the ticket lady, Mrs. Anne Marie Malarchuk. She was married to Clint Malarchuk's brother Garth, who was also a goalie. Anne Marie always hooked me up. Like the mothers in Russell, she was extra nice to me. Some of the seats were nosebleeds, but who the hell cared? It was the Stanley Cup final.

The Canadiens were still off their game. Twenty-nine seconds in, big Joel Otto got a break. He went in alone and Roy went down in a half-butterfly, stopping the puck with his left pad, but it bounced back toward Otto, hitting him just above his glove and—*bam!*—into the net. Otts wasn't the most skilled guy in the world, but he worked as hard as anybody and he was really good defensively. We were up 1–0.

The rest of the game was back and forth, back and forth. Vernie made some unbelievable saves. He was insane. Vernie was five-nine and weighed 155 pounds. For a guy that size, he was as big as a house. Vernie always tested the fittest at camp. He was in awesome shape, and it was really working for him.

We made it 2–0 on the power play, then Bobby Smith replied and it was 2–1. MacInnis kept us out in front with a slapshot from the blue line. I was on Smith a couple of shifts later. He moved out from behind the net, beating me to the puck, and passed it over to my old buddy, winger Mike Keane, who cut the lead to a single goal. Thankfully it did not make the difference, and I headed home that night one win away from the Stanley Cup.

Back to Montreal for game six and a chance to win the Cup. It was just surreal. Before the game, my mind was playing tricks on me. I was saying to myself, "Can you believe you are here? Can you believe this is happening?" I went to the Forum early because I couldn't sleep in the afternoon. Inside the arena, I grabbed all four of my sticks and walked in the pitch-black all the way up past the reds and whites to the blues. I just sat up top, taping my sticks, sipping a cup of creamy, three-sugar coffee, drinking in all the Stanley Cup banners and squinting down at the ice. I could almost see the Forum ghosts moving around the ice. I imagined the old-time goalies, with pads only about half a foot wide and scabby gloves and those funky masks they used to wear. I thought of all those Montreal guys who played there—Jean Béliveau, the Rocket, Guy Lafleur. If I could have held on to that feeling, I would never have touched a drug or another drink. Sitting there was magical. "Wow, man," I thought, "you have gone a long way." That time in the Forum is a memory that will stay with me forever.

I had experienced a major win at the World Juniors, so I knew what the process was. "Don't get too excited, just stay calm. You can't start thinking instead of reacting." My play had to stay instinctive. As I skated out on the ice that night I just wanted to shit with excitement. I was thinking, "Where the hell are my dad and my mom sitting? They must be going bonzo." Fleurys are French—emotional, crazy. I felt an exhilarating anticipation, mixed with anxiety—"Fuck, can we just win and get this over with?"

Colin Patterson opened the scoring for us. He raced into the Montreal zone on a forecheck and stole the puck. Before the Canadiens knew what hit them, it was in the net and we were up 1–0. Claude Lemieux tied the game on a rising slapshot. Then a piece of hockey history: Lanny McDonald jumped out of the penalty box, picked up a pass from Jamie Macoun and snapped it in. Lanny raised his arms in celebration like a 10-year-old, eyes and mouth wide open. It's a highlight you see over and over again on *Hockey Night in Canada*.

Did I care for Lanny? Who wouldn't? When I was 9 years old, he was playing for the Colorado Rockies and Don Cherry was the coach. I won tickets to a game and managed to snag his autograph. First day of training camp with the Flames, I looked for my name on the lockers and who was I sitting beside? The man himself. It was trippy. Now I was his teammate, watching him score the biggest goal of his career. I started jumping up and down on the bench, just losin' it. "Yeahhhhhhh!!!!" Crispy was trying to climb up the glass behind him. The entire team went nuts. What a story! In his last NHL game, Lanny gets a picture pass and fuckin' shelves it on Patrick Roy like it's nothin'!

Vernie continued to play outstanding for us. He took a big hit behind the net. It was a sign of the Canadiens' frustration and it drew a penalty. On the power play, Killer scored a huge goal to make it 3–1. The Habs cut the lead to 3–2 when Claude Lemieux went after Vernie again. He stuck his foot behind Vernie's skate, kicking his feet out from under him, but the goal was counted anyway. Crispy blistered the ref with his opinion, but the goal stood.

When there was about five minutes left on the clock and I knew I was not going to get another shift, I began counting the clock down. But it would not go down fast enough. I would watch a little of the play, then look up—"Aw, whaddya *mean* only ten seconds gone by? What's going on?" Gilmour played the game of his life and put a lock on it with an empty-netter, and then finally—10, 9, 8, 7, 6, 5, 4 ... and helmets, sticks and gloves were flying and everybody washed over the boards into a big dog pile. Crispy picked me up and swung me around. And then I carried the Cup around the Forum ice. I couldn't believe it!

I was one of the first guys off the ice, and there was champagne in the room. So I started shaking one of the bottles, and the cork popped off and hit Rick Wamsley right between the eyes. Wamsley was Vernie's backup, a really good goalie and a great guy in the room. He was one of the funniest guys on the team. He was nearly ten years older than me and I respected him, so I immediately said, "Oh, man! I'm sorry, man." He grabbed the bottle—"That's okay, kid"—and he started guzzling champagne, wearing this big, shit-eating grin while a toe-sized welt grew on his forehead. I got hammered, and was having the best time of my life, but we had to catch the charter back to Calgary. I would not take my equipment off until Bear said, "Hey, everybody's getting on the bus." I showered fast and changed, and we drank and partied some more on the plane and landed in Calgary about four in the morning. I was annihilated. Not just drunk, but exhausted. That night seemed to last for months.

There's a tradition that continues to this day—every player gets to keep the Cup for a day and overnight. Usually, they take it back to their hometown and have a party for family and friends, old coaches, people in the neighbourhood who helped them make it to The Show.

Some of the parties get pretty wild. The Cup has splashed around in more than one swimming pool, and at least once some guy has left it behind in a taxi. I was the last guy to get the Cup overnight because I was the youngest on the team. When I picked it up at the rink in November 1989, I remember saying to myself, "Hey, I could take it to Mexico if I wanted—who would know?" There was no Cup handler back then. Today, a representative of the Hockey Hall of Fame escorts the Cup all over the place. He's like a Secret Service agent guarding the American president, only in this case he's wearing white gloves and hauling the Stanley Cup.

I had a bunch of friends over and took some pictures with it. Then, when it was time to go to bed, I said to Shannon, "I'm sleepin' with the Cup tonight. Out." I put it right in bed with me, one leg over the bottom and arm around the neck—just like one of those body pillows—and slept with it. I remember waking the next morning, running my fingers over all the names engraved on it and finding mine and thinking, "Cool."

10

THAT GOAL AGAINST EDMONTON

IN MY FIRST full NHL season, 1989–90, I had 31 goals and 35 assists for 66 points altogether. Things started out well for me. I remember a game against the Hawks in November when I put up two goals and an assist. Their goalie, Alain Chevrier, was still pissed about the playoffs, so he had a few comments for me each time I skated past. And I had some choice remarks for him too. At the end of the second period, he tried to trip me with his stick, so I fell right into him. He lost it and started to beat me with his blocker. It turned the game into a real war between us. I thought I had one in when Newie made a pass and I sniped the puck toward an open left side, but Chevrier sprawled across and snagged it. The game was 4–3 for the Hawks, with seven minutes left, when I found myself in front. I snapped it in and beaked him, "Take that, you sawed-off little runt." Revenge is sweet.

We had some remarkable games as a team that season. We crushed the Leafs 12–2 on February 23, and toward the end of the year we were on a six-game unbeaten streak and won the Smythe Division title by nine points over the Oilers, finishing second overall in the NHL. It looked like we had a good chance to repeat our Stanley Cup championship. But by the playoffs, things had started to go south. We got knocked out in the first round, partly due to a goal in game six that was clearly in the net but was called back. If that goal had counted, we wouldn't have lost in overtime and who knows what might have happened? But we were eliminated early and our coach, Terry Crisp, got his walking papers that May.

Today, Crispy has the best job ever, as a broadcaster with the Nashville Predators, but back then he had problems with the Flames' owners. They had asked him to hold it down on the bench because fans were complaining about his language. Personally, I liked the guy. Crispy always had time for his players.

No excuses, but I was injured after Christmas—a second-degree sprain of a medial collateral ligament just before Valentine's Day. I didn't get out of the way quick enough when some big Quebec Nordique freight train came at me. It was kind of scary, and as I hit the ice I thought, "Aw heck, I just made it to The Big Show. Is this what it's going to look like for the rest of my career?" I finished the game, of course. I was playing on the best team in hockey, and there was no way I was going to wimp out. By the end of the third period my knee was pretty wonky. I could not put much weight on it, and I could bend it both ways, but I had learned how to block out pain. Go somewhere else.

At the end of the 1990–91 season, I sustained another fairly serious injury. We were in Los Angeles, and I ran into Tony Granato. We were two yappy little guys. I did not particularly like Mr. Granato, so I went out of my way to try to hurt him but ended up hurting myself. I've since met him off the ice and he's a great guy, but I was jealous. He was a college guy. He'd just been named to the NHL all-rookie team, and because I'd started halfway through my first season, my stats weren't good enough to put me in consideration. He was always in my face, most of the time with jokes about my height. This was particularly irritating because he wasn't much bigger than I was. He'd say, "Oh you little fuckin' short shit," and I would respond, "They are going to take you out of here in a body bag, asshole." The usual clever back and forth. What I should have done was grab him and beat the shit out of him—embarrass him in front of everybody.

So it was late in the regular season, and we were getting killed, losing really badly to L.A. Tony was coming up the ice and I was stuck in the railway tracks. He made a move and I went to stop him with my knee out and—*bam!* Knee on knee. Down I went.

It was particularly bad timing for me. I was only three goals away from fifty for the season. Luckily, we had four full days off after that game. I came back to Calgary and did some physio. We were scheduled to play Vancouver next. I was hurt really bad, my knee was super loose, but c'mon, I was three goals away! So I participated in the morning skate and then saw the doctor. I was sitting on the table and he started reefing on it. I mean, the bone was moving from one side to the other. It fuckin' hurt like hell. I acted like I didn't notice. "Feels fine." I *had* to play. I had to get to fifty. He told me to squat down and duck-walk around his entire office. Each step was like a knife ripping up my entire leg. He was watching my face, so I kept it neutral. I shrugged, hopped back up on the table and shook it around. "No problem, doc."

He stared at me a minute, trying to figure out why I could not feel this knee that was so obviously torn up. I kept grinning at him like I was really happy it was all better.

"Okay," he said, "everything is fine. Let's see how you feel in the warmup. Bearcat will tape your knee." He and Bearcat stood at the edge of the boards, watching. Circling, I caught my toe on an edge and my knee was jarred. It Ping-Ponged—crunching bone against bone— for a second and I dropped. Bearcat started out the gate, yelling, "What happened there?" I got up, said, "Aw, I just fell the wrong way," and skated away. Riser got wind that I was on the ice. He was the Flames' GM by this time and he ordered me into his office. The doctor had told him I had a six-week injury, and because I was our best scorer Riser was thinking I should rest in order to be back for the first round of playoffs. "Theo," he said, "forget the fifty goals. This is not about fifty goals, we gotta make sure you're ready for playoffs."

I shrugged. "My knee doesn't bother me, seriously."

Riser didn't believe me. "You gotta think about the team. You can't be playing hurt." I looked him straight in the eye. "Doug, it doesn't hurt. I feel good." That night, I got a hat trick and made my target. God was looking after me.

We met up with the Oilers in the first round, but by that time my knee was hamburger. Thankfully, it didn't *look* injured and when I taped it up, that gave it some real stability. I was going for ultrasound treatments, icing it and using electrical stimulation on it, but during the course of the game I would get a little twang and start hanging on by my fingernails.

It was just an unbelievable series. Edmonton had finished the season twenty points behind us, but they brought everything they had to that series. Each game was like a game of road hockey, like you'd play on the street in front of your house. And it was a dream series for a player like me—an absolute war. Men were men, and if you weren't a man you got put out of commission early. You know how you see players tap each other with their sticks and it's called slashing? What we did was come at each other with full baseball-bat swings. It was nuts. But it was fun, so much fun. Sather put the defence pair of Jeff Beukeboom and Steve Smith on me every shift. Beukeboom was Newie's cousin. He was six foot five, 230 pounds, and Smith was six-three and 215. Every single shift of every game I played, I was up against those two giants, and their sole purpose was to try to wear me down. They used anything they could on me—cross-checks, slashing, elbows, whatever it took. It felt like I was part of the Battle of Falkirk from *Braveheart,* and I loved it. I loved that kind of pressure. These are the situations an elite athlete dreams about playing in, wants to be a part of. I know that there is nothing in my life, with the exception of my kids being born, that will give me another blast like playing in those types of situations. People don't find themselves in situations that spectacular in everyday life.

We split the first two games in Calgary, both by 3-1 scores, then Edmonton won the next two at home, putting us down three games to one. Fifty goals during the regular season and I still hadn't scored in the series. Again, I'm not offering excuses, but my knee was killing me. Back in Calgary for game five, we won 5-3, avoiding elimination and sending the series back to Edmonton.

It was a really, really close game, back and forth, and it went into overtime. Mark Messier circled back and was looking to pass across the ice. I anticipated it, scooped up the puck and skated right between Beukeboom and Smith in a foot race—which was easy 'cause those guys were big and slow. Suddenly, I was one-on-one against their goalie, Grant Fuhr, and as I stickhandled the puck toward the net, it jumped onto its edge. I saw a tiny opening between Fuhr's legs—a gap literally the width of a sideways puck. I lifted my back skate and shot. It went in. In the blink of an eye I had scored the biggest goal of my entire life—on one leg. I felt like I had a rocket strapped to my back as I moved past the net with my stick in the air, then ran down the left side of the ice past our team. I made it to centre ice and went down on my knees, punching the air. Momentum took me sliding into the boards while I pounded on the ice. I could see Newie coming at me full steam, a grin as big as an ass crack plastered all over his face. I flipped over and hit the side boards with my feet in the air while everyone piled on.

Those five seconds made life worth living. No drink or drug that I have tried since—and I'm talking about cocaine, weed, whatever—compares to the feeling I had at that moment. If you tune in the NHL Network, they probably show that goal fifty times a day. I remember being on *Hockey Night in Canada* with Don Cherry and Ron MacLean afterward. I was a little smoother than I had been at Piestany but still out of breath with excitement.

That win allowed us to go back to Calgary for game seven, April 17, 1991. It was a phenomenal opportunity for us. Glenn Anderson was going down the left wing near the boards. I had him lined up, and just as I went to hit him he ducked and I went right over top of him, hitting my right shoulder square on top of the boards. I don't know what made more noise—the sound of my shoulder dislocating or the crunch against the wood. I got up, struggling to get it to pop back in and yelling at Bearcat to come help me. He bent down and had me hang over his back so that gravity would pop it back in place. It did and I skated back into the play.

The muscles in my shoulder had been stretched and torn and were screaming at me. With everything on the line, I allowed the team doctor to shoot me up with local anesthetic. Before the game, he'd asked me if I might be more comfortable if we put some freezing in my knee and I had agreed. Now, with my shoulder on fire, I was like, "Pullllease!!!" He did it right in the dressing room. It was no big deal, and I have no clue what he put in there. All I know is that when I got the shot, I could move my arm around and my knee wasn't full of sharp, broken glass. I would enter a world of hurt by the time I got home, but painkillers and a couple beers took care of that.

But you know, that is the way hockey was back then. That was the old school, and I am damn proud of it. I have more respect for that era than any era that came after. The players were true-blue guys—men. There was something special about the group from the early '80s through the salary cap era. It consisted of a breed of player that you'll never see again. I am talking about Wayne Gretzky, Mario Lemieux, Mark Messier, Steve Yzerman, Ron Francis—so many unbelievable guys. Joe Sakic, Peter Forsberg, Paul Kariya and Chris Pronger. All of them played the same way—creative and hungry. Now you have your top three guys on every team and everybody else is just a Stepford wife. They all look the same, they all play the same. This is how the game has evolved.

We were up 3–0 after the first period, and I had scored one and had an assist on another. The Oilers were even by the end of the second, and they pulled ahead in the third on a goal by Anatoli Semenov. Then, with two minutes left to play in the third, Ronnie Stern put one in for us and we were tied at four. We ended up going to overtime, and at 6:58 Esa Tikkanen banked it in off Frankie Musil—a lucky goal. You go from being on top of the world to the lowest point humanly possible. And for me, emotional pain was a lot tougher to deal with than physical pain. As soon as I hit the dressing room I just started bawling. I couldn't believe hockey was over. Al MacNeil, one of the Flames' great hockey guys, always made me feel a little better. He always had something nice to say. I would wonder what it might have been like to have a father like him. I know things would have been easier, that's for sure.

I look back now and I think, "Fuck, that was insane!" It was all about playing, all about winning, all about the team, and I didn't want to let the team down. Losing to Edmonton was a heartbreaking early playoff exit.

I went on a good drunk for a few days. I started out at a bar, and when it closed I found a buddy's place. I drank everything in his house—beer, whisky, whatever. Then back to the bar. I kept it up thanks to a little help from cocaine and marijuana. It took me four or five days with no sleep to get the loss out of my system. This became standard procedure for me at the end of every year. I set my record for consecutive days partying in 1998, when I stayed up for the entire Calgary Stampede—that's ten days. Hey, as long as hockey season was over I figured I wasn't doing anything wrong. Do you think I really cared that I had someone at home waiting up all night for me? It was the end of the year, man. I was just having fun.

11

LEAVE ME ALONE

MY LIFE WAS HOCKEY. And when your life is built around something you cannot be totally honest about, it eats at you. I had to be tough, never show weakness. A coach would never put you on the ice if you expressed your real feelings. "How you feeling tonight, Theo?" "I'm feeling really blue right now. I feel real sad." You think he's gonna put me on the ice? No way. So I would say, "I'm fuckin' pissed off tonight!" and I could bet I would be on the ice for first shift. "That's awesome, perfect. Keep that feeling!" Underneath anger is sadness. If you are not happy, what do you project? You project anger. What does anger say? It says, "Leave me the fuck alone."

When they traded Brett Hull to St. Louis in 1988, the year before we won the Stanley Cup, I thought, "Great—maybe they're making room for me." Cliff Fletcher said he might go down in history as having made the stupidest trade ever in the NHL, because he knew Brett was going to be a star, but he made the trade to benefit the team. At that time the chemistry was off and the Flames needed more of a veteran presence. And to be honest, I don't think *anybody* expected Brett Hull to score 86 goals in a season like he did in 1990–91. Those are Wayne Gretzky numbers. The players we got in return, Rob Ramage and Rick Wamsley, turned out to be two amazing team guys with a tremendous amount of leadership, so they fit into the puzzle. Did the Flames make a mistake? No, because they won a Stanley Cup thanks to that trade.

We could have brought the Cup back to Calgary a few more times, but the team broke up. Fletcher let Håkan Loob out of his contract so he could raise his family in Sweden. Lanny and Pepper retired and Joe Mullen was traded to Pittsburgh prior to the start of the 1990–91 season. I had come into the organization as a centreman, but when they traded Mullie there was nobody to play with Dougie Gilmour. Riser came to me and said, "What do you think about playing right wing?" I asked if it meant I would get to play with Dougie Gilmour and he said yes, it would. So I told him I would do whatever it took. Paul Ranheim was our left winger, but Ranheim broke his leg in December. Riser switched me to a new line, with Nieuwendyk and rookie Tim Sweeney, which was okay too. I was versatile. If I played with a centreman who passed, I'd shoot. If I played with a sniper, I'd pass. No problem.

I ended up scoring 50 goals that year, my first 100-point season. Being only three years into the league, I was like, "Holy cow, this is really happening fast."

You had to earn your ice time with Risebrough. You had to go out every night and play committed—his kind of game. I was expected to score and to shake things up. So I did. I was fired up when I got my first NHL hat trick on December 5, 1990, downing the Rangers 4–1. I got another a couple of months later, on February 18, 1991, in a 7–4 win against the Blues. I was on a team with Newie, Killer, Sergei Makarov and Robert Reichel, and I was the highest-scoring forward. It felt unbelievable.

A lot of it had to do with intimidation. I had to protect myself, and the best way to do that was to have people believe I was crazy. I wanted them to be looking over their shoulder when I was on the ice. I wanted them wondering, "What is he going to do tonight? Cut my eye out or kiss me?" This was my competitive advantage. I didn't have size, but I was volatile. There has yet to be a player my size in the NHL who played the way I played. What sets me apart from every other little guy who has tried to make it is stamina. Teams found out that they could beat the shit out of me and I would not back down. I would not fold up—in fact, the pressure made me improve. I made the choice to live by the sword. The blood I left on the ice was the price.

Moving into junior, I knew I was going to be tested. In minor hockey, I basically had the puck the whole game. Few had the skill level that I had. It was tough to catch me. But when I made the transition from bantam to junior hockey in less than a year, I found bigger, badder, stronger bullies on the playground. It was a shock, quite frankly. Suddenly, I didn't have the puck all the time. I had to go get the puck. Well, how was I going to do that without getting killed? I found out in a Western Hockey League exhibition game against Brandon.

I was going wide down the boards and this big defenceman closed in on me. I told myself, "All right, you're gonna get smoked. Hard. Do something after you're hit." As I went down, I hung on to the puck and made a hell of a play to one of my teammates, and he went in and scored. On the very next shift, I made sure to dump the puck into that same big defenceman's corner. When he went for it, I jumped up with a little elbow to the chops and he dropped like a sack of pucks. He went after me later but with a little less enthusiasm.

I had a hard-nosed attitude. Instead of shying away from people and trying to avoid not getting hit, I just banged into people. I controlled the hit. Bearcat always said the body reacts a lot differently when it is hitting compared to getting hit. When you are hitting, your muscles are set and the body is gung ho and holding everything in place, but when you are hit, your muscles are not ready so you are not in a strength position. Sometimes, what looked like me being crazy out there and going after everything in sight was simply injury prevention. Other times it was just the unpredictability of my game, which turned out to be my greatest asset. Nobody knew what the hell I was going to do. Half the time it was an act, and the rest of the time I was serious.

Don't get me wrong. Thanks to what I had been through, I was angry and I played angry. Every professional coach I had could see that if you got me pissed off, you would double the threat that I'd beat you. But it was rarely anger gone out of control. I funnelled it and used it. At night, I would visualize my plan for the next game. It helped me sleep. In addition to all my other ghosts, I had begun agonizing over my on-ice mistakes. Elite athletes spend way too much time going over situations and plays and wins and losses—"What could I have done better? What if I had done something different?" Now I know it's just wasted energy. The best thing is to move on, try to do better the next day.

I worked on all kinds of ad libs to throw at the opposition. I was on the ice in junior with my linemates, Kelly Buchberger and Mike Keane, while Dave Manson was playing for the Prince Albert Raiders. Manson was on the blue line, and as we lined up for the faceoff I said, "Do you have any naked pictures of your girlfriend?" Manson replied, "Fuck you. No I don't." "Do you want some?" The puck dropped and Manson started chasing me all over. I was ready to stand up for myself, but there was no way Kelly Buchberger was going to let that happen. Not with a guy like Manson, a legitimate heavyweight, ready to kill me. He stepped in and everybody took hold of somebody and we had a line brawl. Another of my favourites was, "I'm gonna carve your fuckin' eye out," which I would follow with a subtle air jab with my stick. A one-eyed hockey player, even if he is six foot four and 230 pounds, doesn't do anyone much good. My opponent would unconsciously back away a bit as he pictured my blade slicing across his eyeball.

When I first started saying this stuff, players were kind of shocked. They would wonder, "Who the hell is this little fucker?" Then they'd laugh it off and say, "Yeah, yeah, yeah. Big talker, big talker." And so I would do things behind the play to show them I was serious. A little whack in the back of the legs, a nice spear in the crowd, a butt end in the ribs. I used my stick as the great equalizer. If somebody wanted me, I'd put my stick up and they'd have to come through it to get to me. It was a matter of survival. There were a couple times when I didn't have enough time to get either my stick or my elbow up. I took some big hits, but I would get right back up and say something lippy.

It was best to say things that would get under the guy's skin. You had to be sharp, but the right remark could really shut a guy down. We played Chicago on February 3, 1991, when they were the top-ranked team. Their coach, Mike Keenan, had been convicted that December on a drunk-driving charge. I was on the faceoff and Keenan was chirping at me from the safety of the bench, as usual. I turned to him and said, "Hey Mike, do you need to borrow my driver's licence to get home?" His whole bench was laughing so hard they had to bury their heads in their gloves, and Keenan had nothing more to say to me the rest of the game. I guess he didn't want me to bring up his DUI again. It was a good night. I tied it up by scoring our first goal on a five-on-three and set up the second by being the first to the puck at their blue line and sending it to Killer, who fired in a backhander. We won 3–1.

One time in Los Angeles, Marty McSorley and I got separated from the group during a big fight. He could see that the referee and the linesmen were busy, so McSorley, the big dumb fuck, grabbed the collar of my jersey, held me up about four inches off the ice, pulled back his massive forearm and just suckered me. I found myself staring at the ice, trying to remember my name. There were ten thousand hot needles ripping at the front of my brain and tearing a path behind the bridge of my nose down into my top lip. It was the kind of hurt that takes you beyond screaming to something that feels like the sound of a dentist's drill. I forced myself up and sneered at him, "Is that all you got?" Fuck, was he mad.

In another game, I was lined up against Detroit's Bob Probert, the undisputed heavyweight champion of the ice at the time, and I challenged him. "Okay, Probie, you and me, centre ice . . . let's go."

He started laughing. "You crazy little son of a bitch. You would too, wouldn't ya?"

The secret is that if you show the tiniest clue that you are intimidated or afraid, you are finished.

When I was in junior, I had never been hurt, except for the cut on my arm. Then when I was 16, we were playing at the Stampede Corral in Calgary, against the Wranglers. I was standing in front of the net when one of my teammates came out of the corner. His back was to me and his stick was up as he pivoted to go after a pass. *Wham!* He got me right on the gum under my lip. Three front teeth cracked off just liked icicles—gone. I was bleeding pretty badly, so they took me back to the dressing room, sat me down on one of those old shitty wooden and vinyl chairs and shot my mouth up with freezing. There was so much blood, the trainer had to keep seesawing my head back and forth so I wouldn't choke on it as they sewed me up. I made it back for the third period. My lip was out to here, but they were just teeth. I knew something like that would happen eventually.

The next night, we had to play in Moose Jaw, so we bused it all night long right after the game. A couple of hours into the ride, the freezing wore off and those three exposed roots caught fire every time I inhaled or exhaled. This went on for nine hours—no sleep. They had arranged for a dentist to give me three root canals with caps. I went straight from the bus into his chair, and straight from his chair onto the ice that night. I didn't know any better, but you know what? That is what makes the good players great. And then there are guys like Peter Forsberg. He's made of glass—unbelievable talent, but he's made of glass. It's not his fault, it's just genetics.

I HAD ALWAYS taken retaliation penalties, which were usually bad for the team but necessary for my survival. I was unrelenting. If I hit a big guy and he whacked me back, hoping I'd learn my lesson, I would come back even harder. I was ferocious. I had to be.

When Riser was head coach, I'd get called in and he would sit there looking kind of relaxed and try to reason with me. "Look, we can't afford some of these penalties. You are one of my best scorers and I can't have you in the box all night." He said the problem with a bad penalty wasn't just the penalty, it was the way I reacted and pissed off the refs. "Theo, you're going to be looked at as a complainer. You can't get these guys not on your side. You need a little help." He was worried about how long I would last if the refs got so mad they would ignore it when guys went after me. And by the time I played for Chicago, this prediction would turn out to be true.

Other times, I'd open the door to his office and could just *feel* Riser's anger. He'd start by sitting back, arms crossed, trying to resist the urge to reach across the desk and throw me into a wall. I always felt badly, especially if we'd lost, but I would try to explain to him that if I let one guy take me out without doing anything about it, the next guy would be standing in line behind him. So I made no exceptions, even when the game was on the line. I couldn't. Riser was totally about putting the team first, at any cost, so he would get madder and madder, his face getting darker and darker. Then he'd explode, ordering me not to take any more goddamn stupid penalties. In the end, we'd talk it out and reach an agreement, and in the next game I would make it up to the team by playing awesome. He helped me out by boosting my tough-guy image in order to intimidate the other teams. He admitted to the press that I did take the odd bad penalty because when I got hit I answered. Doug Risebrough—toughest guy ever. He had my respect. That's how it was with him.

Most coaches are fucking idiots. Seriously, they are. It's unbelievable. They all think winning will come with some magic system. I guess they're under too much pressure. The key to being a good coach is people management—getting the most out of each individual without breaking them down. It's easy to be in authority and put somebody down. Simple. But can most coaches back it up? No, they can't. So many are wimps, and they're all scared. How do they project themselves? They say, "I'm higher, I'm mightier than you, and I can control you." And out of respect for your teammates, you don't say anything to disrupt the team.

There is so much money involved now that coaches cannot afford to lose. So what do they teach? Defence. They say it is what wins Stanley Cups. Trouble is, it is not much fun to watch a 0–0 hockey game. Five guys skating backwards through the neutral zone—who wants to watch that? If I have possession of the puck, why would I voluntarily give it up? I know there are certain times when you get backed into a corner and there's not much you can do other than throw the puck away. But pros are skilled. I don't enjoy watching hockey as much now.

I played for Dave King between 1991–92 and 1994–95. His idea of a perfect game was a 0–0 tie with a scoring chance in the last minute. I did not care what he said, superstars don't have to listen. That's why I like the Crosbys, Kovalchuks and Ovechkins of the world, because no matter what the coach tells them, they are going to play their way. In the end, they are paid to get the puck in the neutral zone, skate as fast as they can, beat somebody one-on-one and score. It gets the crowd standing in their seats. Hey, that's what it's all about. The team that scores the most goals wins the game, right? So they get four on you, you'd better get five. They get eight, you'd better get nine.

It's all systems today. It's robotic, stupid and boring as hell for the fans. If I were coaching today, my teams would have fun playing. But I probably wouldn't have a job for long, because both sides would rack up the goals. The guys would love playing for me because there would be so few rules, and we'd play the game the way it is supposed to be played—offensively.

The coaches that bug me the most are the ones who've never

played. Some of them come in after a game and take down a guy who is all cut up. One time I had stitches, bleeding all over the place, and King called me in and told me I was ripping the team off. I looked like I'd been in a war, and he was telling me I wasn't fucking working hard. Tell me, Dave, have you ever felt like that? I mean it—have you ever felt like that? No, you haven't, because you have never paid the price. Few have.

Or say a guy sprains his ankle. He comes in before a game and tells the coach he's hurt. Coach will say, "What do you mean you're fuckin' hurt?" The player will say, "I know when I'm hurt. I'm going to give you all I can tonight, but I'm telling ya right now, I'm hurt." Coach looks at him and shakes his head. "Doesn't matter. Get out there. Ankle? Long ways from the heart. Get out there. Suck it up."

There were times I was barely able to walk into the rink—ankle, shoulder, knee, concussion—but I was too proud. I could count on one hand the times I said I was injured, but even then I still heard it—"Get out there. Suck it up."

Coaches who never played break guys down. Guys like me who became superstars, we would laugh at them. Because you know what? As long as I was scoring goals, they couldn't touch me. I had power. At the 1991 Canada Cup, Mike Keenan was the coach. There was so much talent on that team, his job was to open the gate. What's he gonna do? Play head games with Gretzky? Wayne would have laughed and told him to fuck off.

Keenan never touched a star. He'd go after a third- or fourth-line player to make an example of him. And the poor guy had to think about his family. He had to put food on the table.

I saw it all the time with coaches. They'd come up after a game and say, "You're fuckin' useless. What the fuck is wrong with you?" And that's fine, as long as he does it behind closed doors, one on one. But a coach should never embarrass a guy in front of his teammates.

When Dave King was coaching, he was a great teacher, but a sarcastic guy. He'd stir guys up to fight by belittling them. You never do that. I mean, the player knows his job. He knows he needs to go out there. If the other team was having a good game, King would cross his arms and stare across the ice and say something like, "Enjoying the show?" He wanted to change the momentum of the game. But a question for you, Dave: have you ever gone out and fought to change the momentum of a game in your life? Unless you are willing to do it, you can't tell somebody else to go out and fight. You've gotta show it to the team, otherwise keep your fucking mouth shut and coach.

Pierre Pagé was the Flames' coach from 1995–96 to 1996–97, and I didn't believe in what he was coaching. I didn't like where the team was going or the direction it was going in. It wasn't a very talented team, and it wasn't very fun to play in Calgary at the time. The only chance we had of winning was if we outworked the other team.

I knew Pierre from my first training camp. He was probably one of the nicest guys you'll ever meet away from the rink, but it was straight comedy on ice with that guy. He was really out there. His thoughts about how the game should be played, and how you should handle yourself on and off the ice, did not mesh with mine. He has a master's degree in physical education and his thesis was on the biomechanics of skating—in other words, why some people skate better than others. Pierre figured it came down to the angle of the knee. I have it figured differently. My theory is, you skate better when you try harder.

One night in Dallas, it was something like 4–0 for the Stars within the first five minutes. At the end of the first period, Pierre came into the dressing room and said, "Everybody stand up." We looked at each other, but we got to our feet. He threw his arms out wide and said, "Put your arms out like this, tilt your heads back and take some deep breaths." At this point I realized, "This guy has fuckin' lost his mind." I couldn't stop laughing. It was such stupid stuff, man.

One time he came jumping into the hockey room like he was hunting rabbits. He was diving around, hiding behind stuff. He seemed to like to hide, because when we were on road trips he would conceal himself behind plants in the hotel lobby, trying to catch people out after curfew. I'd walk in and wave. "Hey, Pierre, how's it going?"

Pierre was so preoccupied that he would come running out on the ice with his skate guards still on and he'd be falling and flying all over the place. He always had three hundred things going on in his head. We were playing in Montreal one night, and we were going out on the power play and he called up Sundin, Sakic and Nolan. I turned around and said, "Pierre, we're *Calgary.* I wish those guys were here, but . . ."

At the end of the second year, I told Al Coates, our general manager, "Either you fire him or trade me, 'cause I can't go through another year with him as a coach." Pierre was gone that summer, ending up behind the Anaheim bench the next season.

Bearcat Murray was at the Sutter golf tourney in Edmonton, and on his way home he got a call from his wife telling him that Pierre had quit. Bearcat called Brian Sutter, who he had just left half an hour before. Sutter's last head coaching job had been with the Bruins from 1992–93 to '94–95. Brian told Bearcat that he had been getting offers from all over the NHL and that Philadelphia was really being persistent, but he didn't want to go there. Bearcat told him to call up Coatsie. He did, and—*boom!*—he got the job.

From an NHL player's perspective, if you want respect as a coach, you have to be willing to put your stuff on and sit beside me. I will get out there if you are willing to get your head beaten in with me. Dress and go to war with me, I'll do anything you want. Maybe I don't know enough about you, and maybe you have had some struggles in your life. But when it comes to the game, you haven't done any of the things I have been willing to do to get here. So until you show me some quality about yourself that makes me believe you have the right to come in here and degrade me, fuck off.

Lots of guys have what it takes. Risebrough, he was there. Crispy won a couple of Stanley Cups. Sutter played. Those kind of guys I respect because they know how players feel. Who don't I respect? The Dave Kings, Mike Keenans and Pierre Pagés of the world. They are your Xs and Os guys. Technical guys. Pierre was a coach who liked lots of video sessions—video after video after video. The truth is, it's a simple game. If your talent outworks the other team's talent, most nights you're going to win. But if your talent gets outworked, you're probably going to lose.

12

THE TERRIBLE TRADE

IN THE SPRING OF 1991 I was invited to play for Canada in the World Championships in Turku, Finland. I told them, "I am seriously injured. I can't go," and they said, "Well, we need ya. We would really love for you to come and play."

"Yeah, I would love to come and play too," I said, "but I'm really hurt." They said, "Have you been using freezing during the playoffs?" I told them I had. "Well, we can do the same thing here," they said.

"Okay, sure," I said. "Why not?" I don't know if my durability was something I acquired or if it was part of my DNA, but I could play really, really hurt and banged up.

We ended up winning the silver medal. Problem was, we had to beat the USA by five goals, while the Russians had to at least tie the Swedes. We did our part, beating the Americans 9–4 with two goals in the last fifteen seconds. That kept our hopes alive. But then Sweden beat the Russians 2–1 on a goal by Mats Sundin, taking the gold right from under our noses. Canadians don't play for silver, so it sucked. Damn that Sundin. It would have been awesome to add that gold to the collection. Anytime I played for Team Canada was a wonderful experience, and I was very fortunate to play for them nine times in my career.

Cliff Fletcher, our GM, had just moved to Toronto with the Leafs, and Doug Risebrough came up through the ranks to take his place.

Risebrough was old school. So was I, for that matter. In my mind, a hockey team worked like the military. You don't question authority, you collect your paycheque and do as you are told.

Fletcher had mentored Riser, so Riser had a lot of trust and respect for his former boss. But just as Fletcher was tough and single-minded while building our team, he was the same when he moved to Toronto. And Risebrough forgot one very important thing. Hockey is war, and you have no friends in war.

Anyway, Dougie Gilmour was looking for more money, which he deserved, but Riser took it personally. He and Killer didn't see eye to eye. Risebrough had five Stanley Cup rings—four playing with Montreal and one as our assistant coach. He was fearless. He had proven himself to Flames fans during the Battle of Alberta, in a home game in the 1985–86 season. Risebrough, at five foot eleven and 183 pounds, took on the Oilers' big goon, Marty McSorley, who was six-two, 235, and nearly ten years younger. McSorley got the upper hand in the fight, but Riser managed to come away with McSorley's blue road jersey. He took it with him into the box and sat there slashing his skates through it, cutting the sweater to ribbons. Then he tossed it back to McSorley, who was so pissed he was purple.

Anyway, Riser had been an excellent soldier the whole time he played. And he did not exactly approve of what he saw as the new, more glamorous NHL. His teammates had been some of the greatest hockey players of all time—Guy Lapointe, Larry Robinson, Serge Savard, Bob Gainey, Jacques Lemaire, Guy Lafleur, Yvan Cournoyer—and they all did what they were told. Not one of them ever held out for more money. So not only did Risebrough fail to understand the kind of heartthrob celebrity Dougie Gilmour was achieving due to his good looks (Killer spent a lot of time on his hair and stuff, and I don't think Riser knew what to make of that), but he couldn't believe Gilmour had the temerity to walk out and sit on the sidelines just because his contract was not settled.

Killer and Riser were feuding even before Doug was coach or GM. When Riser was an assistant coach before the Stanley Cup, Gilmour was sick and tired of being told, "I want you to be my Guy Carbonneau. I want you to be a defensive player like Guy Carbonneau." Gilmour pictured himself as more than a defensive player. He had both offensive *and* defensive talent, and he was fed up with Doug wanting him to be Carbonneau and not Gilmour.

So when Risebrough became head coach and went on with this Carbonneau business, Gilmour said, "Okay, Doug, you want me to be a defensive specialist like Carbonneau? Then *pay me* like Carbonneau." That very year, Carbonneau had signed a million-dollar contract, a lot of money at the time. But Riser would hear none of it. He was pretty thrifty. He was a novice GM and he was trying to stay within the team's budget, trying to prove himself.

Billy Hay was our new president. Now, Billy was a super-nice guy, and a former hockey great with Chicago, where he was rookie of the year and played on a line with Bobby Hull. After hockey, he went into oil and gas and was very successful. Billy Hay was old school too, so he also refused to up Gilmour's contract offer. The end result was a knee-jerk reaction that gutted our team.

On New Year's Eve, 1991, we beat Montreal and Gilmour had one of the best games he ever played for Calgary. Two days later, on January 2, Riser pulled the trigger on a deal that handed Doug Gilmour, Jamie Macoun, Ric Nattress, Rick Wamsley and prospect forward Kent Manderville to Toronto for forward Gary Leeman, defenceman Michel Petit, goaltender Jeff Reese, tough guy Craig Berube and prospect defenceman Alexander Godynyuk. Killer went on to score 765 more points, most of them as the heart and soul of the Leafs. And he led them through many tough playoff series, giving the Leafs their best years since 1967. Macoun had six and a half great seasons in Toronto and two more in Detroit. Leeman, a former 50-goal scorer in Toronto, played for us for just two seasons and tallied a grand total of

11 goals in that time. We lost character guys, and none of the guys we got in return worked out.

I know that sometimes what coaches and general managers know, players don't know, so chances are there was more going on behind the scenes, but it was a tough time. I really liked and respected Riser, but the Flames had made a terrible trade. It brought an end to the glory years in Calgary. The whole team struggled. I had 25 goals at the All-Star break. Things had been going nicely. Then they traded Gilmour and I scored only 8 more goals the rest of the year. When we lost the core of our team, we lost our identity.

After the trade, everyone in Calgary was pretty mad at Cliff Fletcher. Ian McKenzie and Cliff had worked together twenty-three years. Cliff called Ian shortly afterward and said, "When you come to Toronto, why don't you come and see me anymore?" Ian gave him a shot about the trade. Cliff said, "Look, what was I gonna do? Calgary was determined to make the trade. If we didn't, someone else would have."

THE TRADE took a toll on me. After having had so much success in the first few years of my career, being on a dominant team with so many great players, it was a huge disappointment. But I am not blaming it for my personal problems. By 1992 I was well into partying. In fact, I was such a highly functioning alcoholic that my excessive drinking was a secret. Let me put it this way: when I was on the ice I knew who I was, but I didn't have an identity when I left the rink. I was completely lost, so I did crazy things to try to find out who the hell I was. I had so much money that I could do whatever I wanted, and that ain't right, either. Money is power.

I hadn't touched cocaine since Salt Lake, but on February 11, 1992, after a game against the Islanders, we were at the China Club, a bar near Broadway on West 47th in New York. It was where all the famous people went. I was having a drink at the bar when this very attractive lady came up to me. We started talking and she said, "Hey, would you like to come to my bar?" I'm like, "You *own* a bar?" She was really good-looking, not slutty or anything—dark features, big brown eyes, maybe mulatto, shiny, long, black hair, kind of athletic-looking, tight jeans and a great body. So I said, "Yes, I would like that very much." She said, "Great, I've got a limo outside." I asked if I could bring one of my teammates with me. "Oh yeah, no problem." So I grabbed one of the guys—I can't say who because he's married—and we pulled up to this huge bar.

We went up to her office and she got a couple of lackeys to bring us some booze. We had a few drinks, and she opened up her drawer and pulled out this nice fuckin' kit—a mirror and a gold fuckin' straw. She chopped up a couple of lines, and we partied hard. We ended up going down to her bar, and when it closed we gathered a bunch of random people and went to our hotel, where we rented another room and kept going.

My roommate, Mark Hunter, had been hurt that night and had gone home, so I had a room all to myself. When it was almost light out, this pretty bar-owning chick and I went to the room and did our thing. She left right afterward because I said, "I've got to get to bed. The bus is leaving in a few hours for Washington."

I slept the entire way, got into Washington, and practised with the team. I felt like fuckin' death. Death! Because as much fun as coke was, when you're coming off that shit, you just want to crawl into a hole and die. That feeling, that day, was typical of the way I felt so many times throughout my career. Hung over, either busing it or flying to the next city, getting off the bus and having to practise and watch videos and then go to the hotel and sleep for sixteen hours until the very next morning. Oh yeah.

Toward the end of my career, instead of being just tired, I had periods of really bad anxiety and it got harder and harder to function. It took everything that I had to get through those days. But at the beginning it was so much fun. People wanted to be with me. I was a light, like the fuckin' sun.

13

BIZARRO WORLD

I HAD JUST BEGUN to reach my stride in the mid-'90s. I was
in peak shape, skating faster and had more skill with the puck than
ever. Then one day I woke up with a stabbing pain in my gut that
would not go away. All through 1994 I had had stomach cramps, but
I ate and drank whatever I wanted, so I wrote it off as food poison-
ing or the flu or whatever. Rule number one when you are from a
small prairie town: the only times you see a doctor are when you are
born or you are dying. You might consider getting medical attention
if you're pissing blood or having a heart attack, and childbirth is okay
too. But generally, if you pass a kidney stone—especially during har-
vest time—you do it on the tractor. Besides, I grew up with a mother
who was totally fucked up by doctors, so I did not trust them.

I was in a dressing room in Phoenix after a pre-season game
against L.A.—this was before Phoenix had a team in the NHL. It was
like somebody had taken a knife and jabbed me in the gut every five
minutes, about an inch above my right hipbone. It was so bad it took
my breath away. The team was playing another game in San Diego
the next night, but there was no way I would be able to play. The
Phoenix doctor who was on call for the game suggested I go home
and look into it. He thought it might be my appendix. That night, I
was twisted up in pain on my hotel bed.

I flew home the next morning with Rick Skaggs, our media guy,
and went to the Rocky View Hospital. I stayed there for five days

while they did a whole bunch of diagnostic tests that involved barium enemas. I was having *Dumb and Dumber* dumps every five minutes. They emptied me out completely. The doctors tested my blood and stools and stuck tubes up my ass, shooting dye up there and taking pictures. I found a new appreciation for my insides.

The pain had subsided because they had given me something, but they discovered I had a blockage eleven centimetres long in my large intestine. Thankfully, it wasn't necessary to have surgery. Instead they wanted to make the swelling go down with medication. When you have an ulcer in your intestine and it heals, the scar tissue left behind causes this blockage. It's called Crohn's disease.

Dr. Marty Cole, an expert in the field of Crohn's and colitis, took care of me. He put me on this steroid called prednisone, which is a synthetic version of a hormone called cortisol, which you produce in your adrenal glands. A lot of people gain weight on this stuff, and it's tough on the bones—it can reduce bone mass and make them brittle. This is not a good thing when you're getting pounded into the boards by minivans every night.

For me, my hands and feet swelled up, which affected my touch a bit, but my energy levels increased. I could play sixty minutes in a game and not be tired. My swollen hands and feet really bothered me, so after I'd been on the prednisone for about six months, I just threw it away. I went to a health food store and asked if they had anything for Crohn's. The guy behind the counter sold me about $2,500 worth of fuckin' garbage that I didn't need.

I was doing okay. I did have a couple of small attacks during the season, sometimes during the game, but I just kept it to myself. After a year or so, I was only having periodic attacks—mainly if I ate something that didn't agree with me, like corn, peppers, onions or anything hard to digest. Broccoli or cauliflower would just about kill me. I was determined to ignore it, and eventually it ignored me. Like so many other things in my life, it was just one of those things that went away. I'm not saying it isn't a serious disease—it is. I was unusually fortunate in that my body healed. I swear I am going to donate my body to science someday.

But getting taken down unexpectedly like that made me think I should get something else going and cash in on my name. I needed someone to help me to capitalize on the opportunity, so I hired Shannon's sister, Ryan Griffin. She already had a phys. ed. degree and had just graduated with a marketing degree from Mount Royal College in Calgary. I asked her to take care of the Theo Fleury "brand."

The first idea she brought on board was a hockey school. It was the last thing I wanted to do. "What a pain in the ass *that* would be," I said. But she convinced me. The next thing you know, we were interviewing good, qualified people to work at the school. Richard Gagnon, a trainer from Quebec who had his master's in coaching, put together the curriculum. Then we hired my son Josh's two babysitters. Why? Because of their ability to organize kids. They could learn to teach hockey, but it was more important to hire people with a background in education. We were right. The first week we had a hundred kids, and the second week we had fifty walk-ins thanks to word of mouth. We were sold out for fifteen years. We put through 720 kids per year, and there was always a waiting list.

Ryan was super organized and everything ran smoothly. But for me it was craziness, running two rinks all day plus making sure I got in a workout with my trainer, Richard Hesketh. Rich was a former decathlete, a Canadian champion. In 1988 Rich was working as a personal trainer at Heaven's Fitness downtown, making about a hundred bucks a month. Ryan called him and asked him if he could help me get into the best shape of my life and he jumped at the opportunity. The Flames hired him to train the team and he is still there today.

I had tremendous endurance. I smoked a lot of dope and drank, but it didn't seem to slow me down. There would always be the hangover from the night before. I would show up at workouts and Hesketh would say, "Holy fuck, you stink!" and I would answer, "Yeah, I haven't been to bed yet." He'd ask me if I was sure I wanted to work out, and I'd say, "Yeah, let's go." He had me up to 168 pounds or so and I was benching 300. There are stairs on Memorial Drive across from Prince's Island Park in downtown Calgary that go up the side of a huge hill. I read that if you climb these stairs 130 times you will have climbed the elevation of Mount Everest. Richard would get me to run them ten times per session. Up to the top and back down, take a thirty-second break, then do it again—interval training. I worked out religiously, and I was in stupid shape. I guess you could say in the off-season I used to climb Everest.

On the first Sunday, all the kids would come to sign up for hockey camp, and there would be a lineup. It was just packed. That lineup would go on for hours. I did not leave until every single kid had something signed. The deal was that I would sign stuff that day, but not during the week because that was reserved for hockey. Then on the final day I would sign again. It was a carrot for them.

I tried to show leadership—be first on the ice and one of the last guys to leave. It was my school—my name was on it and I was responsible for it. We had employees who met, married and had kids. We had high school and college instructors—amazing, quality people. Good players like Joel Bond, who went to Union College in Schenectady, New York, or Craig Adams, who won Stanley Cups with the Carolina Hurricanes and Pittsburgh Penguins.

I reconnected with my buddy Pete Montana through the camp. When I first moved to Moose Jaw, Pete was doing play-by-play for the Warriors. Later, Pete told me when I got on the bus for our first road trip to Prince Albert, he saw me and thought, "There is no way this kid is old enough to play in this league." I think I weighed about 125 at the time.

Pete was always good to hang with. We ended up hiring him to coach at the hockey school. Unfortunately, it became kind of a fantasy camp/babysitting service. Parents would just drop their kids off, showing no interest—not even bothering to tie their skates or bring them lunch. I was disappointed in that, so I moved it to Russell after seven years and ran it for eight more. It was a way for me to give back to my hometown. Every cent of profit went to minor hockey in Russell. We donated enough for a new ice plant.

The hockey school had one other added benefit. It gave me an opportunity to spend more time with my son Josh. I made it clear he was to be treated like every other kid—no special treatment—and he had a blast. He was a character, pretty funny and always had a lot of friends. He was a leader, and the instructors would tell me that if we got Josh in line, everybody else would fall in line too.

I was extremely proud of what we had accomplished as a team. Each year when camp ended, Shannon and I put on a barbeque at our home. That first year, the party turned into a gong show. I stood up and started talking about how proud I was of everybody, and then I burst into tears—not sobbing, but crying. The Fleurys are all pretty emotional. So I was hugging everybody and everybody was hugging me. It felt so good to have created this opportunity for others out of nothing. Later in the night, when I was absolutely blasted, I was having a smoke on the front step of my house and Pete was keeping me company. And I just crawled into Pete's lap like a kid. I mean, he was a big guy—six feet, 210 pounds. I thanked him for helping out and told him, "I love you, man. I couldn't have done this without you. This is so great. I am so happy all my friends are here." Suddenly, I needed to take all the guys in the group to the bar. "We need to go out—we're ordering a limo!" Pete said, "No, you're not going to order a limo. I'll call a couple of taxis. We'll be fine." And even though I was hammered, I knew I had found a friend who would not take advantage of our friendship.

BY 1994, it was over between Shannon and me. Our common-law relationship was toast. She tried, she really did. Shannon was very, very protective of me. Once, I mentioned to her that it bugged me that Crispy was calling me Fuckface, Numbnuts, Shithead, Flower, whatever. It felt like he didn't respect me enough to use my name. From then on, God help anyone who did not call me Theoren. Lanny was retired, so at the time I was getting the most fan mail of any player—bins and bins full. Shannon made sure to answer every letter with an autographed picture. We spent a thousand dollars a month on envelopes, stamps and photos. To this day, I still get people coming up to me and telling me that when they were kids they sent letters to their favourite hockey stars and I was the only guy who cared enough to reply.

But it was like living with a mom. She cooked and cleaned and bossed me around. Was she already a mother figure and I was attracted to that? Or did I turn her into one?

My mother was always so lunched on Valium that our home was a mess. You would open a cupboard to get a glass and instead you'd find big plates, Pepto Bismol, Tampax and cups. Next cupboard, a screwdriver, antacid, big plates and last year's mail. Nobody could eat at the table because it was covered in piles and piles of stuff. There were chunks missing from our living room ceiling because my dad and the rest of us practised our golf swings in the house. Shannon was the opposite—very organized. She packed for my road trips and, even though we made a million a year, she would search for the coupons from cereal boxes so we could save thirty-five cents on margarine.

If I wanted to buy a car she would say, "That is a lot of money!" She spent like a sensible, reasonable person, but I felt that it was very restrictive. However, in my opinion, our biggest problem was her family. There was a lot of friction with her dad. I wanted to break off contact, while she was loyal to him. I felt she was choosing him over me.

I would get drunk probably two, three times a week, and I smoked a lot of dope too. I stayed out all night and slept around. At that point, I didn't think I had a problem or an issue—I was still functioning and things seemed to be going really well. I really didn't have problems sleeping at that time, because I'd buried the whole Graham James thing. I thought, "I don't ever have to talk about this. I don't have to deal with it." Meanwhile, Shannon and Graham had become friends. She would call him for advice on how to handle me and they spent hours on the phone together. It wasn't her fault—I still had not told her about what he had done to me.

I was in my early twenties and wanted to live and enjoy my success. Rock stars, movie stars and professional athletes use people. Whoever they are with serves their purpose, and then it's time to move on.

Every time I walked through the door I would get an earful about how selfish I was, what an asshole I was, what a shitty dad I was. Blah, blah, blah. It had gotten to the point where I was with Shannon in that relationship for Josh and Josh alone. I told myself I was done giving and giving and being told I wasn't giving enough. I had never made any decisions for myself. I decided I was going to run my life from then on.

I wasn't used to quitting. So how did I deal with it? By partying. I was out every night and did not come home until it got light out. At that year's wrap-up party, Pete walked into the family room with a beer and sat down. "You look like shit," he said. "Yep, so do you," I answered. He told me he was leaving his wife, Andy. "Really? I'm leaving Shannon." There was silence for a moment. "I guess we should get a place together," I said. "Sounds good," he said. Then he asked, "So where do you want to live?" I didn't care as long as I had easy access to the Saddledome and the airport.

So Pete found a condo for us. The rent was $550 a month. I was happy with it and told him to take the big bedroom because I honestly did not give a shit. All I needed was a mattress and a dresser. Material things just didn't matter much.

I moved a couple of bags of clothing in but had still not officially broken up with Shannon. I had one leg over the fence. She wanted me to go with her to Saskatchewan to see her family and I refused. I didn't want to be a part of them anymore—there was too much dysfunction. Shannon took Josh to visit them, and Pete and I went to the bar almost every night. One night we were at a cowboy bar called Ranchman's. We were standing in a circle, talking, and a guy managed to get next to me. He was staring at my hand and said, "Is that your Stanley Cup ring?" I yanked it off and tossed it to him. "Sure, have a look!" I thought Pete was going to have a heart attack.

As far as women went, there were no ugly ones. I didn't have to do much. Pete would stand in front, screening me, and I'd let him know if I wanted someone to get through. I had to make it tough to get to me; otherwise, fans would be lined up and that might cut down on my drinking time. But women were less intimidated than guys. They would come up and ask me to dance, and Pete and I wouldn't see each other again until my bedroom door opened in the morning and some strange girl would be looking for the bathroom. Sometimes he'd ask, "Who was that?" Most times I wouldn't have a clue. "Yeah, I'm not really sure . . ." And we would both laugh.

One night, we were at another cowboy bar, Longhorns, drinking up a storm and I noticed this brunette sitting with her friends at a table. It was unusual for her to catch my eye, because I always went for blondes. She was petite—way smaller than me, and maybe 110 pounds soaking wet. I thought she was absolutely beautiful, so fresh and natural-looking. I ordered a round for her table and held up my beer to her in a toast. She nodded and smiled, and pretty soon she and a friend made their way over. She had class. "Hello," she said, "my name is Veronica and we just want to say thank you for the drinks."

I was smiling. "Hello, I am Theoren and this is my friend Pete, and you are very welcome." She held her hand out for a handshake. It was tiny. "Feel free to come and join us for a drink at our table if you would like." Then she turned and left, and Pete and I just stared at her perfect little apple ass. She and her friend were not even three-quarters of their way back to their table when I said to Pete, "Do you think I'd look too eager if we head over there right now?"

He held me back for a couple minutes, but it seemed like forever. When we joined them, she and I continued to get to know each other. I asked her what she did for a living and she told me she worked in property management as an executive assistant and that she put in a lot of hours. Then, "And what do you do?" "Oh, I play hockey," I said. Pete looked shocked. Later, he repeated the conversation back to me. "Not 'I won the Stanley Cup and I am a fifty-goal scorer.' Just, 'I play hockey.' Not, 'I play for the Flames.' Just, 'I play hockey!'"

"Do you like that?" she asked. "Oh yeah," I said, "I enjoy it. "That's good, that you like what you do," she said, and I was toast. Maybe she was just flirting with me. You would have to be deaf, dumb and blind to be in that city at that time and not know who I was. I mean, it isn't like my name was Bill or Dave or something. But at the time she seemed to have absolutely no idea who I was or what I did. Meanwhile, everyone else in the bar was like, "Omigod, Theoren Fleury is sitting at a table with eight women!"

Veronica and I saw each other constantly, and just after Shannon returned I moved all my stuff to Pete's. I left Shannon with the house, the furniture, the car, everything.

In the long run, I did her a favour. Shannon was smart—she had graduated top of her class from high school. After I left, she went back to school, got a bachelor of education and a master's in administration and supervision and married a really good guy a few years later.

There was no getting between Veronica and me. She never spent a night at my condo—I didn't bring her to the den of iniquity. In the first two months Pete and I lived together, I brought home maybe twenty girls. I needed someone there with me at night, but they were nameless and faceless. I was really lonely. I wanted someone totally focused on me. And now this girl was it.

ALL OF US NHL players had played the previous year without a collective bargaining agreement. The league was trying to negotiate a salary cap and we said, "Never," so Commissioner Gary Bettman locked us out. It was disappointing, but I wasn't devastated. The Gilmour trade plunged the Flames into a lot of lean years—we hadn't gone past the first round of the playoffs since winning the Cup in '89 and a kind of paranoia had set in around the team. Nobody wanted to be the architect of another trade disaster, so we continued to draft poorly.

When the lockout started, I told my agent, Don Baizley, to shop around and find me a place to play. I was partying every night and losing my mind because I had nothing to do. He found a team in Finland, Tappara. It was Bizarro World there—we had pictures of fuckin' chickens all over our jerseys. The Finns were good to me, and I learned a lot about European hockey, which would pay off in my upcoming international play. But, man—chickens?

Just before heading out to Finland, I went to Pete and said, "Spend as much time as you can with Veronica. Be her friend. I really care for her." When I got there, I missed her so much, I called her pretty much every night that first week. Finally, I asked her to quit her job and move to Europe. I told her, "I know you like your job, but you are an executive assistant. You can always be an executive assistant, but can you always find a person in your life who really matters to you and you love more than anything? Probably not."

That Finnish team hadn't won in forever, and in one of the first games I played for them we went into OT and I scored. It was exactly like the goal I scored against the Oilers in '91—I even dropped to my knees and spun down the ice while everyone piled on. The fans went wild. Veronica and I sent out cards from Finland. Veronica is sitting on my knee and I am wearing that fuckin' chicken jersey. Those Finns loved me, and life was good.

But one phone call was about to change all that.

14

AN OXYMORON

I WAS IN FINLAND for one month over Christmas, and then they
settled the lockout. The NHL ended up playing a 48-game schedule
that year.

I got a phone call from Graham James. When the Moose Jaw Warriors fired him in 1985, he went to Winnipeg and coached a Tier II
team there for a year. Then the Swift Current Broncos hired him as
their head coach. Both times, Sheldon Kennedy followed him. As I
understand it, when Sheldon left Swift Current in 1989, Graham fell
apart. Things started going a little crazy for him. He got careless, getting more boys involved. One of the Broncos, who would eventually
join Sheldon in charging Graham with abuse, punched him in the
nose during a game. In 1994 Graham James was told to leave Swift
Current and not let the door hit him in the balls as he backed out.

Anyway, Graham knew I was doing pretty well financially. When
I was sixteen, Len Peltz, who was like a second father to me, wrote
a letter to a well-known Winnipeg lawyer-turned-agent named Don
Baizley, trying to get some advice about what I should do. Len is a
very smart, resourceful kind of guy. He's one of the smartest people
I have ever met—you play Trivial Pursuit with him, you never get a
turn. Anyway, Don answered Len, and when it was time for me to be
drafted, Don came on board. Don was always creative with contracts.
The whole time I was with him, I never had a contract dispute. He
made sure I was not a guy who went in and tried to renegotiate. Don

always made it very clear to me that you should honour your contract—play it out and then move on to the next one. My first contract
with the Flames ran for three years, from 1988–89 through 1990–91,
and it paid $90,000 the first year, $125,000 in the second and third
years. On top of that, I'd received a $65,000 signing bonus, and a
bonus for games played that first year got me to $110,000.

In 1987–88, my last year of junior, I played for Moose Jaw until the
team was eliminated from the playoffs. The Warriors worked out a
trade for me, to Medicine Hat, who ended up winning the Memorial
Cup that year, but the Flames told me that as soon as my season was
over in Moose Jaw, I was going to Salt Lake. That was more appealing
to me than staying in the Western league. I wanted the quickest route
to the NHL, so I signed my pro contract right after we won gold at
the World Juniors

I did go to Salt Lake, where I played in two regular-season games,
racking up seven points. According to my contract, I could play only
ten games, including the playoffs. Any more than that and 1987–88
would be considered the first year of my pro contract. I played in
eight playoff games and got 7 goals and 5 assists. We won the Turner
Cup, the league championship.

In the third year of the deal, I scored 50 goals, which made me
look extremely valuable. The big money hadn't hit yet: the second
contract was for four years, at an average of $325,000 per year. After
two years, however, I was allowed to renegotiate. I did, and that is
when I signed my first big deal. Don Baizley negotiated five years for
$12.4 million U.S., or $18 million Canadian. I sat out training camp
to get it. At that point, I was one of the best players in the game. The
Flames were cheap, but without me they knew they did not have a
season. It was not all about money. It was also about competing and
being the best I could be. I loved Calgary. I've always loved it. That is
why I am back there today. The Flames gave me my shot, and for that
I was extremely loyal despite what was going on. Let's be honest: if it

weren't for me being the player I was, who knows if the team would still be in this city today?

WITH THAT SECOND CONTRACT I had more money than I knew what to do with. I had bought a house for Shannon and Josh and supported my parents. I was getting some good advice from Dave Stinton, a money manager recommended to me by Tom and Debra Mauro, friends of mine who owned Albi Homes. They helped me through a lot of tough times. Dave had me in secure investments— long-term stuff. I trusted Dave, but I had never had money and wasn't too sure about what to do with it. I was ripe for an "opportunity."

Which brings me back to Graham's phone call. "What do you think about putting a WHL team in Calgary?" he asked.

Calgary had tried bringing the Western Hockey League to town twice before, in 1966 with the Centennials, then in 1977 with the Wranglers. But it seemed that cities that had an NHL team just couldn't sustain a WHL team too. After ten years, the Wranglers moved to Lethbridge and became the Hurricanes.

I didn't tell him to go fuck himself, and it took me a long time to understand why. I guess I felt that, when dealing with Graham, it was a matter of survival. While I was writing this book, I had it explained to me in a way that made a lot of sense by a psychiatrist named Dr. Robin Reesal. He used cannibalism as an example. He said there isn't a person that would say it's acceptable, yet we have heard stories about plane crashes in remote areas where what is normally thought of as wrong is cast aside for the sake of survival. For someone who has been abused, one of the hardest things to learn is that you can go against your abuser and still survive. I know that now. I wish I'd known it then.

Yeah, in the back of my mind I was thinking about the abuse, but it was like when a Catholic Mass starts and there are six hundred people in the building and a couple of new altar boys beside a dirty priest. Chances are there are twenty or thirty guys sitting in the pews who feel pretty bad that they don't have the energy or the strength to talk to those altar boys or their parents about their history with that priest. I didn't consider myself a victim. I blamed myself and thought I had made a stupid, weak choice. I guess I figured that each one of those kids on the hockey team had a chance to make their own choice or to stop it like I did.

I think I believed that I would die as a person if I had to go back and be vulnerable again. Money and position were my protection, and I knew that if I talked about the abuse in public I might lose everything. You might be reading this and saying, "Well, you are writing about it in this book. You could lose everything *now*. What's the difference?" The difference is I am not in the NHL anymore. I have a business, I have a life. I am more secure and I understand that this person cannot control my life. Would I do the same thing today? No. Why not? Because I am no longer trapped by my past. Where is the proof? I don't drink or gamble or mess around in my marriage like I did before. I am not running. I have stopped running.

So when Graham called and said the time was right and that hockey was bigger than ever—in Calgary, especially, since we'd won the Cup—and asked if I wanted to invest in this new WHL team, he still basically had a hold on me. The way I thought, he could tank my career if he wanted. I rationalized that he was a really good coach and manager and that he could put a solid team together.

The team was set up so that there were no majority shareholders. We were all minority partners. We paid $650,000 for the franchise plus start-up costs, which amounted to about $850,000 over two years. I was first in, with a cheque for $125,000. Joe Sakic was next. Joe had also played for Graham. In fact, he was one of the players who survived that terrible bus crash that happened when I was in Piestany.

Sheldon put in $2,000 because Graham wouldn't stop calling him about it. Altogether, Graham rounded up fifteen partners, including himself and John Rittinger. John and Graham were buddies in Swift Current and then in Calgary.

A few partners were players Graham had coached in Swift. Danny Lambert was one. He was a small defenceman, but super, super skilled. A great player and a nice kid. Tyler Wright was a kid from Kamsack, Saskatchewan, a winger. He was the Oilers' first-round draft pick in 1991. Trent McCleary also played for Graham. His career ended after a freak accident during a game on January 29, 2000, while playing for Montreal. Chris Therien of the Flyers let go a slapshot and, when McCleary tried to block it by diving in front of it, the puck hit him in the throat. McCleary was rushed to a hospital and had an emergency tracheotomy. He was minutes from death. Then there was my buddy Tom Mauro, and Rusty James, Graham's brother, who I knew really well. Rusty was also a good friend of *Calgary Sun* sportswriter Eric Francis. I don't think Rusty knew about Graham. I hear they don't speak anymore. Craig Highsinger was a guy I met in Winnipeg. He started out as a trainer for a Tier II team there and now he is the general manager of the Manitoba Moose.

Former NHLer Anders Hedberg was involved as well. Paul Charles too—he scouted for Moose Jaw and Swift Current, and then he became the head scout for the Hitmen. Now he works for the Minnesota Wild. Neil McDermid, a high-profile litigation lawyer in Calgary, was also on board. Graham got a couple of my ex-teammates involved as well. Bob Bassen was on the ice when I broke Al MacInnis's team record for most points. Mark McKay, who was the captain when I played in Moose Jaw, was a great guy—small like me. He wasn't the most skilled player, but he was a hard worker and a huge overachiever. He didn't get drafted, so he went to Germany and became like a god there. He ended up getting his German passport and playing in two Olympics for them. He's a player agent now—very successful. Lorne Johnson, a farmer, and his nephew, an oil and gas guy who would become my best friend, Chuck Matson, were among the businessmen who joined the ownership group.

And finally, wrestler Bret "The Hitman" Hart was involved. Bret Hart was supposed to put in $75,000, but at the last minute he changed his mind and wrote a cheque for $25,000 instead. He felt that his involvement in the team was worth the other $50,000. I really liked and trusted Bret but not the people around him. We licensed Bret's wrestling name, agreeing to pay a percentage on the product we sold. We also used pink, which was Bret's wrestling colour. That was an oxymoron—tough guys playing hockey with pink on their jerseys.

I told Pete I'd bought a Western Hockey League team. He looked at me and said, "Holy shit. Cool." We made Pete our scouting co-ordinator. Graham would end up firing him because he was paranoid and didn't want anyone I was close to on the inside.

Chuck Matson and I met at a couple of owners' meetings and ended up visiting and talking. I think people pushed Chuck to try to strike up a friendship. Everyone saw that I needed more than my bar friends in my life, and Chuck was a really good businessman. A farm boy from Eston, Saskatchewan. Chuck broke his own rule, which is you don't get into business with people you don't know. Ever. But he thought it looked like so much fun, and he says he was mesmerized by all the "stars" who were going to be his partners. So before you know it, he'd thrown $50,000 in the hole without ever reading the partnership agreement. He says that the first time he looked out onto the ice and saw forty 16-year-old kids at camp, he thought, "Oh my God, what have I become involved with? Look at the responsibility and the liability."

Chuck isn't a big drinker, so when he and his wife, Elaine, became family friends with Veronica and me, most of the meals the four of us shared were at one of our homes rather than a restaurant. We had a private relationship, not a public one. But it was known that I really

On my way to my first-ever hockey practice, with my skates in a pillowcase over my shoulder. Who knew this picture would define so much of my life?—cold and alone.

Wally, Donna and me. I look so innocent. I'm sure my parents never thought I'd grow up to be so much trouble.

Wally Fleury and me at Williams Lake. My dad was a heavy drinker at one time. When I grew up and started indulging, he told me I could not drink what had rolled off the end of his chin.

The Russell Atom Team, otherwise known as "The Green Machine." It looks like we should have done some fundraising for new uniforms!

Does this guy look destined for greatness?

Another Manitoba Provincial B Championship with the Russell Rams. What a fantastic group of athletes and parents.

The behind-the-leg goal against the Regina Pats. (Believe me, I'm not always this cocky.)

Reprinted with permission from Roy Antal/Regina Leader Post

Shannon and me at high school grad.
Our son Josh was born eighteen
months later.

Courtesy Shannon Griffin-White

Ede and Len Peltz: integrity and class.

Courtesy Ede Peltz

At the Calgary Flames training camp in Prague, 1989. Pilsner was ten cents a glass.
That's me in the middle of the second row from the back.

Celebrating my most talked-about goal. Game 6, Flames vs. Oilers, 1991.
REPRINTED WITH PERMISSION FROM GREG SOUTHAM/*EDMONTON JOURNAL*

Shannon, Josh and me at the Stanley Cup parade in Calgary, 1989. I don't know how
the little guy slept through the whole thing.
COURTESY SHANNON GRIFFIN-WHITE

Me with "Killer" on a fishing trip in the Queen Charlotte Islands. Gilmour was the best centreman I ever played with.

Joe Sakic (left), me and Trevor Linden. Super Joe was one of the best guys in the game.

With Gary Roberts (right), a great competitor.

One of the best things I ever slept with.

COURTESY SHANNON GRIFFIN-WHITE

With Veronica at Christmas in Finland.
Man, those Finns can really drink!

COURTESY VERONICA HAUGAARD

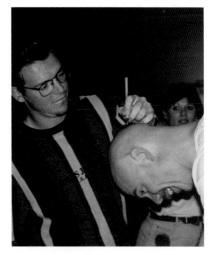

Signing Pete Montana's head. He was a
great teammate and a great friend.

COURTESY PETE MONTANA

One of our infamous after-season trips. Clockwise from left: Chuck Matson, Dwayne Roloson, Travis Fleury, Jamie Allison, Derek Morris, me (back row, centre), Wally Fleury, Cale Hulse, Chris Dingman, Jason Wiemer, Aaron Gavey, Todd Simpson, Joel Bouchard, Paul Naugaard, Jarome Iginla, Ted Fleury.

The hockey school gang: one of the best non-hockey teams ever assembled, with me (centre) as the leader, of course.

Playing in New York: insanity reigned supreme.

Courtesy Dave Sandford/Hockey Hall of Fame

Being traded from the Flames to the Avalanche was the beginning of the end.

Courtesy David E. Klutho/Hockey Hall of Fame

I think it's fair to say that when I
chose to go to Chicago I miscalculated
the outcome.

COURTESY THE CHICAGO BLACKHAWKS

I am one of twenty-three Canadian
players in sixty years with an Olympic
gold medal in men's hockey.

COURTESY DAVE SANDFORD/HOCKEY HALL OF FAME

Paying the price.

Chuck Matson was my conscience when I didn't
have one.

COURTESY CHUCK MATSON

With Wayne Gretzky at the 1992
all-star game in Philadelphia.

COURTESY SHANNON GRIFFIN-WHITE

With Josh and Kelly Buchberger. Kelly
is a great guy to have on your team.

I wasn't always Don Cherry's biggest fan.

Garth Brooks, the biggest star on the planet—next to me.

Courtesy Shannon Griffin-White

Ted (left), Travis and me (in the Harley-Davidson vest), with our dad, Wally. Family is the most important thing in life. Between the four of us, we have 50 years of sobriety.

With Graham James.

This is the mugshot taken in New Mexico when I was arrested for losing it on Steph. The Big Book of AA warns that if you don't get sober, you'll end up either in jail, or in another kind of institution or dead.

With my daughter Skylah at the 2009 Allan Cup. Skylah eased the pain of the loss.
COURTESY KIRSTIE MCLELLAN DAY

Bo Jackson, eat your heart out. Here, I suit up for the first of two pro games with the independent Calgary Vipers of the Northern League in the summer of 2008.
COURTESY KIRSTIE MCLELLAN DAY

Playing for the Steinbach North Stars (Manitoba) versus the Dundas Real McCoys in the quarter-finals for the 2009 Allan Cup. I wore #74.
Courtesy Kirstie McLellan Day

With Jenn at Giant's Causeway, Belfast, Ireland. Serenity at last.
Courtesy Michael Cooper Photography

My wedding to Jenn, August 19, 2006. I finally know how "forever" feels.

COURTESY PERRY THOMPSON PHOTOGRAPHY

trusted Chuck. Even guys like Al Coates would call him and say, "Hey, how's Theo doing?" Chuck and I had a mutual love for golf, and he sold his first company the summer after we bought the Hitmen, so he and I hit the links every single day. This irritated Veronica. She was already upset about the time I was spending away from her. But when I was home it was argue, argue, argue. Our relationship was up and down on a daily basis.

I was a kind of absentee landlord when it came to the Hitmen. I invested and went to a few meetings, but I really had nothing to do with the team on a day-to-day basis. The only decision I headed up as an owner was the logo design—we spent about thirty grand, and we came up with a *Friday the 13th*-inspired cartoon of a guy holding a hockey stick like a weapon, wearing a white hockey mask that looked like a skull. I knew it would sell. I loved it and thought it was unbelievable, but the logo didn't go over with most of the press. They thought it was too violent.

Anyway, the Hitmen was a great name—it had multiple meanings. We decided to launch the logo at the Red and White Club at McMahon Stadium, where the Calgary Stampeders play football. Pete hosted and I was on the phone from Finland. *Hockey Night in Canada*'s Ron MacLean and Don Cherry flew into town just for the unveiling. If you know Ron, he is a really enthusiastic, sweet guy. He pulled off the white cloth and, *ta daa* . . . dead quiet. No applause, no cheering, nothing. For a minute I thought I had lost our connection. Then I heard a smattering of applause and thought, "This isn't good."

Local sportscaster Mike Toth, who went on to become an announcer for TSN and Rogers Sportsnet, went on the air that night on the local sports show on channels 2 and 7. Toth absolutely ripped the logo a new one. The next morning, Graham was tearing his hair out. "What the hell are we going to do?" So Pete had this idea to make the very first Hitmen jersey, and across the logo put one of those Ghostbuster circles with the diagonal bar through it. Then he put Toth's name on the back, and the numbers "2 & 7." Every Friday, all the sports media guys get together and play shinny. Pete used to play with them. He went into the dressing room and handed Toth this jersey in front of all the guys. He said, "No hard feelings. We know you will support the team regardless." Toth was speechless. That night, he wore it on the air and he said, "I want to apologize for everything I said about the Hitmen. They are a classy organization."

The public ate the logo up, but the Flames hated it! They said people were complaining that it was too violent and insisted we change it. The Flames were our landlords—we leased our space in the Olympic Saddledome from them—so they had a certain amount of power over us. We changed the logo to a couple of hockey sticks in a jagged, starburst shape—sort of like a "pow" in the comic books. It sucked in comparison. Whatever the reason, when the Flames bought the team two years later, they reinstated the "Jason" logo.

I should have taken the whole thing as an omen. We had great hopes for the team, and when we started our first season in 1995–96, we thought we were going to beat everyone. We'd sold almost 1,500 season tickets and Graham had all of us investors pumped about the future. We ended up with an 18–51–3 record and a quarter-million-dollar loss. In 1996–97, ticket sales were only half what they were the first year.

But the shit would hit the fan while I was at the very first World Cup of Hockey in September 1996, playing the best hockey of my life.

15

ON TOP OF THE WORLD

IN 1996, the first World Cup of Hockey was held. Basically, it replaced the old Canada Cup tournament. Unlike the Canada Cup, the countries were split up into two divisions—a European group that consisted of the Czechs, Finns, Germans and Swedes, and a North American one made up of Canada, the USA, Russia and the Slovaks. On September 5, we beat the Germans 4–1 to advance to the semis two nights later against the Swedes. In the other game, the Americans played Russia. I will never forget that game against Sweden. It was a single-elimination format, so we had to win. Especially because, when you play for Team Canada, it's not about settling for silver and bronze, it is about winning the gold. It is never about being in or out of the medals, it is about being number one.

It was one of the best games I was ever involved in, in international competition. I didn't play a whole lot because the line I was on was used sparingly. We were the fourth line, although I would say we were probably the best line on the team. I had wrapped up a 96-point season, Stevie Yzerman from the Detroit Red Wings came away with 95 points and Rod Brind'Amour had 87 for the Flyers. But coach Glen Sather had Gretz, Mark Messier and Eric Lindros. Sather had coached Gretz and Messier for years, and he was going to play his boys before he played us. He did put us in and out when his guys needed a break, which wasn't often. We didn't play on the power play and we didn't kill penalties. We were kind of cheerleaders on the bench. Sather had so many players to pick from—Vincent Damphousse, Adam Graves, Claude Lemieux, Trevor Linden, Keith Primeau, Joe Sakic, Brendan Shanahan, Pat Verbeek. It just goes to show you how much talent Canada has.

Although I didn't show it, there were moments during the tournament when I was losing it. I could see that Slats was going to live or die with his boys and that it was getting away on them. It might not have been the choice another coach would have made. I wanted to be out there so badly. But sometimes when you are involved on a team like that, you have to check your ego at the door. And when your name gets called you go out and play every shift to the best of your ability. Whenever I played for Team Canada, whatever role they gave me, I was happy to have the opportunity to play with guys who knew how to win. That tournament established me as kind of a go-to guy for Team Canada. Whether it was the World Championships or the Olympics, I was a guy they could count on. They knew I would accept that role and give it my all.

The game against Sweden was back and forth, the kind of hockey I love to play. The shots on goal were 43-43. A very physical game too. I remember Lindros just laying guys out right and left. Lindros was so physically dominating it was ridiculous. You know that hand-grip test with a dynamometer? In hockey, they use it as part of a rating system called SPARQ—speed, power, agility, reaction and quickness. They test you in each category and the results tell you how you can improve your training. I remember at the 1991 Canada Cup, when he was 18 years old, before he was even drafted, Lindros did this grip test. The results were measured in kilograms, and a score of 64 for a male is outstanding. He squeezed an 80. The next closest was Scott Stevens at 60, and then there was me at 25. Ironically, in 1999–2000 when Stevens was the New Jersey Devils' captain, he gave Lindros his sixth concussion with a crushing bodycheck as he skated over the blue line. Concussions happen when the head has such a sudden movement that the brain shifts inside the skull. They can affect your vision, balance and energy. It is really frustrating because a big, tough guy like Lindros can feel completely wiped, no matter how much rest he gets. That last concussion knocked Lindros out of the Stanley Cup playoffs and he had to sit out the whole next season. Anyway, Lindros was an incredibly talented bull on skates. And I have a theory about how he got into some injury problems. When he was playing as a kid, he was so talented and so big that, when he had his head down while he was carrying the puck, guys would just bounce off of him. But in the NHL guys are equal in strength. So on March 7, 1998, he was coming down the ice with his head down and Darius Kasparaitis saw him and fuckin' put him into next week. After that, he was vulnerable. And yet he didn't lose the habit—he continued to skate with his head down. I never understood why. A guy my size was forced to skate with my head up or be killed.

There was some super goaltending on both ends during the entire World Cup tournament in 1996, but Sweden, Canada and the United States were exceptional in that area. Sweden had Tommy Salo, we had Curtis Joseph and the U.S. had Mike Richter, who was on another planet entirely. Richter had gained a reputation when he held off the Vancouver Canucks in the final minutes of the Rangers' Stanley Cup run in 1994.

The Sweden game was tied 2–2 after sixty minutes, and it went to a second overtime. In the last moments we tried to clear it, but Curtis Joseph had to put three sprawling saves on it. Paul Coffey—a brilliant skater—got hold of the puck and instead of dumping it made one of his trademark Paul Coffey rushes up the middle. One of our guys came off and I skated on, fresh because I had spent the game sitting on the end of the bench. I followed Coffey into the zone and he kind of lost the puck. It ended up on my stick and I shot it, not even hard enough to break a pane of glass. At the same time, Brendan Shanahan was going to the net and nicely cruised in front of Salo, screening him. My shot hit

Salo's stick, and the puck went up and over and in. There was a little celebration behind the net, but nobody said much when I came off. It was expected. That game took us to the finals against Team USA.

Four goals and two assists in eight games. I was on fire and on top of the world when the phone rang in the middle of the night, right before the final against the U.S. Veronica picked it up. She listened for a minute and then, in a tone that made it clear she was totally pissed off, said, "Don't you ever fucking contact us ever again." She slammed the phone down and looked at me. "Graham is being investigated for abuse and he wants you to stick up for him."

I looked at her. "Holy shit, what am I going to do?"

Veronica and I had been married in Vegas less than a month before. About two weeks before the big event, Don Baizley called me up, and when I told him about my upcoming forty-thousand-dollar wedding, he wasn't too thrilled. He said, "I suggest you get a pre-nup." So I told him to draw one up for me. He faxed it over and I handed it to Veronica and said, "Here, I need you to sign this." She was shocked. She said, "What do you mean? Are you saying you think our marriage isn't going to work out?" She said it hurt to think that I was accusing her of being with me only for the money, asked what kind of a person I thought she was and said that if she signed it I was saying I didn't trust her. At that time I was not a mature enough person to sit her down and say, "You know I am protecting myself here and we have only been together for a year. Look at it from my point of view. Are you saying I am the kind of guy who would just leave you with nothing and not take care of you if it does not work out? I *should* be going on the advice of my lawyer and confidant. I have known him for eighteen years, longer than I have known you. He knows me probably better than anybody else."

Instead, I backed off. "If that's the way you feel, then, no problem."

After Graham's late-night call, I had to bury the sick feeling in the pit of my stomach and get through the series. I did what I had learned to do. I turned all my off-ice stress into intense focus on the ice.

It was a best-of-three series against the Americans. Things looked good for us. Everyone was predicting, not a cakewalk, but a likely win for Canada. On paper we were better.

Brett Hull led the USA in scoring. Ironically, as a dual citizen he could have played for us, but I think he was pissed at Hockey Canada for ignoring him when he was coming up. And I'll tell you, without Mike Richter in goal, history would have unfolded differently.

The Americans had a lot of good players on their team. Derian Hatcher was big, slow and dumb with the puck but mean and dirty enough to get the job done. I saw Pat LaFontaine as a guy that had great individual statistics but never led his team to the Promised Land. Gary Suter was one of the best offensive defencemen of his time. Suits and Otts (Joel Otto) were really good guys. I had played with both of them on the Flames' Stanley Cup team. Keith Tkachuk had a lot of talent, big and strong, but never really did a whole lot with it. Brian Leetch was captain. But there were no superstars on that team, unlike our team, which was full of them.

We won the first game in Philadelphia, 4–3 in overtime. The American press was mad as hell. They reported that our win was "tainted" and that Steve Yzerman's goal at 10:37 was offside. I passed it to Brind'Amour, who passed it to Stevie, who broke in on the left side and let go a wrist shot at an incredibly difficult angle. Richter got a piece of it, but it trickled in. It was kind of a cheap goal, but we said, "Hey, we'll take it." Shots on goal were 35–26 for us.

It was an intensely nationalistic series. How many times had I heard the Canadian national anthem in my life? And yet, hearing it in game two sticks with me to this day. Montreal had just opened their new rink, the Molson Centre—they call it the Bell Centre now. The crowd was completely insane. People were going nuts. There were flags everywhere, painted faces, signs. And when "O Canada!" started playing, the hair on the back of my neck stood straight up. It was electric in that building that night. Twilight zone stuff—a long way from Russell, Manitoba. Guys were no longer playing for the NHL, we were playing for our countries.

Otts was a Flyer, and so was Brind'Amour. But in that series they beaked each other big time. It was hilarious. Me, I stood up to anybody and everybody. I saw it as my job to create scoring opportunities and get under Richter's skin. You don't really have to say anything to a goalie to get him going. You hang around the crease, make sure he always has to bend around you to make a save, and after a rebound you're Johnny-on-the-spot. Generally, you make yourself a royal pain in the ass. I got a goalie interference call at 10:32 of the second period, but Richter was unflappable. Team USA beat us 5–2 to tie the series.

The third and final game was on September 14. It was tied 1–1 going into the third. Big Adam Foote finally put one in at the twelve-minute mark and we were ahead. But at 16:42, Hull took a pass from Leetch and tied it up. That goal happened because of a mental mistake made by Claude Lemieux. Our defence rimmed the puck around the boards to where he was supposed to be, but Claude was out of position in our zone below the hash marks. Instead, it went to Leetch at the point, and he aimed at the net and Hull tipped it in.

Hull's goal opened the gate. Tony Amonte came up with the game-winner, assisted by Bryan Smolinski and that big dummy Derian Hatcher, with just two and a half minutes left. Then Hatcher scored into an empty net at 19:18. Twenty-four seconds later, Deadmarsh buried it again. Final score, 5–2.

I've heard the series called "the one that got away," but there was nothing we could do about it. Nobody could score on Mike Richter. He was somehow connected to the puck, as if it was a yo-yo. He knew where it was going as soon as it came off a stick, and he was there for every fucking shot. It was one of the best goaltending performances

I've seen in my life. He made some saves you won't ever see again. Think about it this way: the best players in the world put in our best effort and we couldn't get it past him. Shots were Canada 37, USA 25. Cheers to Mike Richter. Seriously, man.

16

SNAKEBIT

I CAME HOME from the World Cup snakebit. Nothing came together. In my first eight games I came up with maybe one assist.

Coming off a big series is a major adjustment. There's inevitably a letdown. I'd just finished playing high-quality, high-intensity hockey, as good as it can get, and now it was time to rejoin my team, where the skill level was lower and the practices were long and focused on the basics. For weeks, I'd been surrounded by players who could see the ice as well as I could, but now, when I gave my Calgary teammates the same opportunities to score, chances were it wasn't going to happen. We had only two guys who ended the season with more than 55 points—me and Dave Gagner. On paper against the other teams, we never had a chance. Add to that the fact that I was under tremendous pressure, courtesy of the investigation into the allegations against Graham James. I knew the dam would burst, I just didn't know when.

Our NHL season started on October 5, 1996, against the Vancouver Canucks. Vancouver had three top scorers in Alexander Mogilny, Martin Gélinas and Pavel Bure. We lost 3–1. It was a typical result. Each time we went out on the ice, I'd have to play the game of my life in order for us to win. But I figured if I could compete at the level that nobody else competed at, maybe it would rub off on some of the guys. I'd been captain in 1995–96 and 1996–97, and I had to try to do the best I could with what was going on because I hated to lose.

You might recognize five names from the team when I was the captain. I am not saying my teammates weren't good guys, but I *am* saying that most didn't belong in the NHL. We did have some talent that would emerge eventually, like Jarome Iginla and Derek Morris and Trevor Kidd, but most of them were babies at the time. I really loved some of the Russian guys. German Titov, he wasn't a huge guy—five foot eleven, 176 pounds—but he was unstoppable. Very strong mentally. I used to sit beside German every day. Once he started speaking better English, I started having some good conversations with him. I remember asking him, "Teets, man, where did you come from?" He said, "Well, you know I was in army. For four years. I was in army." "You didn't play hockey in the army, Teets?" "No. Fuck, no. I didn't play hockey. I drive tank in the Russian army." "Holy fuck, what was that like?" "Is crazy," he said. "We blowing up things all the time."

He was so funny. Some days he would be dragging his ass at practice and I'd say, "Teets, why are you so tired today?" "Ohhhh, last night we have big party at my house. I drink three bottles of wine . . . a couple bottles of vodka . . . I'm very tired."

In 1995–96 we had Michael Nylander, Phil Housley and Gary Roberts, and we made the playoffs, but as usual the Flames ended up getting rid of all our best players. Fuck, it was frustrating.

Anyway, I was at the start of the biggest slump of my career after the World Cup of Hockey. On October 6, we won our home opener against the Buffalo Sabres, and I set up a couple of scoring chances, but *nada*—no assists, no goals. Then we lost 3–1 to St. Louis at home on October 9. The Blues had ex-Flames Al MacInnis and Brett Hull, which sucked. Two nights later, we beat the Detroit Red Wings with Brendan Shanahan, Steve Yzerman, Sergei Fedorov and Nicklas Lidström, 2–1, and two days after *that* we put John LeClair, Eric Lindros and Rod Brind'Amour of the Philadelphia Flyers down 1–0. But I was pressing—hitting crossbars, fanning on shots, bouncing shots off the post. I was ready to run out in front of a car.

Next up on that road trip were the New York Rangers, who had Wayne Gretzky, Mark Messier, Brian Leetch, Mike Richter and Adam Graves, and we lost 5–4. Then we played Montreal, who had Vincent Damphousse, Mark Recchi, Brian Savage, Saku Koivu and Martin Ručínský, and we lost 4–2. These eastern games are important to a team like Calgary, which is usually out of the view of the national press. I came up dry in all these games. I was past breaking sticks. I needed a goal like a crackhead needs a fix.

When I went through slumps, I made sure I was the first guy at the rink. I'd take a bucket of pucks and pick the corners to get my confidence going. It was insurance so that when I did get an opportunity, I wouldn't bury it in the goalie's belly. Another thing that happens to a player in a slump is that superstitions take a front seat. And hockey players are really superstitious by nature. I had my game-day routine down and did the same thing before every game for thirteen years in a row.

We had to be at the rink at 9 a.m., so I got up at 8, was in the car by 8:13 and in line at Tim Hortons by 8:15, ordering a double-double. I'd smoke three cigarettes on the way, lit at certain stop lights. Drove the same route—Deerfoot, Southland, Blackfoot, past the Cash Casino, up to the Saddledome player entrance. Then there was my rink procedure—I'd get another coffee, get undressed, take a shower, sit in the hot tub for exactly three minutes, go to meetings, practise, shower again, get in my car. I'd head for La Brezza for lunch and eat penne Romanoff and tortellini with soda and orange juice. Then I'd get back in my car, drive home and be asleep by 2 p.m. I'd wake up at 4 p.m., get back in my car at 4:13, Tim Hortons for another double-double by 4:15. I'd follow the same route to the rink, park, shower, spend three minutes in the hot tub, then stretch and tape my sticks—which was another ritual in itself. My sticks were very important to me, as they are to pretty much every hockey player. A stick can make a huge difference to your scoring ability. I would retape my stick between periods too. Always heel to toe, and I'd use a glue stick on my blade to make it sticky.

The glue I used was the stuff that held the stick into the shaft—we used two-piece sticks back then. The brands changed. I was with Jofa for a few years, then Nike and Easton. Jofa and Nike each paid me a hundred grand to wear their stuff—sticks, helmets, gloves, pants. If you look at my hockey cards, you can see which years I wore which brand. When I switched to Easton during my second year in New York, the very first time I shot the puck, it was like, holy cow! That stick increased the speed of my shot by ten to fifteen miles an hour. Today's one-piece sticks are unbelievable for shooting the puck. But for taking passes and handling the puck, it's a completely different feel from the wooden ones. The sticks today are stiffer. In fact, the blade is so stiff that when the puck hits, it jumps off unless you have an extraordinary set of hands. You see guys out there who have trouble with the puck. Why? Because they don't have the hands to control a stick that is that stiff. NHLers pass the puck as hard as we shoot it. So if you have a pass coming at you at eighty or ninety miles an hour and you have a stiff stick, it'll bounce unless you're a very skilled guy.

I decided not to take any money from Easton because I had run into trouble with Nike. I really liked Nike's original stick, but when they came out with a new shaft and a different type of blade, I wasn't as keen. I scored only 15 goals that year. It just didn't feel right. Some of those Nike sticks were okay, but some were heavy, and when I shot the puck it didn't go anywhere near where it was supposed to go. When you pick up a stick, you know whether you're going to score with it. In 1990–91, the year I scored 51 goals, I was using Louisville sticks, and for some reason they were perfect for me. I don't know if it was because I was feeling so confident or what, but when I picked up a Louisville it was like, "Yes."

I didn't like to be around the team before a game. I liked to focus. Gary Taylor, our video guy, would make me an up-to-date video of all the goals I scored, and I'd sit in the back room, put in my tape and watch all the goals. This would get that good feeling going. The coach would have his pre-game meeting and we'd all be there. Next, I would get dressed—always left to right—and make sure I was in line directly behind the goalie for the warmup. I would do exactly the same thing each time: start every drill from the same place (when and where I shot was the same too), go back in, grab a Gatorade and watch the video for a few minutes, put a chew in under my top lip (I don't know how many times management would come up to me and say, "You can't have chew in your mouth during interviews"), then back to the locker room. The ritual would end with me standing in line behind the goalie, coming out for the game, looking up at the flag during the anthem, counting the thirteen points on the maple leaf when I heard, "O Canada, we stand on guard for thee," touching the ice and making the sign of the cross. After all that, I was ready to play.

ON OCTOBER 19, 1996, the pressure was on. We had Edmonton at home the next day and I was tense. Edmonton had four really good scorers—Doug Weight, Ryan Smyth, Andrei Kovalenko and Jason Arnott. They also had Curtis Joseph in goal. I called my dad and he told me that Grampa Fleury taught him that if you are not having fun at something, you will be too uptight to do a good job.

Against Edmonton, I scored my first goal and added two assists in the first period. We won, 6–3. Two nights later I got a hat trick against Colorado. They had a very strong team—Peter Forsberg, Joe Sakic, Sandis Ozolinsh, Valeri Kamensky, Adam Deadmarsh and Patrick

Roy. I beat Roy on a penalty shot that night and we won 5-1. Two nights after that, we beat Pittsburgh 7-5. That team included Mario Lemieux, Jaromir Jagr, Ron Francis and Petr Nedvěd. I was back.

One of the pianos I was carrying around on my back was gone, but there was still another one I had to get rid of.

17

A HEAVY SCENE

THE MEDIA had gotten wind that Sheldon Kennedy was working with the RCMP to build a case against Graham James for sexual abuse. So Graham was frantically trying to get everybody on side. As I said before, one of Calgary's most influential sportswriters, *Calgary Sun* columnist Eric Francis, was a good friend of Graham's brother Rusty James. Eric and I are buddies now, and he says it's kind of hard for him to admit, but he and Graham were friends. He says Graham is a genius—in a "Hitlerian" kind of way—to have pulled off what he did for so many years and not have anybody know. When Eric first heard that Graham was leaving the Hitmen, he couldn't believe it. In his September 7, 1996, column, he wrote, "Whatever lies ahead for Graham James, one can only hope he will be afforded the same type of respect and support he's given hundreds of young players over the course of his coaching career." He added, "hopefully he will remember how much respect he's garnered from coast to coast. I certainly will."

Sheldon said his heart sank when he read that. He said he could see that Graham was trying to look like the victim and that the media was going to paint Sheldon as a drunken troublemaker, just stirring up lies and shit. Fortunately, that did not happen.

Meanwhile, my buddy Chuck Matson had put a lot of time into the Hitmen and was busy with his oil and gas services company, so when his uncle, team president Lorne Johnson, called him and said, "Meet me at training camp in Drumheller in an hour and a half," Chuck refused at first. "Bullshit, Lorne. I have got to get some work done." But Lorne said it was important, so Chuck went to Drumheller. When he pulled up, his uncle, who was a redhead, was so flushed that Chuck thought he was going to have a heart attack. Lorne told Chuck about the accusations levelled against Graham, but added that he figured it was all probably bullshit—just the product of some bitter, pissed-off hockey player looking for revenge—and that the league said it had everything under control. But Lorne and Chuck did not want to take any chances so they called Graham up, told him, "We gotta talk to you," and went to his hotel room.

When Lorne said something like, "There have been accusations of sexual impropriety with a hockey player in the past and possibly more than one," he and Chuck fully expected Graham to drop to his knees in shock and say, "My God, what a terrible thing to accuse me of!" But instead, Graham looked right at Lorne and said, "Well, there may be some things from my past that some people may perceive as improper."

Chuck's heart just fell right out of his chest. He just couldn't believe it.

Lorne told Graham that he and Chuck needed a few minutes together, so Graham stepped out. "We have to put our heads together and figure something out right now," Lorne told Chuck. Chuck's answer was, "We have to remove him from the team today."

"I totally agree with you," Lorne said, "but settle down. We don't want him near those boys again, but we also don't want to trigger a mess or step outside of what the league may want. We need to do this right."

"There are thirty or forty kids on the ice right now that I helped put there and he is never going back to the rink," Chuck said. "I will kill him before he does."

So they told Graham, "Pack your stuff up and go to Calgary." They called all of the owners to let us know what was going on, and there was such shock among everyone.

I was in shock too. I never in a million years thought the truth about Graham would come out.

The next day, Chuck and Lorne fired him. It was a heavy scene. Graham cried a lot. He told Chuck he loved hockey and loved his players. He said the game was all he had in life and he couldn't figure out why people were taking it away from him. Chuck and Lorne told him the owners had to take a strong stand so that the parents and players knew we would protect them.

Believe it or not, there were parents who hated Chuck for that decision. Hated him! We had one kid in particular who didn't play very well after Graham left. His dad was absolutely furious with us.

The ownership group hired a psychologist who specialized in sexually abused children and young adults. Each player was required to attend one interview and return for a second if necessary. The psychologist recalled five guys to meet with him again. He wanted to see three of them a third time, but they refused. We found out later that these three had been going over to Graham's house after he'd been fired and the charges had been laid. One of them was the kid whose dad was angry about Graham's firing. That kid visited Graham a couple of times when Graham got out of jail and went to Spain.

Shortly after all this, I made Chuck aware of my situation. He didn't condemn me. He understood. He looked at me and said, "You don't tell on your priest and you don't tell on your coach. As a society, we have set it up this way." Then he said, "A good story has a villain, and a great story has more than one."

Graham was a villain, but Ed Chynoweth had been the president of the WHL for years. He was the president of the league when Graham got fired in Moose Jaw. He was also the president of the league when Graham had been fired in Swift Current. He allowed us to become partners with that jackass.

When Graham applied for the franchise, I could have done something like phone Ed and say, "For God's sake, you know you can't do this." But I was just trying to survive. So was Sheldon, and so probably were a lot of other guys. We were doing what we'd been taught to do in hockey since we were eleven, listen to the coach and shut up. Well, I can tell you this: Sheldon and I are not the only ones Graham messed with. I'm quite sure there are others, probably many, who are still not ready to talk.

WHEN WE SOLD the Hitmen to the Flames, I was really disillusioned with the way it went down. When our lease at the Saddledome needed to be renewed, we ended up with two choices: sign their lease or leave town. And that is not a very strong position from which to negotiate. We'd invested a lot of money by then. The franchise cost $850,000 and by the time we were all done writing cheques it came to more than a million. We had sixteen or seventeen shareholders, but when times got tough and we faced a cash call, only about 30 per cent of us propped the team up. Chuck and his uncle Lorne, Joe Sakic, Tom Mauro, Neil McDermid and I came to the table every time. No one else that I can remember.

So anyway, we were sick and tired of it. Chuck said he and the businessmen involved had a clear understanding of the liability we faced by owning a team with a sexual predator in our recent past, not to mention buses full of teenagers skidding around on icy roads at three o'clock in the morning. Suffice it to say, everybody's belly was full.

We could have moved the franchise to Edmonton or Red Deer or Kootenay, but we had made a commitment to bring junior hockey to Calgary, and Chuck—who was alternate governor and vice-president at the time—was of the opinion that the Hitmen should stay in Calgary.

He said it wasn't about money or anything like that. So we bit the bullet and sold to the Flames.

The Flames paid us $1.2 million in June 1997. Major junior hockey teams are worth seven to ten million dollars today, but I think we did the right thing for the honour of the sport. The next year, the team turned it around and made it to the playoffs, and the year after that, the Hitmen made it to the Memorial Cup final, where they lost in overtime to the Ottawa 67's.

Part of the deal of the sale was that Chuck and his uncle Lorne, who had built the team, would receive rings if the Hitmen won the Western Hockey League championship or the Memorial Cup. Chuck stayed involved with the team by volunteering to stick around for two more years and guiding the team with advice. When the Hitmen won the WHL final in 1998–99, they called him and said they had the rings and were just waiting for the right occasion to present them, but it never happened.

18

YOU DON'T KNOW SQUAT

WHEN SHELDON came forward about being abused by Graham
James, he revealed there was one other player who he would not
name. Everyone knew I was associated with Graham, so there was a
ton of speculation as to whether it was me or Joe Sakic. I don't think
Joe was molested. He has never acted out and has always been a
very even-keeled, nice guy. Graham did hang out with him and a
lot of other players—it was part of what he did to protect himself.
He took guys like Danny Lambert and Joe to the movies too. They
were friends—just friends. It removed suspicions. It was part of his
game. Friends could testify that they spent nights with Graham,
went out for Chinese food, went back to his house to watch a movie
and nothing happened. I believe Joe never had a clue as to what
Graham was really up to.

In January 1997, Graham was formally charged. It was big, big news.
So every single day for two months I had to say, "No comment." We
had CNN reporters in the dressing room after games. News outlets
tried everything to get me to talk about it. A typical encounter was
the time I was in the hallway after leaving the dressing room, where
I had been asked the same question for almost half an hour. This
good-looking female reporter came up to me and said, "So you are
one of the guys, right?" I asked her what she was talking about. She
said, "You're the other guy, right?"

I said, "I just stood in front of you for twenty minutes and said I can't answer these questions. How do you get 'You're that other guy' from that?'"

"Well, there's a lot of speculation going around right now," she said.

"Yeah," I said, "that's what it is—speculation. Until you hear it from the horse's mouth, you don't know squat."

It became really frustrating and I started hitting the cocaine hard. I had been drinking and partying on a regular basis, but drugs had been kind of like a treat. If coke was there, sure, of course I'd do it. But in my circle of friends, nobody was into that kind of stuff. After the Sheldon thing came up, I bought some for the first time. I was in a bar, I gave a guy some money and he gave me a little packet. I did the drugs in the bathroom cubicle. I'd pull out my car key, pour a little on the blade, stick it up to my nose, sniff. Clean, simple, done.

Coke, drinking and chicks were how I dealt with it on the outside; inside, I wasn't dealing with it at all. I was upset that the whole matter was creating a distraction for my teammates. Here we were, trying to win hockey games, and after every practice and every game there was a media scrum around me. One reporter, Mike Board from the *Calgary Herald,* asked me the same question for two months!

I could not handle the scrutiny. Everywhere I went, I was asked about it. Every media hound in the world wanted to be the one who broke the story, and all I would say is "No comment." Sometimes they asked me openly, sometimes they tried to sneak it in. For instance, we might be talking about the game that night and the next thing you know—*bam!*—they'd hit me with the James thing. But I would totally clam up. "No comment." I knew if I said anything, it would become the focus of every interview, every media story, everything ever written about me again. "Theo Fleury scores his thousandth point despite growing up abused by his hockey coach." "Sexually molested hockey player Theo Fleury sets an NHL record for shorthanded goals."

This went on for more than nine months. I didn't want to deal with it in a public forum. I knew I could get tons of sympathy, but I didn't need that. I needed to forgive myself, because I felt responsible. I'd allowed it to happen. I felt that, in order to get noticed and move forward in the NHL, I'd given up my soul. Both Sheldon and I lost the innocence most kids have. We grew up way too fast. The day I walked out the door in Russell I was on my own, and it was going to be like that for the rest of my life. But carrying it around all the time was wearing me down.

I had zero tools. None. So I looked for an escape hatch. Whenever we were on the road, I started going to strip joints. Sheldon dealt with it by talking about it, through therapy and self-discovery.

THE KEY TO ABUSE is secrecy. Once the secret is out, the spell is broken. If you look back at my story, you'll find that what Graham did was make me believe that if I ever told anybody, there would be serious consequences. It was the same as holding a knife or gun to my head. He held my career in his hands. But now, Sheldon's secret was out, so he was able to start dealing with it. Mine was not. Graham still had control of my life.

At the end of that year, before any of the investigation was made public, we went on a golfing trip to a resort in Phoenix with the guys. One day, Sheldon and I sat down, had a few beers and snorted a few lines. We were in a drunken, coke-induced delirium. We sat in a room and talked for ten hours. I had suspected this and he had suspected that. We even talked about what really went on during that trip to fuckin' Disneyland. It cleared the air between us.

The truth about what Graham did to Sheldon came out in court. Graham called Eric Francis from jail the day after he was sentenced and gave him a worldwide exclusive interview. In that jailhouse phone call, Graham told Eric, "Sheldon and I were in love." He went on to say something convoluted about how he should have been born in Roman times, because back then it was acceptable to have boys as partners. It was the manly thing to do.

Eric called the whole conversation "chilling."

Graham made contact with me once by phone, and I said, "You know what, man? Don't ever call me again. I have nothing to say to you. I'm glad it is finally over. You deserve everything that you are getting. Have fun in jail." I look back on it now, and I know that son of a bitch has to lay his head down on that fuckin' pillow every night and I know he doesn't go to sleep.

Some of my teammates were sympathetic about all the unwanted attention I had been getting, while others were frustrated and disappointed that it had become such a big deal. On the ice, I'd hear comments. Some jerk-off from the other team would say things to get me off my game. It was nasty out there. Really nasty.

Finally, Brian Sutter came to my defence. There was a headline on the front page of the paper: "Leave Theo Alone!" I thought it was a class act because up until then nobody else had stepped up for me. It was a terrible amount of pressure to shoulder alone. I mean, who was putting butts in the seats in those days? I was. Who were people coming to watch? Me. It was just me out there. I was the guy who played with energy, skill and the desire to win. It wasn't right to put all that on a guy who is five foot six.

19

BEATING EACH OTHER
OVER THE HEAD WITH STICKS

BRIAN SUTTER had joined the team as head coach in 1997. I was
ready for a big change after two years of Pierre Pagé, but things ended
up being not quite what I expected. We didn't have a great team—we
had a lot of young, young players—so Brian had to do tons of teach-
ing. I hated defensive drills. Basic, basic stuff. Start in our own zone,
then the neutral zone and then backchecking. Throw the puck in the
corner and the defenceman contains you and doesn't let you get back
to the front of the net with the puck. Hickory dickory dock. Plus, Brian
brought in his own system, which we had to learn from scratch. I wasn't
having a whole lot of fun relearning all of this. Practices were long, two
to three hours, and he used quite a lot of video. Because I was one of
the team leaders, I had to buy into what he was selling to the young
kids. It was very stressful for a vet. Think of it this way: say you had a
Ph.D. in physics and you had to go back and take Grade 9 math.

We weren't going to be a great offensive team, so we were going
to have to win games 1–0, 2–1, 3–1. In order to do this, we had to be
defensively solid in our own zone. I was a high-tempo, offensively
minded player, so my favourite practices were run that way too. Lots
of emphasis on skills—shooting, passing, not too physical. When I
first came to the Flames in 1989 we had a really talented team and it
was exciting and fun. Practices with Crispy were always short and
sweet.

Half the time, Sutter's practices were fuckin' Looney Tunes. There would be two or three fights every time. But he was lovin' it. He had this gravelly General Patton voice—"That's it, boys, that's the way to fuckin' go at it." Because so few had experience, Sutter wanted us to practise as if we were actually playing a game. He was trying to instill an in-your-face work ethic. Every day, we were beating each other over the head with sticks. Michael Nylander and Jamie Huscroft went at it all the time. Mike was a skilled centre and Jamie was just kind of a slug. So Mike would be doing spins in the corner and scooting around with the puck, and finally Huscroft would take his stick and—*wham!*—connect with Nylander's helmet. Then there would be a fuckin' brawl, which everyone would jump in to try to break up. After a while, that gets old for a guy who has been in the league for ten years. Plus, I had all the other shit going on.

Another thing that drove me crazy was that, for all eleven years I was with the Flames, we flew commercial economy. Even after every other team in the NHL had their own charter planes and took care of their players. Why? 'Cause the boys who owned the team were having to write cheques to cover losses at the end of every year, and they didn't like doing that. So they cut corners where they could. We used to say, "Anyone can fly on the Calgary Flames charter if they have 250 bucks." It was ridiculous.

There were rumours all the time. The team was getting sold or going to fold. I always thought, "How is that possible when we have eight owners who are some of the richest people in Canada?" If they hadn't gutted the team they would have filled the seats. And if they had filled the seats, they wouldn't be threatening to move the franchise someplace else. We won games we had no business winning.

In 1995, we were on an eastern road trip and had to get from New York to Boston. We started out at Kennedy Airport, then bused forty minutes through heavy traffic to LaGuardia, where we waited around before getting on a plane to Logan International in Boston.

We couldn't land there because of a snowstorm, so we turned back to LaGuardia, landed and took a bus to Penn Station, near Times Square, and waited for a train.

While we were waiting at the station, we said, "Fuck this," and went to a nearby liquor store to stock up on booze. During that train ride, we got just hammered. We arrived in Boston at around 10 p.m., drunk and tired after travelling for more than twelve hours. So Al Coates told everyone, "Okay, we'll buy you dinner tonight." This was supposed to be a big deal because we got a per diem. Mine had been gone after the first day in New York—some stripper had it. Anyway, we all sat down in the hotel dining room and ordered. Steve Chiasson, who had joined us that season, was really pissed off at how cheap the Flames were. He said, "I've never fuckin' seen anything like this." He'd played for Detroit for seven years and they treated the team great. So Chiasson asked for ten lobsters and went to bed. Never touched 'em.

The next day, before the game, we made up these business cards that said, "Calgary Flames Travelling Fucking Circus." We kept them in our wallets. Can you imagine what would have happened if the media got hold of them?

It is so unfortunate that Steve died in that car accident in 1999. I was sad about it. He had two sons, Michael and Ryan, and a daughter, Stephanie. His ending could easily have been mine. He was a small-town kid too—he grew up in Peterborough, Ontario. When he died, he was playing for the Carolina Hurricanes. The way I understand it, the team took a charter flight back from Boston, where they had just lost the quarter-finals to the Bruins. When you fight a long, bloody, bruising battle, you don't just wave and say, "Okay, well, see you next year." You tip back a few together and talk about how it could have been. They landed at about 1 a.m. and he probably figured, "Well, the kids and the wife are asleep anyhow," so he went with a few of the guys to Gary Roberts's house for a couple of beers. Then, about

4 a.m. he figured he'd better get going, so he said he was taking off. Kevin Dineen was there, saw that Steve was a bit blasted and said, "Wait a minute, I'm going to drive you," and went to get his keys. But when he came back, Steve was gone. Steve was probably thinking, "What the fuck? I can make it. It's only five miles."

Anyway, he hopped in his truck, not wearing his seat belt, and booted it home. He was driving more than seventy miles an hour on this winding road, flipped the truck and was ejected. Some workers spotted his vehicle up on its side against a water treatment plant with the signal light flashing. Dineen had to go and identify the body. Dineen, who is now head coach of the Buffalo Sabres' farm team, the Portland Pirates, was charged with drunk driving in 2006 after a night out with his coaches and players two days after the team was eliminated from the American Hockey League playoffs. (In the end, he pleaded guilty to a lesser charge of driving to endanger and received a sentence of two days and had to pay a $750 fine.) I have heard it said he was next in line to coach in Vancouver and the incident totally fucked up his career. Bonding with your teammates is important, but there are only so many bowling alleys you can go to. For a lot of the guys drinking is a way to unwind after the games.

The list of drunk drivers in the NHL is long. Former Oilers coach Craig MacTavish was a 26-year-old forward for the Bruins when he killed a young woman. Former Chicago Blackhawks defenceman Keith Magnuson was killed with one of my former teammates—and former Toronto Maple Leafs captain—Rob Ramage at the wheel, and now Rob is appealing a four-year sentence. Alexei Zhamnov got a DUI when I was with the Hawks. Ex-Oiler Dave Hunter has three impaired-driving convictions. Bob Probert was arrested five times for impaired driving. Pelle Lindbergh died when his car hit a wall after a team party. Tim Horton was driving drunk when he was killed. Other drivers that have been charged or convicted are Peter Worrell of the Florida Panthers, Sergei Fedorov, Eddie Shack, Dominik

Hašek, Chris Pronger, Bobby Hull, Paul Holmgren, Mike Keenan, Petr Klíma, Mark Bell and Miroslav Fryčer. You think it doesn't happen today? You think some players on every team in the league don't go out and smoke dope or drink and party and get behind the wheel? Maybe in an alternative universe, but not in this one.

We won the game against the Bruins, 1–0. I scored. That is how it was with the team at that time. I took it upon myself to win, and it was really tough. The Flames had traded away every star player from our Stanley Cup team. I was the only guy left, and now I was playing with bargain-basement Europeans. There were a few times I lost it on the guys in the dressing room, trying to get them to buy into the system we were playing. But for the most part I tried to lead by example on the ice. It wasn't their fault we were so shitty. It was management's responsibility for drafting poorly and getting clowns who were not capable. For instance, they drafted Niklas Sundblad. They claimed he was the Wendel Clark of Sweden. When he came over here, absolutely everybody kicked the shit out of him in camp to see how tough he was, and he folded. He never became the player they thought he was and skated in only two NHL games. Jesper Mattsson, another guy from Sweden, never played a game in the NHL. Like fuck, I don't understand it, unless the scouts were drinking while the games were on. If I were running an NHL team I would draft only guys from Canadian major junior hockey. That's it. No college guys, no Europeans. My team would all be juniors. They are tough. They get it.

We banked on Trevor Kidd being a superstar, but Kidder was never in very good shape. He didn't eat well, and even though he was six foot two and 190 pounds, he played like a little goalie instead of a big one. He put himself out of position all the time. He should have looked at Patrick Roy and how he played and copied his style. Kidder could have been great, because he had fantastic talent. He had one of the best glove hands I have ever seen. If we'd had an overachieving goaltender in those days it might have made up for the shortage of talent elsewhere.

Kidder was a different bird. We were roomies and we got along—both from Manitoba. Once during the playoffs, Kidder and I were in San Jose and some morning DJs somehow got through to our room and woke us up at around 8 a.m. They were screwing around and said they were with the hotel and that there were two midget hookers in the lobby, and could they come up. We both thought that was pretty funny.

I was close to Al Coates. I love Al Coates, and to this day he is really the only guy who still calls me to see how I am doing. At the time, I told him straight out what Graham did to me, and on a personal level he said, "Well, if I can help in any way . . ." But I was very happy that Brian came out publicly and said, "Fuckin' leave this guy alone. He's had enough shit without having to deal with you guys." That helped me turn the corner. I got through it. It died down. Sheldon took most of it on himself with the trial.

The police didn't approach me, never questioned me, nothing. I don't know what I would have said. I probably would have 'fessed up, because I needed to. I needed to tell as many people as I could, because that's where the healing is.

One night in a drunken stupor around the fall of 1996, I did make my way over to Shannon's at about four o'clock in the morning. I sat her down and finally told her the entire story. She was in complete shock because she had leaned on Graham to help her through our breakup. She considered him one of her best friends. When I left a couple of hours later, I signed her guest book. "I was here and only you know who I was." It was true, she knew who I was before I was anything.

I KICKED into survival mode. Drinking and partying. When I was having fun, I wasn't hurting. You can ask anybody, and they'll tell you partying with me is probably the most fun you'll ever have in your life.

I had a routine. Monday night was Smugglers, Tuesday night was Claudio's, Wednesday was Cowboys, Thursday was Ranchman's, Fridays and Saturdays after games we went anywhere, because every bar was packed on the weekend. And then, just like the Bible says, Sundays were a day of rest.

20

LEADING THE BOYS ASTRAY

FOR A DECADE, the Flames had been a team that could usually finish with 90 or 100 points in the standings. But in 1995–96, we began a long run as a team that obviously wasn't good enough to make the playoffs very often. That year, by some fuckin' miracle, we finished a point ahead of Anaheim and ended up facing off against Chicago in the first round. We didn't have a prayer.

The series opened in Chicago, and we lost 4–1. Two nights later, Kerry Fraser was the ref, and I seriously wanted to kill the guy. In the third period, we were trailing 3–0, and Fraser kept us two men down with penalties to Trent Yawney and Ronnie Stern (a double minor) about a minute apart. Yawney's penalty had just ended—we were still on the kill—and I was going for a puck in the corner when Murray Craven absolutely fuckin' ripped my helmet off with his elbow. I looked around, but no penalty was called. I guess Fraser was busy thinking about his plans for dinner or something. So what did I do? I took my stick and started tenderizing Craven. Of course, that caught Fraser's attention and he called me for slashing. This put us back to a three-on-five for another three minutes.

I just lost it on him. "I'm gonna fucking kill you! I don't care who you fuckin' think you are. Let's meet outside in the parking lot, you fucking shitbag asshole!" He immediately gave me a ten-minute misconduct, throwing me out of the game. It was too much. I took my helmet off and threw it at him.

Eddie Belfour shut us out in game two, and the Hawks continued to dominate in the early stages of game three. By the three-minute mark of the second period, they were up 5–0. I scored at 12:24, and again about a minute and a half into the third. We also scored the next two, so we were back in, but ended up losing 7–5. Game four was scoreless until Iggy slipped one in during the second period, but Jeremy Roenick tied it up with just nine seconds to go. We went into triple overtime and at about the ten-minute mark, Trent Yawney came back for the puck, got hold of it behind the net and turned back. Meanwhile James Patrick lost Murray Craven, who came up from behind, caught up to Yawns and slipped his stick in between his skates, loosening the puck and chipping it up to Joe Murphy, who was in the slot: 2–1. It still stands as the longest overtime game in Flames history—fifty minutes, ten seconds.

Most years, I would give my brother Travis a heads-up before the season ended. "You might as well fly in 'cause I'm gonna take the team golfing for a couple days out in Kelowna."

We would rent Winnebagos and recruit a couple of volunteer drivers. Travis did not drink. He had developed a serious habit when he was a teen, and by the time he was 20 the doctors were telling him he'd be dead within a couple of years if he kept it up. He had lost a lot of his stomach lining, so he gave it up. My dad was sober too. He made up his mind to quit drinking after he almost killed my younger brothers Trav and Teddy. The last year I played junior in Moose Jaw, he drove Teddy, who was 14, and Travis, who was 11, up for the year-end awards banquet. As usual, he stayed out all night and partied and then climbed behind the wheel with the boys in the car. When they were about thirty miles outside of Regina, he pulled the car over and looked at Teddy. "I can't go anymore," he said. Teddy and Travis were scared. "What are you talking about, Dad?" Teddy asked. But my dad was so out of it he made Teddy get behind the wheel. Later, when he sobered up, he realized they could all have been killed, so he quit. Just like that.

I had a cabin at Shuswap Lake in British Columbia. The lake has about 620 miles of shoreline and is considered one of the most beautiful glacial lakes in the world. People go there to water-ski, houseboat and camp. It really is something to see.

In 1996, twelve guys came with me up to the cabin to go golfing. We spent five days and had a blast. Word got out and the next year, 1997, there were sixteen of us. Travis, Teddy and my dad were our drivers again.

The night before we left, I called the Molson rep and said, "I need beer." "How much do you need?" he asked. "As much as you can give me," I said. So we picked up twelve flats of twenty-four. We also picked up a Texas mickey—one of those 66-ouncers of whisky—and I found a source who sold me a bag of weed the size of a toddler.

Anyway, the idea was to go to Invermere, which is 238 miles from Calgary, to golf and then to my cabin at Sicamous in the Shuswap that night. We went golfing as planned, but by the time we got to the lake, which is only four hours from Invermere, all the liquor was gone. Two hundred and eighty-eight beers and the mickey. That was just the start. For five days we were baked.

My dad would look at me, shaking his head, going, "What the fuck is wrong with you?" When you are sober, it is hard to remember how much fun it is to be drunk. By the end of the trip, as we hit Calgary city limits, we rolled the last joint and smoked it.

The third year, there must have been twenty of us, including Dwayne (Rollie the Goalie) Roloson, Cale (Hulser) Hulse, Jason Wiemer, Todd Simpson, Jarome (Iggy) Iginla, Joel Bouchard, Rick (Tabby) Tabaracci, Chris (Dinger) Dingman and Dave (Gags) Gagner. Generally, if players were married they weren't on the trip, and there were no Europeans allowed.

On our way home, we stopped at a lake. We walked along the beach and there was a buoy a hundred yards or so offshore. Iggy was a second-year player and the boys made a bet with him. They said, "We'll bet you whatever we've got in our pockets that you can't swim out to that buoy and back." It was April and the ice had just melted, so the water temperature was about 40 degrees Fahrenheit, absolutely freezing. Before we knew it, Iggy was buck-naked and running into the water. He started swimming out.

I was laughing at him and yelling, "You are going to make thirty million bucks someday and out there swimming around for a hundred bucks, you idiot." Obviously, he made it back. I remember he got out of the water and his skin was absolutely white. The boys only had about three hundred bucks between them. Iggy was disappointed. He thought he was going make at least two grand, but we were tapped from partying for days. It was pretty funny.

Next stop was a go-kart track. I gave the owner a little cash under the table and we all grabbed a car. It was more of a demolition derby. We had a blast. Somebody T-boned Chris Dingman. Dinger is a huge guy, six foot three and 250 pounds. What a kid he was. I asked him one time, "Dinger, how did your year-end meeting with the coach go?" He said, "Fuck, I dunno. It was pretty bizarre. I went into Sutter's office and I was sitting across the desk from him, and he gets up and points his finger in my face and goes, 'You know what, Dingman? You're either fuckin' stupid or you're fucking scared!'" Dingman looked at me confused. "I didn't know what to do, man. Sit there, or fight the guy?"

I almost pissed myself laughing. He was cocky, despite the fact he was so bad. He needed a pail to carry the puck. He was a tough guy and had been a really good junior player. He was captain of the Brandon Wheat Kings and when they won the WHL championship in 1996. In junior, he scored 83 points in 66 games one year. And to give him props, he has two Stanley Cup rings now—from 2001, with the Colorado Avalanche, and 2004 with the Tampa Bay Lightning. But in 1997–98, his rookie year, all we got out of him was three goals and three assists in 70 games. Yet if he scored three or four in a row during a shooting drill, he would get really pumped and say something like, "Fuck, I'm on fire!" Yeah, okay Dinger, now do it in a game.

Anyway, Dinger's go-kart spun around and skidded into a stack of tires. He hit them hard and they flew everywhere. I will never forget the sight of that great big moose in a teeny little car, spinning through those tires.

My buddy Chuck Matson was one of our Winnebago drivers that third year. He used to say that hockey players are so coddled in life, they have no idea how to do anything mechanical or physical. We came back into Calgary very late at the end of the week, after playing golf in Kelowna all day. Most of us were sound asleep after four days of vigorous activity. We had all been drinking and using the head in the Winnebago. The whole way back, Hulser kept bending our ears about how he was going to help with emptying the sewage. Another thing he had boasted about was that he hadn't vomited since he was 15 years old. He must have said that about a hundred times. We pulled into a Shell station on the edge of Calgary and Hulser climbed out with Chuck and Jason Wiemer to watch them work the hose into the sewer. Hulser's nose was right in there like a dirty shirt when Chuck opened the valve to start it draining. The hose began bouncing a little bit and Hulcer asked Chuck, "What's happening there?" And Chuck said, "That's all of Theo's shit going down the hole there, buddy." Hulcer started gagging. But to this day he claims he never puked, so his record is intact.

My dad said something funny to me that year when it was all over. "Son, you can party, but you couldn't drink what rolled off the end of my chin." And you know what? That was true. When he was partying, he could go harder than anyone. His capacity for alcohol was endless. Once, when I was two years old, we were living in Williams Lake, British Columbia, a real cowboy town. The population is around fifteen thousand. The town is famous for its rodeo every July 1 weekend. My dad had a job managing three Indian cowboys on the rodeo circuit. Well, it was fall and the rodeo tour was over, so he dropped the cowboys off where they lived, in Vernon, B.C. Meanwhile, he had made a whole bunch of money—enough to cover us for three months or so. He called my mom and said, "I'll be home in four hours." Then he headed for the liquor store and picked up twenty-four 26-ounce bottles of whisky and a case of beer for the drive. We didn't see him for four days until he pulled up in front of the house and cracked the last beer.

AT THE END of 1997–98 the Flames were out of the playoffs, but we had a couple of regular-season games left, including one in Los Angeles on March 28. When we touched down, Brian Sutter gave us the day off. He said, "Make sure you are here on time for practice tomorrow and be ready to fucking play hard."

The weather was outstanding. L.A. in March is usually pretty nice, about 71 or 72 degrees, but 1998 was the hottest year in the country's history, so it was almost 80 with a light, warm breeze. Ironically, nine days earlier on St. Patrick's Day, Calgary had had its worst snowstorm in 113 years—about a foot and a half fell in my back yard. I remember going out and plunging my boot into a drift and it came up to my knee.

I turned to the boys on the bus and said, "Who wants to go golfing?" And about sixteen guys raised their hands. I called a golf course up in Newport Beach and booked four tee times. We rented a big Budget van, and when we got off the plane from Calgary we drove straight to Newport from L.A. International Airport. We had a great day playing and getting wasted on beer and whisky then, we headed back. I was at the wheel, and we were passing through Orange County about half an hour from our hotel. I had just merged onto Highway 73 and was headed for Interstate 405 when out the window we spotted John Wayne Airport. Suddenly Iggy, who was sitting way in the back, piped up, "You don't have the balls to go to Vegas!"

I had two credit cards, with $50,000 limits. I could go anywhere I liked, and I liked Vegas. I didn't even respond—I just cranked the wheel and the whole fucking van took a mean right tilt as I crossed eight lanes of traffic. Everyone was wired from nearly biting the big one as we pulled into Budget Rent-a-Car. The guys were buzzing— each had a comment for me as they piled out. "You fuckin' fucker, I thought we were dead. Seriously." "I swear to God, I saw the light." "I bent over to try to kiss my ass goodbye, but I couldn't reach it so I kissed Iggy's ass instead." Six guys headed back to L.A., while the other ten of us boarded a flight to Vegas. We got there and took a limo to the Hard Rock Hotel. Andrew Cassels was my roommate at the time. He and I sat down at a Caribbean Stud table, got just hammered and played cards all night long. I like the game because it is mindless but exciting. You get five cards, and if you have a pair of twos or better you're in. I can't say what anybody else did, but we all showed up at the airport at 8 a.m.

Unfortunately, the flight back to California was cancelled. This was not a good situation. I looked over, and people were boarding at the next gate, so I asked the agent, "Where are you going?" "LAX," she said. "You got room for ten hockey players?" "Sure," she said, "come on over." We exchanged our tickets and got on the plane. When we landed, we got the taxis to boot it to the hotel and we pulled up just as the bus to the Staples Center was loading for the pre-game skate. We won 5–2 that night. Fuckin' A.

21

BEGINNING OF THE END

THE PRESSURE was getting to be too much. All the problems I was having in my marriage, plus carrying the team and the whole Graham James situation, were causing me a lot of anxiety. I was winging it. There were demons in my closet and when they were triggered I had to shut them up. Throughout my life, I used several things to do this—drugs, alcohol, gambling, sex, anything that numbed me or took me out of the moment. I was always attracted to the dark side.

There were bright spots. Veronica and I had a baby, Beaux Destan Fleury, on May 26, 1997. What his name stood for in our minds was "beautiful destiny." We wanted to bless him with a great future, starting with his name, but my own future wasn't looking so rosy. I was carrying around a lot of shit I had no answers for and didn't know how to deal with it. I would be faithful for a while, then when I was on the road, I'd go out and have a few drinks. Inhibitions would go down and self-confidence would go up. When a pretty girl made eye contact, instinct would take over. "Hey, you wanna go back to the hotel?" "Yeah, sure." Back in my room, the guy I was rooming with was usually sleeping. If not, sometimes he'd get up and sometimes he'd just roll over. I switched up roomies fairly often, but most of the guys didn't care.

Chuck used to try to encourage me to recognize that marriage to Veronica was a good thing. He tried to tell us to change our relationship because it was up and down all the time. He told us to replace the words "I love you" with "I respect you," and eventually we would mean it. That never happened.

We used to go to Vegas every year for our anniversary, and we would take friends with us. One year we asked Chuck and his wife, Elaine, my teammate Andrew Cassels and his wife, Tracy, my brother Travis and Veronica's brother Carson. We stayed at Caesars Palace. In those days it was one of the most upscale hotels in Vegas.

On the third day, we played thirty-six holes of golf. Whenever I wanted to go out and party, I would pick a fight with Veronica and she would respond the way I wanted—by telling me to get lost. So I would. Chuck kept warning me, "One of these days you two are going to kill the other. This relationship is totally out of control."

So on the way back to the hotel after golf, I said, "Shower up, boys, we're heading out for the night."

"No we're not," Chuck said. "I ain't going anywhere with you tonight, Bones. I can smell a rat." And Andrew said, "Nah, I think I'll take a rain check too." They stayed back and took the girls out for dinner, while Carson and Travis and I went partying. As usual, we ended up at a strip joint.

We made it home, just wasted, at about 5 a.m., and Veronica was livid. The front desk kept calling and telling us to turn it down or get out. I crawled into bed, pulled the covers over my head and crashed. She called Chuck, waking him, and said, "Chuck, you won't believe what your little effing buddy has been doing! You'd better get up to this room right now!"

Chuck got out of bed and said to Elaine, "By golly, today could be the day."

He came up to our room and saw me passed out. I was semi-awake and could hear the conversation. Veronica was yelling, "That guy has been screwing around!" Chuck tried to calm her down. "Now, Vern, you don't know that. You can't just say that." She said, "He came in and sprayed himself with cologne before he went to bed, and

I know he is screwing around." And Chuck said, "Listen, Vern, you can assume that, but for Godsakes, he is out with your brother! He is not going to be screwing around." "Yes he is, I can smell it on him!"

I knew Chuck was incredibly homophobic. So when she said, "Chuck, smell it—smell the sex on him," I almost lost it. I heard him say, "Vern, you are like a sister to me. I would do almost anything for you, but smelling his cock is not something I am going to do." Well, that was too much. I started laughing so hard the bed was shaking. Now Veronica was really mad. She packed up all her stuff and left for the airport. That day was our anniversary.

Chuck and Elaine had a flight out that morning, so they looked for her all over the airport, but she wasn't there. Chuck told me he worried all the way home, but Elaine kept saying, "Chuck, they will have kissed and made up by the time we get to Calgary." He didn't think so. He was sure it was over between Veronica and me.

They got to Calgary and called me on my cell phone to say they hadn't heard from Veronica. They caught us as we were in a limo, headed back to the hotel from dinner. "Aw, Chuck, she's not at home, she's here with me! We had an unbelievable dinner and I got her a great bracelet and she loves it!" Chuck later told me that he learned from that incident not to worry about me, because *I* was not worried about me.

I think the Flames were the only people who had a chance to rein me in. If you go back to when I was 23 or 24, if I had been suspended and told to piss in a bottle once a week, my problems might have been nipped in the bud.

In 1999, I went out after a game in San Jose with some of the guys from the team. We went to this bar we always went to. I got wasted—as usual—and thought, "Fuck, I need some coke." Cocaine kept me straight. I started talking to this guy at the bar—"Hey, where can I get some shit?" He said, "No problem. I can make a phone call." *Bang!*

It was there in twenty minutes. Out of respect for my teammates and friends, I did not do coke or anything stronger than weed in front of them. So when the boys on the team went back to the hotel, I went into the bathroom, dug my key into the coke and snorted it.

Wham! This stuff hit me hard. Like a brick in the head. This was about 2 a.m. My new friend and I went to a party. We were snorting and smoking when I looked at my watch—and it was 7 a.m. Holy fuck. I called the hotel to tell my roommate, Andrew Cassels, to pack my bags and take them downstairs so I wouldn't miss the bus. I made it back in a taxi just as the last person was boarding. We got on the plane and my whole body was numb. Hours later, I was driving Cass home and I began to feel really weird. Something was going on. I dropped him off at his house and made it home. Later, I was sitting on the floor, playing with Beaux, when all of a sudden I jumped up and started pacing back and forth. I was thinking, "I have finally accomplished what I have wanted to accomplish for a long time. I am going to die." My heart was just pounding, and the more I started pacing, the more freaked out I got—which made it pound faster. Finally I said to Veronica, "Will you please call an ambulance? I think my heart is going to explode." She was frantic and assumed someone had spiked my drink. Veronica had no clue I was doing cocaine. No clue. But I thought I was going to die, so I made kind of a deathbed confession about my drug use. She was shocked.

The paramedics arrived a few minutes later. Elite athletes have slower heart rates. My heart would usually beat about fifty times per minute at rest and maybe 140 at peak exertion, but they clocked my pulse at 190. That's not good. It's okay if your heart races for a little while, but you run into trouble if it continues. They said, "Just see how it is for the next little while," and left.

I was sure I was going to die. I had been up for almost two days, played a hockey game, hadn't drunk a whole lot of water—so I was dehydrated—*had* drunk a lot of booze and had a ton of what I thought was cocaine in my system. I was in a full drug-induced panic. I could not sit still for one second. The more I thought about dying, the faster my heart started to pound.

Five minutes later, I couldn't take it anymore. I called 911 and said, "The ambulance has gotta come, *now!*" This time they gave me an IV full of the tranquilizer Ativan, which is like Valium, and I calmed down. The emergency room doctor asked me what I was on and I told him I'd been at a party and done some cocaine. He said, "It wasn't cocaine. You overdosed on crystal meth." Oh, great. Perfect. Not that cocaine is a health food, but crystal methamphetamine is bad shit. You can find the ingredients under your sink—drain cleaner, battery acid, iodine, paint thinner, lye, acetone and kerosene. Basically, I had ODed on fuckin' nail polish remover.

We just happened to have four days off after that. I slept the entire time. The first twenty-four hours, I never even woke up. And you know what? I have never been the same since that episode. I have had panic attacks ever since. They are more manageable now, since I have had counselling and gained some tools. I think it was a sign from God saying, "You know what, man? You are not invincible anymore."

And to compound things, earlier that season I had been cross-checked behind the right ear by Bryan McCabe while playing Vancouver. I was standing in front of the net and he got me with his stick. I got really dizzy after the next several games. And I had vertigo and all kinds of freaky shit, and I didn't tell anybody that I was concussed. I had to keep my mouth shut. Can you imagine what the Flames would have looked like without me at the time? But even when I got to New York with the Rangers, I didn't feel right. For instance, bright lights gave me trouble.

It was par for the course in my life. I couldn't sleep because I had so much anxiety. I would lie there, staring up at the ceiling, thinking, "Okay, I know I am going to die. Please make it soon rather than later." I was obsessed with dying. Drugs made the worry go away.

22

NAGANO

THE OLYMPICS IN 1998 were the first time that NHL players were allowed to participate. Canada hadn't won a gold medal since 1952, so everyone expected that we would build a dream team and just cream the competition. The roster was going to be announced on national television on November 29, 1997. It was like the Oscars. Every NHL player in the country was sitting on the edge of his seat. Well, almost every player. Patrick Roy, Gretz and maybe Eric Lindros would have been sleeping just fine.

The night of the big announcement, the Flames were scheduled to play Anaheim, and I had to get to the rink, but I was glued to the TV in my McKenzie Lake house in Calgary along with the rest of my family. My mom and dad were there, Josh, Veronica and Beaux. It was a big family gathering. There were TV and newspaper reporters set up in my living room. The whole city was so supportive.

I had been playing mind games with myself for weeks. *I know I belong on the team, but what if I'm not picked? . . . There's no way they'll go with a guy from the Flames, the worst team in hockey . . . Yeah, but that might work in my favour, and I'm from the west—they need a guy from the west . . . I performed at the World Cup last year . . . Yeah, but we didn't win . . . Wasn't my fault—if Slats had played me . . . Yeah, but he had Gretz and Mess and there are so many guys who belong on the team . . .*

When my picture appeared on the screen, everyone was cheering so loudly we didn't even hear my name. Joshy was always a pretty cuddly guy, so he had his arms tight around me and his head buried into my neck, squeezing hard. He was my best buddy, my biggest supporter, just a great kid. It was a huge relief. I'd never been cut from any team, except when I was sent down for half a season the first year in Calgary, and even then I wasn't really cut. To be considered one of the best twenty-three hockey players in all of Canada was incredible. It was something I dreamed about as a kid. I've played for my country at least nine times in my career, put the maple leaf on my chest and gone out to win for Canada. It's a huge deal, a big honour. Not everybody gets to experience what I've experienced, that's for sure.

That night, I went out and scored the goal that broke Joe Nieuwendyk's team record for career goals scored. Quite a night.

Knowing I might be drug-tested, I had taken myself off everything a full month before we left for Japan. Well, not alcohol—they don't test for beer—but I did slow it down. The whole team met in Vancouver, and we travelled on the Rolling Stones' private jet to Nagano. It was pretty cool. A huge plane—it had a bedroom upstairs. Every seat was first class.

THE GAMES OPENED on February 7, 1998. The Japanese don't do anything small-time. They had built a cherry blossom–shaped stadium just for the Olympics. There were seventy-two nations participating. We arrived the day after the opening ceremonies. There was tight, tight security around us, because of the bombing at the 1996 Summer Games in Atlanta and the terrorist killings in Munich in 1972. The Japanese government did not want any of that kind of bullshit to disrupt their Olympics. I remember reading an article about the Nagano police asking local high schools to lock up their baseball pitching machines because they shot balls at ninety miles an hour and that meant they could be used as weapons. All three thousand of us athletes were under twenty-four-hour guard and there were metal detectors everywhere.

The NHL had shut down for two and a half weeks to allow us to compete. Eight lesser hockey countries played in a preliminary round, and the best two—Kazakhstan and Belarus—joined Canada, the U.S., Russia, Sweden, Finland and the Czech Republic in the run for the medals. We played a three-game round robin to determine the seedings for the medal playoffs. Canada went undefeated, winning 5–0 against Belarus, 3–2 against Sweden and 4–1 against the Americans. We beat the Kazakhs 4–1 in the quarter-final, extending our win streak to four.

So what happened? One word: Hašek. He did not let in more than two goals in any game he played. I don't know if you've ever seen him play, but he looks like he's having some kind of seizure when he stops the puck. You could not score on him on a breakaway. If it were not for him it would have been 25–0 for us. Instead, we ended up in a 1–1 tie. Jiří Šlégr scored first, and Trevor Linden got it back for us with 1:03 left in regulation. A ten-minute overtime settled nothing.

Which set the stage for a fuckin' shootout. The game—which had repercussions on the medal standings—was decided by an individual skills contest. My point is, how can you decide who wins a team sport by the actions of one or two individuals on slushy ice? The Czechs basically played just for that shootout—they did not forecheck. Once they got that 1–0 lead, they just lined up at the blue line, and when we tried to enter their zone they were like a fucking brick wall.

I was the first player called out to shoot. I came in on Hašek, and not to take anything away from him, but it was so frustrating because the ice was totally shitty. I could not get the puck to lay down. If you expect to score, the puck has to be lying flat on the ice. When the ice is hard and cold, you can control it and it has speed, but when the ice is soft the puck bounces and rolls all over the place.

In the end, the Czechs won the shootout and the game. They went on to beat the Russians, 1–0, in the gold-medal game. The Finns beat us, 3–2, to take the bronze.

I think that Nagano was the first time things started to change on the ice for me. You cannot drink and do drugs and then suddenly stop and not have it affect you. I wasn't as fast as usual, and when I shot the puck it didn't always go in the net, which would drive me fuckin' crazy. I was used to shooting the puck and have it go in the net, now it took me two or three shots. And rage was starting to affect me, not just off the ice. When someone came near me, I wanted to stick him in the face, or cross-check him in the neck or spear him in the stomach. I didn't because it was the Olympics, but I was starting to get really frustrated.

23

RETURN TO JAPAN

MY LAST SEASON with the Flames, 1998–99, began with another trip to Japan—this time to Tokyo. The Olympics in Nagano had raised hockey's profile, and the league was trying to build some goodwill and secure sponsorships with some of the big Japanese companies. So we went halfway around the world to open the season by playing a two-game set against the San Jose Sharks.

This time, I had a lot of fun there—I think. All I remember is being in some fuckin' strip joint in a place called the Roppongi district. Well fuck, why not? It was full of drugs, booze and hot South American women. I never had sex with any of them. I was so fuckin' high and wasted, there was no chance of that happening. But I loved hanging out with them and partying. I remember being just stoked when we landed in Tokyo. We had a couple of days off to explore before we played. I said to the concierge, "We are just looking to go have some beers and have some fun. Can you help us?" And he told me to go to the Roppongi district. A couple of guys from the team came along, and sure enough there was a ripper joint. This group of girls was hanging around at the front. Every one of those girls was good-looking. A little hard around the edges, you know, but hey. This particular strip club was a shady place, full of tourists. The Japanese people were more into geisha, not hookers. I walked in, picked one and tipped her a thousand bucks. Money was not an issue. I liked the company. I needed the company. I was number one on the team, the most famous and the most alone. I was at the top and I fucked it all up because I had no idea what to do once I got there.

Each night I would choose a different girl, but we would have the same conversation. "Where are you from?" "Oh, I'm from South America." "Well, what do you do down there?" "My father is a fisherman." "Why are you here?" And she would tell me her story about how she was a victim of some kind of abuse, neglect or abandonment. Every one of them would tell me about the kid she'd had back home when she was in her early teens. How was she supporting that kid? By being a stripper. It is great money.

I have a theory as to the reason I could not stay out of strip joints. Finding the hottest girl and keeping her beside me all night, and then adding booze and cocaine to the picture, made me feel like a rock star.

Except for game nights, my routine in Japan was to arrive at the club after dinner and make sure to be back at the hotel by 6 a.m. I was so fucking loaded that whole trip that I hardly remember it. The first night, I went right from partying to practice, wasted. Two days later, we played and tied. In the next game, I scored a hat trick. I was on fire—high and drunk and I was incredible.

In fact, I was having a great season. By Christmas I'd scored 17 goals and 20 assists in 33 games. On January 24, at the 49th NHL All-Star Game in Tampa, Mark Recchi and I were wingers on a line with Wayne Gretzky. The format matched North America against the rest of the world. Our line combined for seven points in the 8–6 win for Team North America. Gretz talked to me about the Rangers, told me how he loved living in New York and that I should think about going there when I became an unrestricted free agent that summer.

On February 20, I scored two goals and assisted on a third in a 6–3 victory over the Anaheim Ducks at home. That night, I passed Al MacInnis to become Calgary's career points leader. It was weird—I had played almost eight hundred games in the NHL, yet that night

I had butterflies. I tied Al with an assist in the first period, and then, fifty-two seconds into the second period, after picking up the puck in my own end, I cut through the neutral zone, made it past their defence and slapped one in. That gave us a 3–1 lead and my record—824 career points (362 goals, 462 assists in 787 games), including 28 goals and 35 assists to that point that season. As the puck went in, the crowd went nuts, and for a minute and a half, the game stopped as everybody stood up and yelled and whistled and clapped and cheered. I circled at centre ice, pumping my right arm up and down. It was a rush that is hard to describe. The feeling that comes over you when sixteen thousand people are screaming your name is unbelievable. Most of the rest of the world will never know what it is like, but trust me, it is addictive.

After setting the record, I waited for the other shoe to drop. There was no one else left from the Stanley Cup team. It's tough to keep a good team together, especially on a tight budget. You could see the same thing happening with the Pittsburgh Penguins in 2008–2009. They are going to have to make some tough decisions about who to keep and who to let go, because they have got too many good, young, talented guys who are going to need to go elsewhere to get their money.

At the very beginning of February, Harley Hotchkiss, one of the owners, called me in and basically asked, "Is there any chance you would take less than market value when you become an unrestricted free agent at the end of the year?" He offered me $16 million over four years, an average of $4 million per year. I said, "Look, I think this is below my market value. But I *will* take $25 million for five years, or five million per year." In NHL terms, we weren't far apart. And as it turned out, I was already leaving millions on the table with my counteroffer, but Harley said no.

I picked up the paper the next day and the headlines screamed that I had said no to five years and twenty-five million. I felt fuckin' sick to my stomach. It wasn't true and made me look bad to alienate my fans. I saw the writing on the wall. Three weeks before the trade deadline, I sat down with Coatsie. I said, "Veronica wants a new house, and the one she is looking at is across the lake from where we are in McKenzie. Coatsie, I am not buying a new house if I am getting traded this year. So what the fuck is up here?"

"No, Theo, we are not trading you," he reassured me. "We definitely are not going to trade you." So I said, "All right, I am buying her the house."

Our friends came over to move us. You might wonder why, making millions of dollars a year, I'd be asking my friends to move me. Why not just phone a moving company? Because of who we really were— we were small-town kids, and moving was just something friends did for each other. You can change your location and salary, but you can't change who you are. Chuck and a few of the boys helped me push my hot tub across the frozen lake. We just had a blast doing that, skidding it across. It took us the better part of the weekend to move.

Fast-forward to Sunday morning, February 28, 1999. My buddy Chuck Matson and his wife, Elaine, were sitting having breakfast and their phone rang. It was Al Coates. He asked if Chuck had my new address. Chuck figured it out right away. "Coatsie, you prick, you've traded him!"

"Listen, Chuck, I need you to do me a favour," Coatsie said. "Don't call him. Don't say anything for an hour. I owe it to him to talk to him in person. What is his address?"

I was at home, getting ready to go to practice, when I saw Coatsie's champagne-coloured 1943 BMW pull up into my driveway. He'd never been to my house before, ever. I knew then and there I'd been traded. I think it was tough for him. I could see it in his eyes, which were watery, and hear it in his voice, which was cracking. He said, "This is one of the hardest things I've ever had to do. I traded you today."

My heart was pounding so hard I was afraid he could hear it, but I just shrugged. "Okay, cool," I said. He said, "Theo, I made sure

I traded you to a place you have a chance to win a Stanley Cup—
Colorado."

I started to feel excited, because Colorado really did have a chance
to win. Coatsie left and I called Chuck. "These bastards just traded
me," I said. "I know," he said. "You're going to Colorado." There was
a silence while I took this in. I said, "How do you know that?"

I GET FRUSTRATED when I hear the Flames and the Calgary
media make comments like, "Poor Theo. He got traded because he
wanted too much money and went to the big city and his life went
downhill." I was always a very loyal employee and felt I had earned
the right to stay in Calgary. At that time salaries were skyrocketing
and there was a lot of pressure on me from the Players Association
not to consider a hometown discount. Nobody wanted that kind of
precedent. But in reality, I was so messed up the Flames probably saw
a huge problem about to happen. On the other side of the coin, when
I was there, if the Flames had invested in me, Calgary wouldn't have
had so many lean years.

At the time of the trade, the Flames were two points out of a playoff
spot. I was proud of where we were as a team, considering we had a
shortage of talent. Basically, there was me and Phil Housley. Coatsie
was quoted as saying, "We know Phil is a one-dimensional player, but
it's the dimension we don't have." German Titov was a great guy, but
as I said, he drove a tank for four years in the Russian army. They just
picked him up late in the draft and he turned out to be a pretty good
player. Michael Nylander was skilled, but he was young and he was
hit-and-miss. They traded him in January. We had Cale Hulse and
Derek Morris, and Iggy was a comer, but he was inexperienced. For
us to be that close to making the playoffs, and to have them fucking
pull the rug out from under me and trade me, I was pissed off. The

team left me out on my own for five fuckin' years, answering the journalists' three million fuckin' questions, and with no talent on the ice, and here we were, about to turn it around . . . and what did they do? Traded my sorry ass out of town.

I WAS UP AND DOWN. One minute, I was looking forward to the opportunity that playing in Colorado presented. The next, I was devastated, absolutely devastated. I called Chuck back a little while later and said, "There's a news conference at 2:30 p.m., and then I'm on a 5:00 p.m. flight to Colorado. You have to come with me."

"Bones," Chuck said, "I've been running around with you so much, I've been neglecting business." He called me "Bones" because I used up a lot of energy, and if I didn't eat enough I lost weight. One time he stood back and looked at me and said, "Holy cow, you are skin and bones!" And that was what he called me from then on.

"No, Chuck, I need you. I don't just want you to come. I *need* you to come."

So Chuck agreed. We went down to the news conference, which turned out to be a terrible time. So many emotions went through me. I tried to be strong and hold it together, but I lost it at the first question. I couldn't hold back the tears. Up until that time, it hadn't hit me that I wasn't a Flame anymore. The Flames were the only team who had given me the opportunity to be who I was. In the next twenty-four hours I would experience every emotion a human being can feel. And the next day, when I put on the Colorado Avalanche jersey, it was an out-of-body experience.

I was traded for René Corbet, a forward, defenceman Wade Belak and future considerations. Belak was huge—six foot four and 225 pounds. He played in 72 games over two years, racking up just three assists but 224 penalty minutes. In February 2001, the Flames put him on waivers, and the Toronto Maple Leafs picked him up.

When Corbet hit town, he told the papers he wasn't going to try to be me, and he kept his word. He scored 9 points in 20 games the rest of the '98–99 season, and 14 points in 48 games in 1999–2000 before they traded him to Pittsburgh.

The real value for Calgary in the trade was the "future consideration," a big (six-three, 230) defenceman named Robyn Regehr. He was Colorado's first-round pick, nineteenth overall, in 1998 and an all-star in the WHL. His tenure as a Flame got off to a rough start. He was riding in a car when another car crossed the centre dividing line and hit him head-on. Both his tibias were broken, and he had to work his ass off to rehabilitate his body. And he succeeded—he played 57 games for Calgary in 1999–2000. I heard Regehr is a good guy. His parents were Mennonite missionaries in Brazil and Indonesia who ended up in Rosthern, Saskatchewan, about a six-hour drive from Russell. Anyway, he is one of my favourite Flames today, a hard-working horse with talent.

Eric Francis later told me that at that press conference he was thinking, "Theo will be back here and play one or two more seasons, because this is where he became famous. This is where he became rich. This is where it all started."

That would have been a happy ending.

24

CLARK KENT AND ME

CHUCK MATSON travelled with me to Denver—the Avalanche paid for his ticket. On the plane, we were still in shock, going, "Holy fuck." We had no idea what to expect. Veronica didn't come with us because she was eight months pregnant. She wasn't thrilled about the move, especially with the new house in Calgary and trying to settle the kids, but when you buy a red car, there is no point in wishing it was blue. NHL players move around. I got off the plane and walked to the terminal and there were eight million cameras and bright lights on me. Reporters asking about *hockey*, mind you—not one question about my past personal history. I took that as a good sign.

We had to arrive at the rink early for practice because I had to do all these medical exams and formalities. Chuck didn't leave my side. It's funny how I could be perfectly at home wandering the streets of any city late at night, totally fearless, but in this situation I really needed a buddy. Anyway, the team started to arrive because we had to play Edmonton that night. It was like watching an all-star team walk into the dressing room. There was Paddy Roy and Adam Foote, Peter Forsberg and Joe Sakic.

Then Claude Lemieux walked in. I've heard people say Claudie is the biggest asshole to ever put on a pair of skates. The meanest guy ever. After he sprayed Kris Draper's face all over the boards in Detroit during the 1996 Western Conference final, he had to have a police escort everywhere he went when he played in that city. Chuck

185

was sitting beside me in the dressing room when Claude came up to him and said, "Hey, bud, you're in my spot, move over." Chuck told me that he was thinking, of all the guys to walk into that room, this was the guy he would least like to meet. So Claude sat down and said, "You're Chuck Matson." And Chuck said, "Yeah, how do you know?" "I read it in the paper. You came down with Theo. I wanna tell you something. I know how Theo feels. I know what it is like to be traded from your first team and the team you love. And the only reason you are here is because you're Theo's buddy, and I love that about you."

Well, Chuck was blown away because it was such a kind thing to say. Claude gave him his phone number and said to call him.

Chuck figured Claude was just being nice, so that was that. Well, that summer for his birthday surprise, I flew Chuck down to Sherwood Oaks, a highly exclusive private golf course, to golf with his all-time hero, Wayne Gretzky, and one of Wayne's best friends—Claude Lemieux. Claude got into the cart and said, "Chuck, you never call me. What's wrong?"

Claudie was one of the nicest men I ever met in hockey. We ended up being good friends. I used to call him Thurston Howell III because he always dressed so well, had nice cars and fuckin' went to spas. He was like, "You gotta go get one of those pedicures. They're the best!" Goes to show you, you can't judge what a person is like from his performance on the ice.

Colorado really was a good group of guys, a close-knit team. They had won the Cup in 1996, but I hadn't played beyond the first round of the playoffs in ten years and wanted it badly. The Avalanche were struggling a bit that February, despite the talent. I think management thought I could do for them what I did for the Flames in '89—ignite them a little. I wasn't traded alone. Chris Dingman came with me to add some toughness.

Peter Forsberg was the team's god. A different bird but a really good player. Europeans are sometimes a bit timid, but this guy was really tough. And he had insane skill. He could pass the puck and work the power play like nobody I have ever seen. Peter was a bit of a rock star. Girls loved him. He always had that scruffy beard and messy hair and that great Swedish accent. He was fun to play with and a super-nice kid.

Joe Sakic and I had known each other since we were kids. Whenever I was around, in junior or in the pros, he knew it was not going to be a fun evening for him. I'm sure when he looked at the schedule and saw me playing against him, he threw his head back and squeezed his eyes shut and said, "Fleury. Fuck." I kind of kicked it up a notch when I played against Joe. I was always aware of the fact that we were tied for the WHL scoring championship our last year of junior, and yet he was a first-round draft pick while I was an eighth-rounder. I was very physical with him and constantly worked to intimidate him physically. I made sure he went home with several black-and-blue tattoos each time we played. We called him Clark Kent because away from the rink, he was just a nerd. Then he'd go into the Colorado dressing room and put on his Avs jersey, and all of a sudden he was Super Joe.

I loved playing with Super Joe because he was so sound, but we could not have been less alike in personality. I used to bug him all the time about how he didn't react when he made some unbelievable move. On April 24, during the first game of our first-round playoff series against the San Jose Sharks, I fed Joe the best pass I have ever made in my life. Joe picked it up and shelved it, putting us ahead 1–0. He just skated around the net as if nothing had happened. I was losing it, especially because the fans in San Jose were giving me grief, as usual. I grabbed him and was hugging him and pounding him, "Holy fuck! What a goal!" And he just shrugged. I asked him, "Joe, fuck, what's your problem?" And he answered, "I just don't get excited. That is not who I am." "I know, man," I said, "but that was fuckin' amazing." He said, "Yeah, I know."

Adam Deadmarsh was a good player, a first-round draft pick when the Avs were still playing in Quebec back in 1993. His problem was he got hurt all the time. His first concussion came in November 2000 after dropping the gloves with Vancouver's Ed Jovanovski. Then in a game in Phoenix in December 2002 he got another one when he accidentally connected with his teammate Craig Johnson's knee. The next Remembrance Day, when he was almost recovered but still on the injury list, he and another teammate, Jozef Stumpel, backed into each other during a shooting drill, and this time it affected Adam's balance big time. In hockey, balance is super important. Think about it. You have to balance on a skate blade for like, fifteen feet per stride, going thirty miles an hour while manoeuvring a three-inch piece of rubber at the end of a five-and-a-half-foot stick. He was still working on his recovery during the lockout in 2004–05, but he never made it back. He was 27 when he played his last game in the NHL.

Milan Hejduk was my roommate. He was a Czech rookie, barely spoke any English at all. Milan was so skilled and talented. He won the Rocket Richard Trophy as the NHL's top goal scorer in 2002–03 with 50 goals. He was a great kid.

We were in Dallas during the playoffs, the night before a game, and we were sitting in the hotel room watching TV when the phone rang. I answered. This girl was on the other end and she was slurring her words a little—"Theo, I'm your biggest fan. I sent you my panties and I sleep with your poster, you have no idea . . . I just have to come up . . . da-da da-da da-dah . . ." Always. I think most guys in the NHL will tell you that.

She walked into the room, and she was hot. A redhead. Gorgeous and built. She immediately started taking off her clothes, but not the way a professional stripper would. In fact, she had been drinking, so she was stumbling a bit.

Milan was lying in bed with his eyes bulging and his bottom lip somewhere around his chin. He looked at me, then looked at her, then me, then her, and I started laughing, almost pissing myself. "You know this girl?" he asked. "No," I said. "You don't know this girl?" Nope. "You know this girl?" No. "You don't know this girl?" No, Milan. I don't know her.

When she was totally naked and I realized how hammered she really was, I tried to stop her. "Lookit," I said, "you really need to leave." She got really mad and started swinging her purse at me. "You motherfucker! You fucking asshole!"

I grabbed up her clothes, opened the door and threw them out into the hallway, and when she ran to pick them up, I closed the door behind her. Click.

Milan looked like he had been hit in the head with a fry pan. "What just happened here?" he asked. I was still laughing. "I don't know."

Chris Drury was a super guy and an awesome player. The bigger the game, the better he played, even when he was a rookie. Whenever we needed a big goal, Chris would score it somehow, some way. He could dig deeper than anyone. That kind of guy is really rare.

Adam Foote was a big, tough defenceman. Hard to play against. In fact, he was a prick to play against because he was always in your face. When I played for Calgary, I played against Foote every single shift. If I tried to intimidate him, saying something like, "I'm gonna cut your fucking eye out," he would come right back with something just as tough. He was one of the few players I knew who was willing to go as far as I was to win. When we finally played together on the Avs, we would laugh about all the times we used to hack and whack each other. There was mutual respect.

Patrick Roy—I always had his number when I played against him. Always scored. But he was a total competitor. He just hated to lose. He was the king of the Avs. We were golfing buddies—Paddy, me and Claudie Lemieux. Some mornings, Patrick would look outside and it would be a breezy, sunny day and he would go into Bob Hartley's office and say, "No practice today. See ya." Then he would call me. "Come on, Tee-yo, let's go play some golf."

Playing with this team was like having a full-body orgasm. Calgary had not seen a lineup like this since the Cup in 1989.

I was pumped to play my first game with these guys. Colorado had acquired me to put them over the top and I knew I could do it. But after missing just seven games in eleven years with the Flames, I was injured in my first game with the Avs on March 1, 1999. It happened in the third period against the Oilers, just after I scored. I was behind the net and my skate got caught in a rut and I got hit at the same time. My knee went one way and I went the other. I finished the game, but in my head I knew it was fucked. It was hurting, I was sore and I was really down.

That night, Chuck and I went to this bar and I saw this girl I knew from the last time I'd been through there with Calgary. She said to me, "Hey, you wanna go do some mushrooms?" "Yeah!" I said. "Perfect." So I took some, and about an hour later they kicked in. I was feeling rosy while I had reality on hold. Chuck was pissed off that I was cheating on Veronica again, so he left. I made it back to my hotel and turned on the TV and the highlights of the Flames game were on. I watched for a minute and just broke down and started crying. Absolutely sobbing. It was like somebody close to me had died. I called Chuck, who came down to my room. Good friend that he was, he felt just terrible for me. We started talking about how I needed to be a better husband and father. Chuck has a strong faith and he said, "I think we have to pray about this." That was hard to do because I had a big ego, but I knew he was right so we did. I was emotionally drained and we stayed up talking until the sun came up. I was taking baby steps toward bringing God back into my life.

The next morning I went to the doctor and he told me I would be out a couple of weeks. The team was leaving for a road trip, so I went along with them to get to know my teammates. I liked everybody.

They were experienced. You didn't have to work to convince them to win. Instead, we all knew we were there to win the Stanley Cup and we all knew what it took to do it. I got to golf every day on the most beautiful courses you can imagine and it was fun. It was a long way from Brian Sutter meeting me as I walked into the rink on game day, drilling me in the arm, going, "Are you fuckin' ready? Are you fuckin' ready?" And me showing him my watch and saying, "Well, it's 8:30 a.m. I will be ready by seven tonight, but first I need a coffee." Sutter wanted his players to eat, sleep and drink hockey twenty-four hours a day. I was beyond that. I had fought to establish myself. I was already there.

25

THE AVS

THANKS TO MY KNEE INJURY, I got to see my daughter Tatym born on March 15, 1999. I have seen all four of my kids born. It was exciting. If anybody needs a midwife, I'm your man. We always liked Tatum O'Neal's name, and when we found out it meant "light-hearted" we thought it was perfect. We picked a different way to spell it, like we had done with Beaux. What is special about Tatym is that she is exactly like me. She is kind of laid-back and doesn't get too excited about too many things. But when I watch her ride horses, it's amazing. You see this cute little quiet girl, and yet when she gets on her horse she is totally focused, just zoned right in. I love that about her. She is serious when it comes to competing. She hates to lose—like, *hates* to lose.

I went back on the road with the Avalanche, playing in Phoenix a couple of nights after Tatym was born. The doctors there were shooting up my knee, no problem. I played 14 more games with 24 points (10 goals, 14 assists) before the end of the regular season, and I think it's fair to say I contributed. Our record was 10–3–2 in the final fifteen games, making us the second seed in the Western Conference behind the Dallas Stars. I was doing what the Avs had hired me to do. In our final game against Dallas in the regular season, I scored my 40th goal with thirteen seconds to play in the game. We won 2–1. We were pumped and ready to take home the Cup.

Then, on April 20, 1999, the massacre at Columbine High School happened. Two students shot and killed twelve other students and a teacher, and wounded twenty-three more before committing suicide. This all happened in Jefferson County, Colorado, which is a quiet, middle-class suburb of Denver, where we played. It was an awful, awful thing and just devastated the entire city. The playoffs were delayed by three days, and we moved the first two games to San Jose. It was all we talked about in the dressing room. In fact, we wore CHS patches on our jerseys and went to the hospital to visit some of the kids who had been wounded. I didn't know what to expect, because they had been severely traumatized. Seeing their schoolmates killed—I couldn't imagine it. For us to be able to go and cheer those kids up and let them know that we were all behind them was really important.

We all had sympathy, we all had compassion, but it was time to play, and we focused back on hockey. We were one of the favourites to win the Stanley Cup.

In the first game, I had two assists and drew a four-minute high-sticking penalty against Vincent Damphousse when he cut me on the nose. We came away with a 3-1 win. Those fuckin' Sharks just hated me. During a timeout they showed a feature on the Jumbotron called "Celebrity Look-a-Likes." It showed the bugs from the movie *A Bug's Life* and then my picture next to them. It was hilarious. The fans went crazy.

I loved getting to the San Jose guys. When the ref was busy I'd give someone a face wash with my glove, or tap their goalie, or peck at the back of a guy's calves, where there's no padding, with my stick. Guys hate it when you do that. And when I scored, I made sure the fans ate it with lemons by pointing at the crowd and riding my stick. Those laid-back California hockey fans would absolutely lose it.

My rookie roomie Milan Hejduk scored at 13:12 of sudden-death overtime to clinch the series in six games. I hadn't been past the first round of playoffs in ten years. It was an unbelievable feeling! I raced over to Milan and jumped on top of him. He gave me that stunned look again, and I started laughing. He killed me, that kid. Things were looking good for me. I had 11 points (3 goals, 8 assists) in our six-game series victory over San Jose.

In the next round against Detroit, the press had us pegged as the underdogs. The Red Wings had taken home the Cup for the past two years. Chris Dingman, who had been playing for the Avs' affiliate, the Hershey Bears, was called up. Detroit and the Avs had developed a rivalry a lot like the one between Calgary and Edmonton. It all started long before I got there, in game three of the Western Conference final in 1996, when Slava Kozlov of Detroit drove Adam Foote's face into the glass with his fist and there was no penalty. Foote needed twenty stitches to close his forehead. So Claudie Lemieux punched Kozlov in the mouth.

In the parking lot after the game, when Claudie and his wife and new baby were walking to their car, Red Wings coach Scotty Bowman just went nuts, swearing and calling him all kinds of names. In front of a wife and baby? No matter what has happened during a game, you just do not do that. Not ever.

That kind of disrespect toward his family obviously did not sit well with Claudie, because three games later he cranked Kris Draper into the boards from behind. The problem was that the player's gate was open and Kris crashed into the hard edge of the open door. Draper's face basically caved in. As Claudie stood there watching the carnage, Detroit's Darren McCarty sucker-punched him and they went at it. Then, almost a year later, on March 26, 1997, McCarty went after Claudie again, just beating the shit out of him. Patrick Roy tried to intervene and ended up scrapping with Mike Vernon, who was now Detroit's goalie, at centre ice. Things got uglier during the Western Conference final that year, when Avs coach Marc Crawford, the same calm, cool and collected guy who had stood behind the bench for us at Nagano, was fined ten grand for calling Bowman out during game four. He got so mad he tried to climb the partition that separates the benches.

So there was bad blood between the Avs and Detroit, and when Detroit beat us the first two at home, our fans booed us out of the building. But we were a team of disciplined veterans. We took responsibility and responded with two wins on their turf—we were a great road team. We swept the rest of the series. I was winning about 64 per cent of my faceoffs, and in the two rounds I had 14 points in the play-offs, tied with Joe Sakic for third in the league. The Denver press was screaming for the team to sign me, and that suited me fine. I loved it there. I thought that if we could beat Dallas in the conference finals, I might be buying another home in the Rockies.

We jumped out to an early lead in the series, stealing the opener in Dallas. It was hard fought all the way, but my buddy Valeri Kamensky scored the winner late in the third to seal a 2–1 victory.

We were confident, bigger, younger, maybe faster and more skilled, but they wanted it more. We played two strong periods in game two and were tied 1–1. But in the third, they threw everything at us, out-shooting us 15–1. Mike Modano and my old Flames teammate Joe Nieuwendyk scored, and they took the game 4–2.

The series moved to our home turf, McNichols Arena, but Dallas just kept coming. Newie, who was just incredible in the playoffs that year, had a goal and two assists and they blanked us 3–0. I was frustrated. I wasn't getting into the slot. Sakic and I were both pressing.

Game four was one of the most intense games of my career. Roy stepped up as the team leader and became more vocal than ever. He challenged us to "get it the fuck going." We were all a lot more physical. Milan was steered into the boards by Dallas defenceman Richard Matvichuk and ended up with a broken collarbone. Matvichuk put a tough hit on Forsberg, injuring his shoulder too. We were already missing Kamensky due to a wrist injury—this is why depth is so important. I put up a fuckin' tent in front of Eddie Belfour, screening him like crazy. Joe scored the first goal off me and Hejduk. We were tied 2-2 at 19:29 of overtime when Chris Drury shelved it over Eddie Belfour's right shoulder. Shots were 45-all. Heck of a game.

Then I came down with a wicked flu. I never got sick. Never. I think I missed seven games in my eleven years with the Flames. On May 30, as we were ready to go into our game five against the Stars back in Dallas, I literally could not get out of bed. Despite the speculation later on, this was not due to partying or any bullshit like that. I was just sick, period. Thankfully, we ended up winning 7-5 with two goals from Drury and two from Kamensky. The next game could decide it for us.

But it didn't. I dragged my ass out of bed and watched Eddie Belfour come up huge, stopping 26 of 27 for a 4-1 win. We had three days to get ready for a seventh game.

I knew that game seven would create an opportunity for one great individual effort to make the big difference, and I wanted that effort to be mine. The new owners of the Avalanche, Bill and Nancy Laurie, were not paying me to finish one game short of the final. I was making $2.4 million, and knew I could get three times that as a free agent. Basically, winning game seven would be a big step toward convincing the owners to sign a big-number paycheque for me next season.

It didn't happen. Mike Keane, my old friend and teammate from the Moose Jaw junior days, did the damage with two goals. Dallas won the series and went on to face the Sabres and win the Cup on a disputed goal by Brett Hull, whose skate was clearly in the goal crease while he swatted in a rebound. Everybody on our team was disappointed, Patrick Roy maybe most of all. He could not get over game six. He took it very personally.

When we lost, only one game short of the Stanley Cup final, I knew

I wasn't going to be re-signed by Colorado. They were just carrying too much payroll. Peter Forsberg made $9 million, Roy took home $7.5 million, Sandis Ozolinsh was at $4 million, Adam Foote made $3.1 million and Claudie $2.5 million. It wasn't in the cards for me.

Losing fuckin' sucks. Big time.

26

THE RANGERS

JULY 1, Canada Day, is the start of hockey's fiscal year, which means the beginning of free-agent season. I had turned 31 two days earlier. I was in my prime, I was considered one of the biggest prizes in hockey and I could pick and choose. I'd played 15 games before the end of the season for the Avalanche and scored 10 goals and 14 assists, then another 5 goals and 12 assists for 17 points in 18 playoff games.

I had given the Flames my heart and soul, and they had rewarded me by making me one of the lowest-paid franchise players in the league. Salary-wise, I didn't even crack the top fifty. Detroit's Sergei Fedorov was number one, at $14 million, and he scored 63 points in 1998–99. He was on a team with Steve Yzerman, who was paid $4.8 million with 74 points, and Larry Murphy, who made $3 million with 52. That same season, I had 93 points in the regular season on a $2.4 million contract.

The New York Rangers had made it clear to the media that they wanted me, and that felt good. The Rangers' general manager, Neil Smith, and Dave Checketts, the president of Madison Square Garden, flew to Winnipeg on the team's private jet to negotiate with Baizley on the very first day of free agency. I was at my cabin in the Shuswap. Within five hours, I got a fax that had to be a mile long. When I got to the numbers, I said, "You gotta be fuckin' kidding. They want to pay me *this* much?"

The contract said that I had three hours to decide, and if I didn't sign with New York they "were going in a different direction." Wayne Gretzky, who had just retired after playing his last three years with the Rangers, had called me earlier in the year and told me how great it was to live in New York. I discussed it with Veronica. "What do you think about me going to New York?" She supported it. It's hard to say no to $28 million over four years. So I ended up taking the contract and going to New York.

The Rangers were looking forward to having me on their team because they thought I could get some of the apathetic New York fans to quit sitting on their hands and at the same time needle the Islanders fans. But looking back, it was probably not a good place for me to be. Take a kid to a candy store and what does he want? Candy. And there's plenty of candy in New York. I wasn't prepared for what came next, and I didn't have the tools to deal with it.

Bearcat Murray had worked as the Rangers' equipment manager in 1980. He used to say that the people who hung around the rink in New York were absolute animals. Later, when things went to hell for me, he said he wasn't surprised. "It's full of just terrible people, happy and patting you on the back with a knife in their hands. It's a tough spoonful to take living down there, and you have to live there to understand it."

The Rangers were like an army of mercenaries. In a two-week period during the summer of 1999, Neil Smith handed out millions in contracts. He went for every top unrestricted free agent in sight. In addition to me, there was Valeri Kamensky and Stéphane Quintal, goalie Kirk McLean, Tim Taylor and Sylvain Lefebvre. Finally, just before the start of the season, he acquired a tough and talented defenceman, Kevin Hatcher, from Pittsburgh in exchange for Peter Popovic—that cost another $2 million. The team's payroll was not just the highest in the league, it was the most any hockey team had ever spent: $59.4 million. But mercenaries do not always beat guerilla fighters. Why? Because guerilla fighters form a brotherhood. New York had a different feeling—it was all about the money. On every other team in the NHL, players hang out together. They golf together, their wives know each other and they have dinner together. In Calgary, we knew what the other guys had for breakfast. The problem with the Rangers was that the single guys lived in the city, near Madison Square Garden, and the married guys lived out in a place called Rye, near the team's Playland practice rink. I mean, it was like playing on two different teams. Very dysfunctional.

Veronica and I flew to New York and met with the real estate agent the team had lined up for us. We looked around at different properties and decided on a house in Greenwich, Connecticut, right next door to New York's Westchester County. It was ten minutes from the practice rink, and forty-five minutes to the Garden in my brand-new BMW 740 IL. Fully loaded. Greenwich, along the coast overlooking Long Island Sound, has beautiful beaches and meadows. It has woods and fields with lots of wildlife.

It was a big two-storey house, and it was pretty nice, newly constructed on a great lot, but believe me, relative to the homes around us, it was not spectacular. Greenwich has one of the most exclusive zip codes in the United States, and at $1.6 million, ours was the cheapest house in the neighbourhood. We were located in the hills along with Tommy Hilfiger, Diana Ross, Mel Gibson, Ron Howard, Jack Nicholson, Regis Philbin and Oprah's buddy, Gayle King. Sprinkled in between were big-time stockbrokers.

Madison Square Garden was this incredible meeting place where every celebrity in the city seemed to meet up at one time or another. There was a green room where family and friends went before and after the games. The girls, our wives, also got to know unbelievable people. I met a whole new group of deviant fellows like me. Jason Priestley became a really good friend, and still is. The Rangers would stage an exhibition hockey game once a year before the All-Star Game, where we'd split the roster in two, rounding out the two teams with celebrities who played hockey like Alan Thicke, Michael J. Fox, the Barenaked Ladies, Mike Myers and Chris Reeve. It was all part of what made New York so cool.

I tried my hardest to bring the Rangers together as a team, but money changes people. Sometimes the guys who lived in the country had to stay home with the kids so their wives could go shopping. NHL wives come from small towns all over North America, and suddenly they have limo drivers and Fifth Avenue charge accounts. It changes their values. You don't see too many marriages last, and if they do it's purely materialistic. I got caught up in the whole thing. Relationship-wise, playing in New York made things very complex. It was impossible for Veronica to know where I would be from day to day. So I could indulge in my addiction all I liked. I could say, "Hey, we're staying in the city tonight because we've got practice at the Garden tomorrow morning and then we are leaving for Philly." And I would take off wherever. There was just no accountability.

On top of everything else, the media in New York were like pit bulls. They segregated us to a point where we could hardly function as a group the way a hockey team needs to. Guys like me score goals partly because tough guys take care of us. Look at the relationship between Marty McSorley and Wayne Gretzky. McSorley always had Gretz's back. If the media had made McSorley out to be a nobody and a zero, while pumping up Gretzky as a world-class hero, Marty might not have been so interested in keeping Mr. Gretzky from getting hurt.

The New York Times wrote some flattering things about me in the pre-season, building me up, making me out to be the hardest-working player in the NHL and a folk hero. Every story ever written about me said that I was an underdog because of my size. I told the *Times* the same thing I told every reporter—"I don't play small. I don't act small. Small is just a word."

We got off to a decent start, but then it went downhill. Coach John

Muckler was a different cat. He was another one of those old-school guys. I'd finally escaped Brian Sutter and his two-hour practices, and now here I was in New York, playing for Muckler, who was basically the same guy. I was just, like, *fuck!* I think Muckler respected me as a player, but our personalities clashed. He wanted me because he said he hated me when he coached in Edmonton and I played for Calgary. He thought I could replace Gretz. But I wasn't Gretz, I was Theoren Fleury. And I wasn't the 21-year-old Theo Fleury of 1990 that Muckler wanted me to be—an instigator out to prove himself. I was so far past that. I was so tired of being mentally burnt out due to coaching from the ground up. Learn this system and that system, watch this video and on and on. I had become a totally different player. I played with finesse, and I was smarter, older—*and* bigger. I weighed 178 now, which was twenty-five pounds of muscle that I didn't have at age 18.

Muckler was a bag-skater. Every day we were bag-skated, which means you skate till your bag falls off. Some guys would puke, everyone got dehydrated. Sometimes he would bag-skate us the day of a game. Muckler did win a few, like the Cup in Edmonton in 1989–90, and in six years coaching the Oilers and Sabres he'd made the playoffs every year, but I just don't know how guys like him keep getting jobs over and over and over again.

Adam Graves, one of my linemates, was my roommate—a fantastic guy, great guy, and the ultimate team player—but I didn't click with Petr Nedvěd. He was all over the place, really hard to play with. He wasn't very good in his own zone, which meant we would get scored on, which meant my line would sit on the bench.

Overall, it was just a nightmare, just a fucking nightmare.

THERE WERE REALLY GOOD GUYS on the team. John MacLean, a longtime New Jersey Devil, signed as a free agent the year before I did. He was a great addition to the Rangers. He'd won the Cup with the Devils in 1994–95, and he scored a lot of clutch goals. A great team guy. Funny, quick-witted, a veteran who had been around the block, an honest player and a good family man.

Jan Hlaváč was a talented guy, big-time talent, although he was a bit lazy. We called that group—Hlaváč, Nedvěd and Radek Dvořák, who joined us in December 1999—the Czech mafia. They didn't worry about coming back into their own zone too often, they just liked to score goals. For them, hockey was all about offence. They would not backcheck. But sometimes you have to play defence. I found them frustrating to play with because they stayed out way too long on their shifts. Often, they would hurt the team by not playing along with the team concept. But most of the time, the Czech guys really loved to laugh and have fun. They were very easy going and laid-back off the ice.

Alexandre Daigle, what a beauty, that guy. He was a strange cat. Probably one of the fastest guys I ever played with. He had all the tools, but no box to go with it. Dumb as a post—he didn't get it. He could have been a superstar, but he was too dumb to realize you have to work hard and not blame everybody around you for your failings. Guys who use excuses and place blame on others don't get it. In that respect, he was like Gary Leeman, who played in Calgary in 1991–92 and 1992–93. He told Doug Risebrough, "You never gave me a chance." Riser said, "You are playing on a line with Theo Fleury and Joe Nieuwendyk, what more of a chance can you have?" Anyway, Daigle was on one of those whirlwind tours, trying to find his place in life. He made it more difficult for himself than he had to. Super-cocky dude. He always made it out that he was better than he was. Muckler didn't like that kind of guy.

Tim Taylor was very serious and steady. He would chip in with the odd big goal. Tim wasn't hugely talented, but he had a great work ethic. He was one of those unsung heroes that you have to have on your team. A quiet family man.

Mike Knuble was a big, strong winger. Hard worker, great forechecker. He found his game when he went to Boston and got to play with Joe Thornton. Eric Lacroix was a hard worker too. He didn't have a lot of talent, but, man, he could hit. He could knock you into next Tuesday.

Kevin Stevens had won two Stanley Cups in Pittsburgh. He ended up in the NHL Substance Abuse Program too. He was arrested near St. Louis in 2000 and charged with soliciting a prostitute and possessing drug paraphernalia. He was ordered to complete an eighteen-month court-supervised drug program. He is doing all right now, scouting for his old linemate Mario Lemieux, which is nice to know. Back then he was a big, incredibly strong kid from Boston. He had the accent, you know like the joke, "Khakis—what you need to start your car in Boston." He was phenomenal playing with Mario. He had back-to-back 50-goal seasons.

Todd Harvey was a happy-go-lucky guy. He wasn't the greatest skater in the world, but he worked really hard and was emotional. He played with his heart on his sleeve. He would fight every once in a while. He really would do anything for the team. A character player. I played against Rob DiMaio in junior when he was in Medicine Hat. He was tough for his size. Pretty quiet off the ice.

Valeri Kamensky was a scary-talented dude, but by that time he was playing out his last few years and making big money. He was a typical Russian player from the Central Red Army team. There was no joy or passion for hockey there. That had been beaten out of them in Russia. When they came to North America, it was all about Versace and Mercedes-Benz.

If you look at our defence, on paper it was probably the best in the league. Kevin Hatcher was a huge dude. Talented but near the end of his career. He wasn't as hungry as he once was. Nice guy, though. I hung out with him sometimes. I never really got to know Mathieu Schneider. Let's just say he and Muckler had a difference of opinion of how one should play and one should coach. But he was a real steady defenceman. Good on the power play, great passer. Kim Johnsson had a lot of talent, but he was a rookie. Playing defence in the NHL takes a while to learn. He was a quiet guy.

Stéphane Quintal was one of the free agents brought in that year. He didn't handle the pressure in New York very well. He played like shit all year and his plus-minus was minus-10. That's bad. Great players like Nicklas Lidström in Detroit end up with a great number, something like plus-40, year in and year out.

Sylvain Lefebvre came from Colorado with me. He was a nice guy—not a flashy player but steady. He played well on defence with Brian Leetch, but things went sideways for him in New York.

Rich Pilon had a kind of a lisp. He always got dehydrated, so they were always trying to restore his electrolytes, which are basically salts that carry an electrical charge. You lose electrolytes through your sweat, mainly sodium and potassium, and that causes you to dehydrate. So the trainers gave him Pedialyte, which is normally for children. He was always seizing up because he wasn't in very good shape. But it was hard to play against him because he was tough and mean. He wasn't overly quick, but he was a hacker, whacker and slasher. Back then, you could hack and whack all you wanted.

Dale Purinton was a tough guy. He had more ink on his body than a newspaper. He had his name tattooed on his back.

Our trainer, Jim Ramsay, was a real character. Very funny in a perverted way. He didn't hold anything back, was always making comments about guys' wives. He might say, "Man, your wife has a tight ass." He was a big flirt with the women.

Kirk McLean, his nickname was Weird. He had *Weird* embroidered all over his goalie equipment. I have never met a goalie who was normal. McLean was even more eccentric than usual and had kind of a perverted sense of humour. Nice and funny but different, for sure. He was probably the last stand-up goalie that played in the

NHL. You would rarely see him flopping around, but he was effective. Great glove hand and good technically, and very smart, but out there. When you talked to him he would give you this intense stare. You never knew what he was thinking.

I can describe Mike Richter in two words—great guy. Quickest feet on a goalie I have ever seen. His career ended due to knee injuries and a skull fracture and concussion, but he was the first Ranger with 300 NHL wins. Mike tore the anterior cruciate ligament (ACL) in his right knee in 2001, the second time in one year, but he played through his troubles and saved our asses more than once. His last few years of hockey were not a whole lot of fun for him. He wound up going to Yale and getting a bachelor's degree in ethics, politics and economics. Really smart guy.

Brian Leetch was the captain. He was a hero to the fans because he played on Team USA. But I thought Leetch did not recognize how much talent was on our team. I think if he could have seen it, he might've been able to bring the team together. That is the captain's job. He always seemed pretty cozy with the coaches and management, and I figured he would finish his career in New York and then become a suit after hockey. Instead, he retired after playing eighteen years, but he finished his career with the Bruins and apparently he blames Slats for that.

The biggest issue that first year in New York was that we did not buy into what Muckler was selling. Muckler had a defensive system, but nobody really played it. It was the standard Buddy Ryan system, named after the 1985 Chicago Bears defensive coach. It is a defence system that eliminates the passing. As a result, we gave up way too many goals. Secondly, we were not committed as a group. Our guys were not willing to work that hard. The play in our zone was horrendous. Guys would get out-muscled. It's never just the coaches that are to blame, the fault is the group's collectively. I have since told my wife that if I ever think of coaching, she should kick me in the nuts as hard as she can. It's an ulcer waiting to happen.

We tried to fix our problems with a lot of team meetings after practices and games. It was like group therapy, everybody airing out their differences. I was trying to bond with my team, so I would go out to the bar with them, and when they all went home I would take off and find another place to keep partying. Most nights, I was happy with booze and a nice comfy bar stool in Greenwich, near my house. I didn't advertise that I was snorting and rolling in at dawn, but I did not make any secret out of what I was doing either. I always trusted my teammates 100 per cent. I mean, these guys had my back. They were fighting a war in the same foxhole with me, day in and day out. Anyway, around February, as I was packing for a game against the Leafs in Toronto, I got a call from Dr. Brian Shaw, who represented the NHL Players' Association in the NHL Substance Abuse Program, and Dan Cronin, who was the program's director of counselling. Dan was the liaison between Dr. Shaw and Dr. David Lewis, who worked for the owners. "We're concerned about you, Theo," Dr. Shaw said. "There are a whole bunch of rumours around about you taking drugs and staying out late. What is going on?" Dan said, "When you get to Toronto, why don't you come and have a meeting with us? We will talk."

So I met with them. They knew that I was partying and doing drugs. They said they could see it in my play. They wanted me to sign up for the substance abuse program. They told me that all I had to do was take the odd drug test so they could protect me. They suggested I play out the season and then go to rehab that summer. It all sounded reasonable, so I signed up. But once I was in it, I thought it was one of the worst mistakes I made in my life, because it took away my freedom, my coping tools (drugs) and left me unhigh and dry.

How could the program know what I was up to? Someone on the team had told the coach about me, that's how. I thought I could hide in New York, but it turned out someone was spying on me. I figured out who it was, and to this day I have no time for this person. But I won't mention his name because unlike him, I am not a rat. After that, I think the Rangers had me followed by professionals, though I guarantee that you will never get anyone from that organization to admit it. I can't blame them—I was an $8-million-per-year investment.

Right after that, I became extremely secretive. I would go for a couple of beers with the guys, just to make an appearance, hire a limo to meet me out front, get in and have the driver take me around the block. Then I would get back out of the car and go back into the restaurant. The limo would drive around a bit. Then I would head to the back of the restaurant, through the kitchen and escape into the alley, where the limo was waiting. They wanted to play their game, I would play my game.

New York is a city that never goes to sleep, with bars that never close. For an alcoholic it is an all-you-can-eat buffet.

VERONICA WANTED STABILITY for our kids and she was eight months pregnant, so when I played for Colorado she stayed in Calgary until our daughter was born. But with New York I was on a multi-year contract, so she came with me. When we first got there, she had Chuck's oldest daughter, a really sweet kid named Christa, and Christa's boyfriend there to watch the kids and for company. Veronica, like most NHL wives, was crazy about clothes and loved to shop. Having that much money changes you. I was wearing Versace shirts and she was carrying Prada and Louis Vuitton. We had two credit cards with $50,000 limits on them.

I spent very little time at home. The strippers and cheating were not new behaviours for me, but I think in New York when I was on the road I wasn't as careful about hiding it as I was in Calgary and

Colorado. So Veronica started to ask a lot more questions. This is how it is for a lot of the hockey wives from the bigger teams. But a lot of hockey players have a different view of women than the rest of the world. Chuck put it this way: "Wrong as it is, hockey players view women like cars. You have your own car and you love your car and you want to take care of your car, and you want to take your car to every important meeting you have, and you want it to be beautiful and shiny and sometimes with new headlights. But you love other guys' cars. You love looking at their cars. You don't want to have their cars, but you would love to take them for a drive once in a while, and it's a horrible premise for a relationship."

27

SLATS

NEW YORK felt really strange. For the first time, I didn't achieve what I thought I could do. I would wake up every day and start over, but nothing went right. I never got a break. I was snakebit. And so I laid a big egg. In 80 games I scored only 15 goals, less than half my usual performance (in the 806 games I played before signing with the Rangers, I scored 374 times). Eight million for 15 goals. Through the 1998–99 season, my career shooting percentage was 13.7. In 1999–2000, I took 246 shots, for a success rate of only 6.1 per cent. Like, fuck! I bet I hit 25 or 30 goalposts that year.

An example of a typical frustrating game was on Friday, February 18, against Colorado. I had always had Paddy Roy's number. He had a lot of confidence—in 1996, Jeremy Roenick tried giving him an earful and Roy told the reporters he couldn't hear J.R. because he had two Stanley Cup rings in his ears. But Roy's weakness was between his ears. If you got it into his head that you could beat him, then you could. He was so superstitious that if he stepped on a line on the ice, it would bother him. Certain things would shake him up.

So I was looking forward to this game, because I thought I would bury a few on Roy and the curse would be lifted. In the first period, with the score tied 1–1, I came in on a shortie and deked, then deked again, then faked a backhand, turned and shot . . . and somehow, his glove was there. I was so fuckin' frustrated, I made toothpicks out of my stick against the boards. In the third period, Colorado was leading 3–2 and the door opened up twice on the left side, but it didn't happen. It didn't help that the New York fans were all over me, booing and calling me down. And of course the media could not believe that I'd flipped them off on my way into the tunnel. It wasn't the best way to bring the fans onside. In Calgary or Colorado if you came up dry the fans weren't happy, and I had been booed by opposing teams since I was seven, but to be called out in your own building—I mean, who *does* that?

Muckler was frustrated with the way I was playing. Any coach I have ever had had high expectations. Day after day, I would hear, "We need you to play better. We need you to contribute more."

The New York press was all over me for the shitty first season we had. They were absolutely brutal. I mean, you meet these basketball-bellied reporters who are dandruffy, armchair nerds in their short-sleeved plaid cotton shirts and whose biggest decision that day is deciding between chai and orange pekoe and you cannot believe they have the nerve to write shit about you. But this was the first time the Rangers had missed the playoffs three years in a row since 1966, so they felt entitled. Valeri Kamensky and I were called big-money disappointments. I was scratched for the final game, against Philly. By that point I had been around long enough to realize you can't dwell on the negative.

Despite the $61 million payroll, we ended up in eleventh place in the Eastern Conference, with a record of 29 wins, 41 losses and 12 ties. Everybody was blaming everybody. Dave Checketts blamed Neil Smith, our general manager, and coach John Muckler, and fired both at the end of March after Detroit took us to the mat, downing us 8–2 and 6–0. Rumour had it Smith tried to pin the team's failure on Muckler and ownership, and I felt Muckler blamed me. I took some responsibility, saying that I had not met the expectations I'd set for myself. But my expectations were different from Muck's—he was looking for the hell-bent-for-leather guy I'd been when I was a kid, and he wouldn't accept who I was or the way I played now.

The interim coach, John Tortorella, and the acting GM, Don Maloney, were on me too. "You are not trying, you are not playing hard enough." I was so fucking sick of these wannabes calling me a slacker. If that was supposed to be their idea of help and motivation— well, fuck. I did have 49 assists, leading the team, and played on a line with Mikey York, who was a contender for the Calder Trophy as the NHL's best rookie. Obviously, I was doing something right.

I had a no-trade clause so I was protected, but still I felt like shit. We were all waiting to hear who our next coach would be. Would he be able to help us with the team's chemistry? Would he be the glue we needed so much?

On May 31, 2000, the owners of the Rangers found the president and GM they were looking for in Glen "Slats" Sather. Slats got it. He had five Stanley Cup rings from his days as coach and GM of the Oilers between 1984 and 1990. Slats started turning things around right away. First, he hired Ron Low, his former backup goaltender and head coach in Edmonton. Ron was from Dauphin, Manitoba, twenty minutes from Russell. I was a kid when he made it to the NHL, and I looked up to him. He provided a lot of inspiration to every kid in our town. He was great. I went to his hockey school, the one he had with Butch Goring.

In one of his first player moves, Slats re-signed Mark Messier, the leader of the Rangers' 1994 Stanley Cup team and captain of the 1990 Oilers team that won the Cup, for two years at $11 million. It was a ballsy move. Messier was 38, and no one was sure what he had left. In his three years with Vancouver, Mess had averaged only 17 goals and 54 points. Then Slats signed Vladimir Malakhov, a talented Russian defenceman who had broken in with the Islanders, then moved on to Montreal and had just won a Stanley Cup with the Devils. He cost $17.5 mil for five years.

A couple of days after he was hired, Slats gave me a call. I think he was genuinely concerned, and Slats isn't fuckin' stupid. He had coached Grant Fuhr, Dave Semenko and Dave Hunter, who all partied hard. He mentioned the Graham James issue right off the bat. Basically, he said, "I understand what you have been through. Most of it is due to that fucking bastard. That fucking asshole. But Theo, I know what kind of player you are and I know what you can do for our team. Some don't think you can do it. I do." He said, "Get yourself in the best shape of your life."

But first, I'd agreed to enter the substance abuse program that summer.

28

ATLANTA STRIPPERS

AS PART OF MY TREATMENT under the NHL Substance Abuse Program, in the summer of 2001 they sent me to Cottonwood, a rehab facility in the desert near Tucson, Arizona. Don't get me wrong—I knew I had a problem, but I didn't want to get sober just so I could feel pain. It was my first major stint in rehab. I was scared shitless because I didn't know what to expect or what other issues were going to be exposed. One thing I know for sure, I needed to go for a year and work on everything. You can't just go for thirty days and expect to be better, because you only gain a couple of tools rather than the whole set, and when they run out you inevitably go back to drinking and drugging.

Back at that meeting in Toronto, when everybody was saying I needed to enter the program for my own protection, I had a buddy who was in the program and said, "Whatever you do, don't go in the program. You're fucked once you enter it. You're finished—done." There were so many times over the next five years I wished I had listened to him, but now that I am straight, I can see that I really needed help.

The substance abuse program had the power to control my career. I was constantly being made to sign "contracts" for aftercare, and if you violated one of the points set out, you were gone—maybe to rehab, maybe forever. A lot of these "contracts" would start with "I, Theoren Fleury, understand and agree to the following," and then they would put in all the shit they didn't want me to do, like "I agree to maintain total abstinence from all mind-altering drugs and alcohol. I agree not to enter or frequent strip clubs, men's clubs or establishments where there is partial or full nudity," followed by "I understand and agree that failure to meet the conditions of this aftercare plan may result in fine, suspension or movement to the next stage as provided by the NHL/NHLPA Substance Abuse and Behavioral Health Program at the sole discretion of the Program Doctors."

Anyway, once I signed on, it was the start of constant pee tests and sessions with psychologists.

There are four stages to the program. If you're caught violating your "contract," you move on to the next stage and the penalties get more severe. At stage one, you receive in-patient treatment but no suspension. But if you violate the terms of stage one, you advance to stage two, where you're suspended without pay while you get further treatment, after which you're eligible to be reinstated. Fail another test and you move to stage three, where you're suspended without pay for at least six months before you can be reinstated. Violate your stage-three treatment plan and you're out for at least a year, with no guarantee you'll be reinstated.

Basically, it meant they could order me not to drink, go to strip clubs, use drugs, gamble, whatever they felt like. And if I didn't do what they asked, they might or might not pull me out of hockey. As far as I was concerned, I could turn in ten dirty pee tests and as long as I was scoring—nothing, no consequences. But if I was playing shitty and gambled one night, or—God forbid—went to a titty bar, they could order me into a rehab program for a month. The program had total discretion to do whatever it wanted.

Another one of the program mandates was that I had to continue to see my therapist. I am sure some psychologists will try to help you if you are honest. But I wasn't ready to be honest, I was suspicious. What is this guy's intention? Does he really want to help me, or is he just collecting the two hundred bucks an hour? The sessions were like a game of cat and mouse, me trying to outsmart the expert. You know, I can barely watch *One Flew over the Cuckoo's Nest* because there are scenes in there that remind me of my own life.

I had nothing against any of these therapists, but I saw them as the representatives of those who had forced me into being there. From the time I was five years old until today, I have made every decision, every choice on my own. So when somebody tells me what to do, I really have to trust them before I will listen. I have a handful of people who I trust—Ede Peltz, Chuck, my wife Jenn, Don Baizley. End of list.

When I entered the office of the first psychologist, I looked around and thought, "This ain't Bob Newhart's place, that's for sure." It was four walls and a bunch of books. The guy looked a bit like Graham, to tell you the truth. He asked, "Why are you here?" I was thinking, "Let's see. I am fuckin' hung over. The money I make has corrupted everybody, every single person around me. I have completely lost sight of who I am. I have a job to do and I need to focus on doing that job, but I am being pulled in all different directions by home, the team, the NHL, the fans, you name it. I am no longer a person, I am just a commodity, a piece of meat. The little boy in Russell, Manitoba, who grew up an honest kid, a talented kid, a trusting kid, is gone. I am in survival mode and I want to quit hockey." Instead, I said, "I think I might have a drinking problem. I'm not convinced yet, but it is possible."

He said, "Tell me about where you grew up. What were your parents like? How did your mother treat you?" The typical bullshit. "I had a great childhood," I said. "It was awesome! I had loving, supportive parents. Can't recall anything that threw me off track."

WHEN I GOT BACK, I had the whole summer to get myself into the best shape of my life, as Slats had ordered. And I did. I built a gym out at the cabin in Sicamous and bought all kinds of fitness equipment: a squat rack, bike, bench press, elliptical walker, weights. A couple of thousand dollars' worth.

The way I saw it, after that disappointing first season in New York the world was saying I was done, so I took it as a challenge, an opportunity to shove it up somebody's ass.

The team had given me a training manual outlining every detail of everything I needed to do, so each morning I would get up, have a coffee and a smoke, walk into the garage, crank up Céline Dion on the ghetto blaster and start my workout. Why Céline Dion? Well, when I was on my first road trip with Colorado, we played the Florida Panthers, and after the game, in the green room, there she was, in the flesh. It turns out our GM, Pierre Lacroix, and Céline's hubby, René Angélil, were buds. She came up to me and said, "Oh, how's your knee?" Good Canadian girl that she is, she's a hockey fan. It was such a shocker—one of the biggest music stars in the world asking about my knee. She was super nice.

A while later, I bought one of her CDs and started using it to work out. Not every NHLer listens to Metallica, although I have to admit they're good too.

We had training camp at the University of Vermont, where Marty St-Louis played his college hockey, and we went through the fitness testing. I had improved in every area. One of the tests measured our VO_2 max, which is the maximum rate at which you can use oxygen when you exercise. It's expressed in millilitres of oxygen per kilogram of body weight per minute, or ml/kg/min. An elite athlete should test at between 55 and 65, but I was closer to 65 or 70, which is what marathon runners, professional cyclists and Olympic athletes test. In other words, in terms of fitness, I was in Lance Armstrong territory.

THERE WAS A BIG STORY in the paper that fall about some of the Knicks basketball players getting blowjobs at an Atlanta strip bar called the Gold Club. The owner of the club had apparently been linked earlier to Mafia families, money laundering and all kinds of racketeering. The whole Knicks thing eventually went to trial and *Sports Illustrated* reported that a week before the incident they heard that a hockey player had been in the club and spent thirty grand on strippers in one night. Guess who?

Okay, here is what happened. We had a pre-season game in Atlanta on September 21, 2000. I didn't play that night and I was feeling antsy, so I went out by myself to the Gold Club. I've been to every strip joint in North America. Twice. The waitress who was looking after my tab started bringing girls into this private suite, one after another. It was like *Project Runway*—they were climbing all over themselves to get in there. One would go to the bathroom and say to her girlfriend, "I got this guy spending money like crazy, you have to come in there." Eventually, there were fifteen girls and me in the private suite, partying all night. These were good-looking ladies—huge, fake breasts, evening gowns, jewellery, makeup, and they smelled good too. We ordered champagne, and I paid the bouncer to dial me a dealer. He came back and said, "Okay, the guy is outside." So I picked up some blow and things got even rosier. Every hour my waitress would bring me a new Visa receipt to sign. I had two cards, each with a $50,000 limit. When you're getting a paycheque for about $400,000 every two weeks, you just don't worry about a bar bill. There were cameras in these rooms, so it was a no-sex zone, but I was far too high anyway. We would turn our backs away from the cameras when we went into the corner to snort. The lights were low. There was some cool hip-hop music for dancing. We were having a great time, just hanging out.

I got back to the hotel at 9:30 a.m.—just in time, because our bus left at 10:30. My cell phone rang at 9:45, as I was stepping out of the shower. It was Veronica, and she said, "I am at the mall and I am trying to use the credit card and it's maxed out." And I said, "Well, I don't know what that is all about." She said, "There is some charge on there for $36,000 from a car wash company." And I said, "Well, I dunno." I knew exactly what it was, because as I was talking to her I was pulling all these Visa receipts out of my pocket and thinking, "Holy fuck."

She said that if I didn't know what it was for, she was going to phone the credit card company and stop payment. I had to 'fess up. What was I supposed to do, lie? How could I get out of this one? Couldn't. So I told her, and she went ballistic. Veronica was in full detective mode all the time. When I came home, she would check my cell phone to see who I'd called. As soon as the phone bill came in, she would underline every phone number and ask, *Who's this? Who's that?* She would sometimes call the numbers. She was so unhappy.

Don't get me wrong. I am not saying the way I behaved as a husband was acceptable, but it's weird that, as soon as we moved to New York and the money started rolling in, it became all about *things*. What had attracted me to Veronica was that she seemed so unpretentious. I got sucked into the stupidity of caring too much about material things too. One day Veronica needed the van to drive the kids somewhere because it had child car seats, and I argued with her because I wanted to take it. Veronica said, "Why don't you take your Viper?" I had a really cool Dodge Viper that I had bought right before the playoffs in 1994. Some little old lady won it in an auction and a car dealer called me and said, "Hey, I got a car you might want to look at." So I test-drove it, wrote him a cheque for seventy-five grand and drove it away. Anyway, I said, "No, it's raining." Today, would I care if my car got wet? Absolutely not.

We tried marriage counselling. That was hilarious. After five minutes of hearing about my behaviour, the counsellor told me I was completely fucked and there was nothing wrong with her. I said, "The NHL is paying you five hundred bucks an hour to come up with this scenario?" and I walked.

The only place I felt good when I was sober was on the ice, but when I left the rink I didn't have a clue who I was. And I think it went back to the dark room and waiting for that fucking guy to come and molest me. Because that's what it fuckin' felt like. That is why I could not go back to the hotel room after games and sleep inside those four walls. I couldn't. And I couldn't go home, either. I just couldn't deal with my marital problems on top of everything else.

So I went out, and stayed out, for days at a time.

29

GATORADE PEE TESTS

I STARTED SLOWLY during the 2000 training camp but was out of the slump by the middle of October. In our third game of the season, I scored twice against the Pittsburgh Penguins. We lost 8–6, but it was a high-tempo contest. Our coach, Ronny Low, made you earn your ice time, and he was giving me more than any other forward, about twenty minutes per game. He also put me on the right point on power plays. My confidence was building.

But by the end of the month, I was in Low's doghouse. During another game against Pittsburgh, we were down 3–1 and I got called for slashing. Low told the *New York Post* he was concerned about my taking penalties in the offensive zone and he put me on the fourth line. I mean, shit, nine games into the season and I already had five goals and he was worried about penalties? I had to survive out there somehow. I went out in the next game against the Bruins and scored a shorthander and chipped in an assist. We won it, 5–1. On November 1, I scored three goals and assisted on the game-winner against Tampa Bay. Then we beat Montreal a couple of days later, and I opened the scoring. That goal gave me 11 in 13 games and made me the sixtieth player in NHL history to score 400 regular-season goals in his career.

On November 18, we played the Flames at the Saddledome—only my second time there since leaving. It was Josh's 12th birthday, so we arranged for him to bring his friends to a skybox. I assisted in the first period and scored on a shorthanded breakaway at the start of the second.

The game was tied at four and we were headed for overtime when, with five seconds left in the third, I got called for roughing. I just snapped. I wanted to choke the ref, Dan Marouelli. Throughout the game, Toni Lydman had been hooking and holding because that's the only way you could stop me, and Marouelli was oblivious to it. Of course, I got frustrated. I saw him as a typical NHL ref, wanting to control the outcome of the game. He added a ten-minute misconduct, so I was done for the game. Fortunately, Valeri Kamensky scored at 2:44 of OT, so we won.

MEANWHILE, as per the substance abuse program, I had to provide urine samples from time to time, but since I was still out partying, they were consistently dirty. I was putting Gatorade in the test samples. Sometimes I'd use other people's pee, sometimes even Beaux's. Dr. Shaw and Dr. Lewis kept warning me. Countless times, I would get the call—"If you continue this behaviour, we're going to have to pull you out." Did I believe them? No. I was one of the highest-scoring players in the NHL. What were they going to do?

Occasionally, I'd ease up. If my buddy Chuck Matson came to visit, it helped. Slats used to love it when Chuck was around, because I always played better. I got two goals and an assist in one game, and Slats stopped Chuck in the hall and said, "Hey, Matson, you should come by more often." And then I got a goal and an assist in the next game, and Slats saw Chuck and said, "Hey, Mats, I think you should move down here and live with Theo." Chuck said, "Yeah, you can tell my wife that's gonna happen." In the game after *that*, I got three assists. Slats walked past Chuck and me as we were leaving, then turned around and said, "Matson, what's your wife's number?"

But most of the time I didn't have any friends like Chuck around for support. I was alone. Number one and alone. And every time I got to the top, I fucked it all up because I didn't like being there. Maybe I felt that I didn't deserve it. And I had huge problems with being alone—it was like I couldn't have a relationship with myself. The funny thing is, the higher I rose in society, the more alone I became. Why? Because I was treated differently and dehumanized. I knew that half the time people were nice to me because I had money or I was a hockey star. I had become addicted to cocaine. The only days I wasn't doing it were game days. My new routine was sleep, play the game, party till 6 a.m., go to practice, come home and sleep around the clock till the next day. Alcohol and drugs stopped the anxiety attacks and took away the worry, shame and guilt. When I was blasted I was happy, and when I was happy I played great hockey.

And I was playing awesome. On February 12, 2001, *The New York Times* wrote an article with the headline "Fleury Continues Impressive Comeback." The article said, "There can be no argument that Fleury, who is in his second year with the Rangers, is critical to any chance the Rangers have of salvaging their playoff hopes." Mark Messier, who had been on my line for the past couple of games, was quoted as saying, "That's the kind of year he's had, though. He's played hard, scored big goals for us, played in every situation, and played unbelievably consistent for us all year. He had another big goal for us tonight."

WITH SIX WEEKS left in the season, we were eight points behind Boston and Carolina for the last playoff spot in the Eastern Conference, but still hoping to catch up. I was fourth in the NHL in scoring with 30 goals and 44 assists for 74 points, trailing only Joe Sakic,

Jaromír Jágr and Alexei Kovalev. Then the fuckin' NHL Substance Abuse Program decided that thirteen dirty pee tests were enough, and it was announced that I had voluntarily entered the substance abuse and behavioral health program run jointly by the NHL and the players' association. Voluntarily? Well I guess that depends on your definition of the word.

The pee test guys showed up after our game against Ottawa on February 26, and I was still out partying. Dan Cronin was trying to get hold of me. Finally, he called and said, "Pack your stuff, you are going to L.A." My season went tits-up.

Everything had been going so well on the ice. I was playing great. I guess it was just another example of me self-sabotaging something that was good. And I'd been warned, I *had* been warned.

I went home and sat on our bed and cried and howled like a wounded animal for six hours straight. Just raw emotion. Thirty-two years of everything that was shitty kind of poured out all at once. I loved playing hockey so much—when you took that away, what was left? And I had let the Rangers down.

Glen Sather called me before the flight. I am sure he felt like he had been hit in the side of the head with a baseball bat, because he didn't see it coming. Why hadn't I turned to him? I felt really badly, and I think he would have helped me if I had gone to him. And to top it all off, our goalie, Mike Richter, was out with a blown anterior cruciate ligament (ACL) in his right knee.

I needed to be able to deal with pain without using drugs, so I was sent for treatment at the Promises Westside Residential Treatment Center in California. I found it interesting that Dr. Lewis worked for the NHL Substance Abuse Program, yet he was also on the staff of the facility he sent the players to. The facility was garbage in my opinion—crappy, bland food, ugly, cheap furniture and the beds were shit.

One day, Dr. Lewis came in and said, "You need to start working out." Fuck you, I thought. He said, "There are a bunch of us going boxing tonight, why don't you come along?" He was such a dickhead. We just didn't get along—I rubbed him the wrong way and he rubbed me the wrong way. I don't know which one of us had a bigger ego, but I thought he was such a poser. He had your typical California tan with a full head of beach-boy blond hair. He was in his late 40s, but to me it looked like he had work done on his face.

I said, "As long as you put the headgear on and go three rounds with me, I am in. I am all in." He said, "Well, I won't be doing that." Fuckin' chickenshit. Not that I blame him—I would have killed the guy. Still, since it meant a chance to earn some brownie points, I said okay. They put me in the ring and I was hitting the guy holding up the punching pads so hard that I was lifting him right off the canvas— I was that mad. Dr. Lewis was looking at me, and I figured he was thinking, "What the hell? This guy is a psycho."

I WAS SICK with guilt over letting my team down. And on March 6, 2001, when I had been in treatment for a week, I heard about the Rangers' embarrassing 5–2 loss to the Islanders at the Garden. We were out of the playoffs.

MEANWHILE, I would check my bank statement every day to keep track of where my money was going. I called home, and Veronica was not there. My brother Travis was babysitting the kids. Veronica had gone on vacation. First she went to the Bahamas for her birthday, then she went down to Florida with all the wives for the April 7 game against the Panthers. "Fuck it," I said. I couldn't worry about it. I had to concentrate on my own shit.

At the treatment centre, Dr. Lewis started me on the antidepressant Effexor. I was already overstimulated, not depressed or suicidal, so the Effexor just ramped everything up. I felt like I was on speed. I worked with the therapists on why I was so good at beating myself up. We did some inner-child stuff. In one exercise, they put a pen in my right hand—I had become ambidextrous after the skate blade accident when I was 13, but I usually write left-handed. The stuff I wrote represented my inner child, and it was talking to the adult in me. It said, "I'm okay, I've always been okay, you have always taken care of me." It was an exercise that truly put into perspective what kind of person I was, despite all the shit. At my core, I'm a caring guy. If I see a weaker person, I try to help them. So the doctors wanted me to learn to be that way with myself. In our society, we don't teach people how to like themselves. I had to learn that.

And then I did equine therapy. We went on a field trip to a big farm with horses all over the place. You go into a ring with a horse. The idea is that you have to get the horse to trust you. So the first thing you do is stand right in front of the horse so that it picks up on your energy and whatever. Before it was my turn, we had a chance to sit in the grandstand and observe what was going on. The first couple of people were tugging on the reins and the horse wouldn't move. And then it was my turn, and I swear to God I could have walked back to the treatment centre and that horse wouldn't have left my side. I didn't have any trouble getting him to trust me, I just started walking. I didn't even touch the reins. We just walked around the circle and he put his nose over my shoulder, nudging me, kissing me. It was pretty powerful stuff. It gave me such positive affirmation that I was a good guy. One worth trusting. Once you surrender, the sky is the limit.

The next stop was a treatment centre that specialized in trauma. It was called the Life Healing Center of Santa Fe. There, I broke the record for going to the most AA meetings. In thirty days, I'll bet I went to ninety meetings. You could go at lunch *and* you could go for two meetings at night, so I was hitting three a day. I felt it was my duty to try to get my shit together, because I had let a lot of people down in New York.

Some of what they told me was helpful, and some was just fuckin' ridiculous. They told me that I cheated on Veronica so much because I had a "sex addiction." They said it was triggered "when client is alone after games on the road [and] he and his wife would argue." Well, if that is true, then it turns out a lot of sex addicts play hockey.

Chuck came down to visit. He had never been to a treatment centre before. Dan Cronin picked him up at the airport and they spent half a day together. Chuck thought I was one of a random few guys in the NHL who had trouble, but when he saw that Dan had two cell phones, with two lines on each, ringing nonstop he realized I was not alone. Chuck said to me, "Bones, you would not believe who was on the other end talking about their troubles—the whole freakin' league!"

At the centre I introduced Chuck to a super-rich guy. Cocaine had made him so paranoid he was found holed up in the master bath of his humungous home with a lampshade on his head surrounded by cornflakes so he could hear anyone who tried to break in. His nose had an actual hole in the cartilage and he would slip a straw through it to make us laugh. Before coming to the centre he had had diplomatic immunity so he was making regular flights in his private jet to Colombia to pick up coke. The place was full of characters.

The substance abuse program "contract" required that I have a sponsor—"I will obtain and work with a twelve-step sponsor in my hometown." There was a meeting at a church on a Tuesday night. I loved going to the meetings. There was lots of good sobriety there, lots of great people. I was outside having a cigarette, and this little fat guy comes walking by and he's got a Detroit Red Wings hat on. I thought, "We're in Santa Fe. The only ice here is in a glass." So I walked up to him and said, "How're you doing?" I didn't tell him who I was. I said,

"You're a big Detroit Red Wings fan?" He said, "Oh, I'm the biggest Detroit fan. I love Steve Yzerman." And I stuck out my hand, "Well hi, I'm Theo Fleury." He fuckin' lost it! He said, "I read about you! This is where you are? You're here!" I said, "Yeah, I'm in the treatment centre on the south side of town." He introduced himself. His name was Jim Jenkins, JJ for short. We talked hockey for quite a while, and at the end of the conversation I said, "Okay, man, one of the requirements is for me to get a sponsor while I'm in treatment here. Are you willing to be my sponsor?" He refused. I said, "What do you mean, 'No'?"

"Are you ready? Are you really ready?" he asked. "Because I've seen guys like you. Lots of guys like you." Jim had done all kinds of things. He had been a professional race-car driver. Honest to God, he was fuckin' crazier than I was. He told me a story about how he had his four kids in his airplane while he was fucked up on Quaaludes and blow and all kinds of shit. They were up in the Rockies, and he looked over at his 12-year-old kid and said, "Take over, I'm done," and passed out. And his kid landed the fuckin' plane.

He finally agreed to be my sponsor. So he met me at the treatment centre the next day and we started reading Alcoholics Anonymous's Big Book together, and we hung out and made sure we were at the same meetings.

I had a therapist who tried to help me one on one. I had told her about what Graham had done to me, and whenever she brought it up I would just check out. She literally had to shake me to bring me back into the room. So they put me in a group. This group really opened my eyes to the crazy shit that people do to each other. There were people who had serious, nasty awful things done to them, and the only way they could face life is by shooting ecstasy, taking heroin or becoming obsessed with relationships and sex.

It was the first time I had ever dealt with the abuse head-on, the first time I could sit in a group and talk about anything. I was hearing some pretty fuckin' wild stuff, so when I told my story it didn't feel so bad.

Toward the end of the thirty days in New Mexico, I was getting ready to go back to treatment at Westside for two weeks to complete the program. But I found that I had connected with Santa Fe—I loved the desert. Jim and I drove out to a community called Las Campanas. It was gorgeous—two Jack Nicklaus golf courses, equestrian facilities, a spa. It was like walking into a picture of Heaven.

I got out of the car and stood at the edge of the road feeling a sense of peace I hadn't experienced since serving Mass at St. Joe's with Father Paul. The hills were covered in cactus and purple and green sage. But the thing that really got me was the light. The sky was big, it met the ground in the distance and the clouds looked like bags of feathers. I remember taking a deep breath of that cool, dry mountain air, and suddenly something clicked in my head. I said to myself, "You've got to move here. You feel safe. Everything is going well. You've got a good program started. If you leave, what might happen?"

I asked JJ, "Do you know a real estate agent?" and he said, "Yeah, my sister-in-law." I called Veronica, and she flew down the next day. We found a place. It cost about $1.2 million and it was an awesome place—one of those adobe-style homes, with heated brick floors and a 600-square-foot guesthouse. Just gorgeous. You could see the San-gre de Cristo Mountains from the front of my house. I had two acres that backed onto the sixth hole of the Sunrise Golf Course, which was 7,626 yards of golf from the longest tees.

I called Don Baizley and said, "I'm moving to Santa Fe!" He said, "What the hell?" I said, "I feel safe here and I've got a sponsor." I was feeling pretty good about myself and was determined to get ready for the next season as I settled into my new place. It was a retirement community, and I was probably the youngest member at that golf course by about thirty years. I met this really cool guy named Claude, who had been in the insurance business. We became good friends and golfing buddies. I got into a really good routine. I'd get up in the morning, work out, have lunch, Claude would pick me up and we would play thirty-six holes. From there, we'd have a bite to eat and then I'd go to a meeting that night. It was perfect.

Veronica came back and stayed with me in Santa Fe for two weeks, but she couldn't handle it. We were in the middle of the desert, with no friends, no family, no nothing. I thought we could start to repair the damage by getting away from her family and just being together with the kids. But there was too much history between us. She said, "I'm going back to Sicamous," and I said, "Well, I'm staying here." I was getting better, and she was used to chaos.

I had a second motivation for getting better—the Olympics. I wanted to be a part of the team that would represent Canada in 2002 at Salt Lake City. I was on the team that had failed in Nagano and wanted another chance. Due to my recent history, it was going to take an extraordinary effort for me to make that team. One morning, I was sitting at the big granite island in my kitchen when the phone rang. I said, "Hello?"

"Hey, Theo, it's Wayne."

"Wayne who?"

"It's Wayne Gretzky."

"Oh, how's it going, man?" I said.

"Well, good," he said. "You know I'm running the Olympic team for 2002. I understand that you've had a really good summer and you've got some things straightened around. I think it would be a pretty good idea if you came and joined us in Calgary for the camp."

"What? You want me to come there?"

"Absolutely. We think that you're going to be a huge part of the team this year at the Olympics." And I said, "Holy fuck," you know?

30

DRY DRUNK

THAT PHONE CALL really meant a lot to me. After getting pulled out of commission before the season ended, I was embarrassed. And to get that phone call from somebody I really looked up to said to me, "Okay, there are a lot of people who still believe in you. There are a lot of people that still want to see you succeed and see you do well."

I was in ridiculous shape, honest to God. I was ripped, big time. My weight was back down to 155 and my body fat was around 6 per cent. When I showed up at the four-day Team Canada mini-camp on September 4, 2001, they couldn't believe it. Al MacInnis was there and Joe Nieuwendyk, all those guys, and they said, "Holy fuck, man! What have you been doing?" And I told them, "Hey, I've got my shit together."

Or so I thought at the time.

I had not seen NHL ice since the Ottawa Senators played the Rangers at Madison Square Garden on February 26, so I was stoked. The camp also gave me chance to play with Eric Lindros. Slats had just acquired him from the Flyers by giving up solid prospects Jan Hlaváč, Kim Johnsson and Pavel Brendl. Lindros was nearly a foot taller than me and almost a hundred pounds heavier. He had scored 659 points in 486 games, for a per-game average of 1.35, fifth-best in NHL history behind Mario Lemieux, Wayne Gretzky, Mike Bossy and Jaromír Jágr. Slats wanted a Cup.

Lindros had not seen NHL ice since the 2000 playoffs. He played eight seasons for the Flyers, took them to the Stanley Cup finals in '97, and when he couldn't make a deal with them and sat out, he was the asshole, right? I think he got a bad rap in Philly. I think Bobby Clarke didn't like him from day one, and then there were all his fuckin' concussions. I know him, and the guy is a fantastic human being.

I was cleared to play by the league and the players' association the same day camp started, and I started hanging on by my fingernails. Although I was clean and working out and going to meetings, I was still a dry drunk. You don't turn fourteen years around in one summer.

After the Team Canada mini-camp in Calgary, I left for the Rangers' training camp in New York. We were scheduled to stay at the Marriott Hotel at the World Trade Center, next to the Twin Towers. We were to report for physicals at Madison Square Garden on September 11. Camp would begin the next day, with the public invited. We never practised at the Garden, but Slats wanted to get us pumped up for the season. He was really happy to see me in the kind of shape I was in. I wanted to do well for the Rangers and I wanted to play for Team Canada in February, so I had to keep it going.

Two weeks before camp, plans changed and the team moved our reservations to a boutique hotel a couple of miles from the Twin Towers, closer to the Garden. I was rooming with Sandy McCarthy and we fell asleep watching TV the night of September 10. We woke up just as NBC was showing the first plane crashing into the South Tower. I assumed it was a movie, but the next thing I knew, Katie Couric came on.

We started making calls, trying to figure out if we were still supposed to go down to the Garden for our fitness testing. We couldn't reach anyone, so we walked from the hotel to the Garden, and you could see the smoke in the sky and hear the sirens. It was just chaos on the streets of New York. People were running and screaming and yelling, everyone hysterical. It was surreal.

The guys that had played in New York for a while had friends that worked in the building, so they were a little more freaked out. Two of the most prominent buildings in all of America had gone down. What was next? We were all walking around thinking, "Okay, when are they fuckin' dropping the big one?" I was calm because at that time I really didn't care all that much whether I lived or died, as long as the end was quick. When I look back at my life and some of the places I've been and some of the significant historical incidents I've been close to—the brawl at Piestany, Columbine, 9/11—I wonder why. Why was I there?

We were at the rink by the time the second plane hit the North Tower, and I called Veronica to let her know I was still alive, then tried to get hold of my brothers, but the lines were jammed. We walked back to the hotel through Times Square and it was like we'd entered the twilight zone. All those millions of people in the city, yet there was nobody around. All the stores were closed. It was trippy.

In the end, training camp was moved from Madison Square Garden back out to Rye, but we couldn't even get out of Manhattan for two days.

On September 17, Slats re-signed Petr Nedvěd for three years at $4.2 million a season, but because of the restriction on flights, there was no way to get him to New York from Prague. We managed to arrange a flight on the Rangers' private jet to Detroit for the preseason opener that day, and there was no one else in the sky. When we took off, you could still see the smoke rising where the Twin Towers had been. It was sad, so sad.

During the third period of that game in Detroit, Chris Chelios made a comment in my direction—"Oh, you'll be around for a couple more months, then you'll be back in treatment." There is no place in the game for that kind of remark. Play hard against me, slash me if you want—that is part of the game. But there's a line, and he crossed it. I just fuckin' lost it. I'll bet I got him at least ten times on the back of his legs with my stick in that one shift. He was so mad he elbowed me against the boards and just started pounding me. Meanwhile, Martin Richter, a rookie, was behind him, scoring the tying goal. I got a roughing penalty, while Chelios got an instigator penalty, another for high-sticking, plus a misconduct and a game misconduct—29 minutes of penalties altogether. Chelios and I had shared a few brewskies on occasion, but after that game I would not say we were the best of buds.

Ron Low tried to have Petr Nedvěd play wing with Lindros and me, but he gave up on that, saying, "It was too fuckin' ugly to watch." After a little more experimenting, he put Mike York with us and the FLY line was born. When you have skilled guys together, it's a matter of knowing where each guy is on the ice. Mike worked as hard as anybody out there, and Eric was one of the best in the game. I loved playing an up-tempo, fast-paced kind of hockey. Mike was small—five foot ten, 185 pounds—but so fast. Quick and gritty. A solid player. I remember telling reporters how good he was. "He doesn't say a whole lot. He just gets his lunch pail and hardhat and goes to work every night. And along with all that, he's got great skill." We were on fire. It was fun. It was like back in 1991, playing with Dougie Gilmour again—that's the kind of chemistry that we had.

On October 27, I set Yorkie up for two and reached 1,000 career points. It was a special night for me. The Rangers surprised me by flying my parents in and presenting me with a silver hockey stick in a pre-game ceremony. I was in shock because I had no idea my parents were in town.

HOCKEY is like any other form of entertainment. If you want butts in the seats, you have to stir things up a little. There was a fierce, long-standing rivalry between the Rangers and the New York Islanders. On November 8, my roomie and good buddy Sandy McCarthy, who was six foot three, 225 pounds, went after Isles defenceman Eric Cairns (six-six and 230) at Nassau Coliseum. Cairns backed off. Then Sandy scored a goal on a rebound and Cairns high-sticked him in the neck. I started doing the chicken dance. I cannot tell you how much the blue-collar, lunch-pail crowd hated me for that. Cairns was in a press scrum after the game, and when I walked past on the way out, he couldn't help himself—he turned and called me a motherfucker in front of the reporters. He claimed he didn't fight Sandy because he had a bad hand. I laughed, "He's had a bad hand for three years now, I guess." Cairns and Sandy did mix it up just before Christmas. And on January 30, Cairns and Mariusz Czerkawski tried to take out one of our defencemen, David Karpa. I grabbed Cairns and he dropped his gloves and just drilled me. The whole fuckin' Islanders business would come back and bite me in the ass more than a few times.

By November 13, approaching the quarter point in the season, we had won seven games in the last nine. The FLY line had 34 points in that time. A month later, on December 15, when we were getting ready to play the Sabres, I got a call just before the morning skate from Wayne. He was always so great to me. He said, "Hey, Theo, we picked you for the Olympic team." I said, "Thanks, man," I was a little choked up. I said, "I didn't think I was going to have another chance to play for my country." And he said, "You know what, man? I believe in you. Just go out and play the way that you and I know you can play." That put my mind at ease and gave me the motivation I needed. I knew that Gretz had taken some heat for that decision, and I was determined not to let him down, even though it wasn't going to be easy.

Gretz had lined up an amazing team. I had played with so many of the guys, like Eddie Belfour, who was playing for the Dallas Stars at the time. We were together at the 1991 Canada Cup. Eddie had tons of idiosyncrasies. His skates had to be sharpened a certain way, and they had to be sharpened at the rink at a certain time. He had to eat certain types of food before a game. I mean, I know *I* had a routine, but it was nothing compared to this guy. Eddie was a strange dude. He's three years older than me, and he comes from Carman, Manitoba, a four-hour drive from Russell. He was really partying one night in Dallas toward the end of the season in 2000, and someone called the police. Eddie put up quite a fight, spitting and kicking until finally they pepper-sprayed him. It was all over the papers that he offered one officer a billion dollars to let him go. Six years later, when he was with Florida, the Panthers' rookie goaltender, Alex Auld, got cut above the eye trying to help out when Eddie was bounced from a club during a road trip on Long Island. I guess he didn't want to leave.

I had played with Martin Brodeur of the New Jersey Devils in a couple of All-Star games. You've got to have great goaltending. Cujo, Curtis Joseph of Toronto, is a fantastic guy, but he's never really won anything. When he's had the opportunity to be "the guy," he's never really lived up to it. It would be the same at the Olympics. The first game, we got lit up 5–2 by the Swedes, and then Marty went in and we won.

Our defencemen were Rob Blake from Colorado, who I played with at the 1991 Canada Cup and 1996 World Cup; Eric Brewer from Edmonton; my old buddy and ex-teammate Adam Foote from Colorado; and Ed Jovanovski from Vancouver. He is a funny guy. We were in Whistler, B.C., for the 1996 World Cup training camp, and there was this big corporate golf tournament. So Eddie and I came strolling up to the check-in, and the lady at the table asked Ed for his name. He said, "Ed Jovanovski." She said, "How do you spell that?" He answered, "E-D."

The other defencemen were big Al MacInnis from St. Louis (I'd teamed up with him on the Flames' power play in our Stanley Cup season), Scott Niedermayer from New Jersey, who has won at every level through his career, and Chris Pronger from St. Louis. I'd played with them all at Canada Cups, World Cups, All-Star games.

Besides me, the forwards were Simon Gagné from Philly, my buddy Jarome Iginla from Calgary, Paul Kariya from Anaheim, Owen Nolan from San Jose and Mike Peca from the New York Islanders. There was also Mario Lemieux from Pittsburgh, Ryan Smyth from Edmonton, my linemate Eric Lindros from the Rangers, Joe Nieuwendyk of Dallas—another of my Stanley Cup teammates from the Flames—and Steve Yzerman of Detroit, who'd been on my line at the '96 World Cup. I had played with Joe Sakic in Colorado, and Brendan Shanahan of Detroit had played on a line with me at the Olympics in Nagano in 1998.

So here I was, named to the best team in hockey for the most important event in my life, and I was white-knuckling it. Basically hanging on for dear life. If I drank again—no Olympics. So I held it together for as long as I possibly could. Some times were tougher than others. On December 17 against Florida, I got 27 minutes in penalties. In San Jose on the 28th, Lindros was put on the injured reserve list after having his bell rung. The same night, I got a match penalty for kneeing Mark Smith, who had made some remark about my being in treatment. On my way down the tunnel, Sharkie, the San Jose mascot, was standing in my way. He could see me steaming, but he refused to move. He was doing his Sharkie thing, so I brushed past him. Seriously, I barely touched him. The next thing you know, it was reported in the Knight Ridder newspapers that I "broke S.J. Sharkie's ribs in a scuffle after being ejected from a game." Typical American bullshit.

In our New Year's Eve game against Phoenix, I had 20 minutes in penalties—five minors and a misconduct. In my opinion, the league seemed to want to take the toughness out of the game. But for me, it was kill or be killed. On January 5 against Pittsburgh, I got a slashing call—my third of the game—with 7:37 left, so I walked. I showered and got on the bus. In six games, I had no points and 40 minutes in penalties. Don Cherry said, "I think [Theo's] going a little wacko. In fifty years, I've never seen anyone walk off the ice

like that. Somebody better get that guy under control." As far as
Cherry goes, I don't understand what gives him the right to say the
things he says about some of our greatest players. He won some
minor-league championships. I know he won the Calder Cup four
times as a player, and the Western Hockey League championship
in 1969 with Vancouver, but he talks about winning like he's experienced it in the big time. If you've won a few Stanley Cups, like Yvan
Cournoyer or Henri Richard, then be my guest to say whatever you
want, 'cause you've been there. But to be mouthing off every Saturday night about a whole bunch of stuff you haven't experienced,
well that just stinks of fantasy hockey.

There were a million stories about what was really going on at that
time. The papers kept saying that I was dealing with personal problems, family problems. But at the time, I thought the real problem
was that I had put my trust in the NHL and its substance abuse program. I refused to take responsibility for any of it. Veronica was upset
and unhappy and frustrated, so the program "helped" her. But at the
time I thought what they really wanted was for her to keep quiet and
show up smiling and for me to score goals. It didn't feel to me like
they gave a shit about what was best for Veronica or Tatym or Beaux
or me. The program was telling me that it was providing the best
counselling in the world, so I figured we should do what they said.
They prescribed clonazepam for me and tried to do some of the stuff
to her that the doctors had done to my mom. But Veronica wasn't
somebody who took things lying down. She left me and took the kids,
and I was out of my mind with worry. I went to the doctors for help,
but I was told to shut up, take my clonazepam and score goals.

After the Sharkie incident, Slats asked me, "What the fuck is
wrong with you?" "Well," I said, "my wife has disappeared and
there's nothing I can do about it—you won't let me leave. What
would *you* do, Slats, if Ann was gone?" Didn't matter. If I left the
team, I would be fired.

Our marriage was over for the millionth time. I had started seeing a stripper named Drea, who I met at Lace, a strip club near my home in Greenwich. She was really messed up, big time. Bad shit had happened to her as a kid. Everybody has an idea of what strippers are like, and they are usually wrong. All strippers are not hard. Some are college students just trying to pay their tuition. The smart ones invest their money and live in nice places. The dumb ones put it all up their nose.

I MOVED into my buddy Jason Priestley's place, a loft in Soho. I used to walk home from the Garden at night. I continued to try to keep a lid on things, not only for the sake of the Rangers, but because I knew Team Canada was watching me. But on January 22 we were back at Nassau Coliseum, and some low-class Isles fans were wearing Rangers jerseys, with my number, 14, and "CRACKHEAD" on the nameplate. For the record, I had never done crack in my life. Every time I touched the puck, sixteen thousand people would yell, "Crackhead!" What would *you* do? I think any normal person would react.

New York is a tough place to play, real tough. No matter whether you're in New Jersey, Long Island or the city, those people are ruthless. They will take your biggest flaw and expose it. These are the guys who take their lunch pails to work every day, go home, have twenty beers and kick their dog. So when we shoved a 5–4 win up their asses, it was sweet, especially because it ended a nine-game slump for me. In fact, I scored the game-winner in the third when I took the puck off their defenceman Marko Kiprusoff and made it all the way down the ice to put it in low on Garth Snow's stick side. When we were skating off, I smacked the inside of my right elbow with my left fist and bent my right arm up, giving the fans a wrestling salute. The league fined the Rangers a grand for my "obscene gesture." The NHL had no problem with the jerseys or the name-calling—just my gesture.

Our first game at the Olympics in Utah was scheduled for February 15, so I knew I didn't have to hang on much longer. If I could just make it through the last four games, against Detroit, Atlanta, the Pens and the Stars.

In Detroit on February 6, I got into it again with my old pal Chris Chelios, who had been named captain of the U.S. Olympic Team. All night he had been tapping the side of his nose, a dig about my using cocaine, and I let that go. Then Dominik Hašek covered up after making a save, and I took a poke at the puck. The normal response would be for Chelios, a defenceman, to give me a warning shove, which he did. Then he said, "Hey, Theo, aren't you due back at the clinic?" I called him a "fuckin' brain-dead motherfucker," and he called me a "sensitive fuckin' asshole."

Naturally, the media was all over me about how I overreacted. Not one mention about how the captain of the U.S. Olympic Team showed such unsportsmanlike behaviour. I couldn't imagine *our* captain, Mario Lemieux, acting like that. It would never happen. Never.

31

GOING FOR GOLD

I AM AN EMOTIONAL GUY, so each time I reached a milestone in my career, I really felt it. But I have to say that the 2002 Olympics were probably the absolute highlight. I remember being four years old in my living room with my dad and watching Paul Henderson score the greatest goal ever scored—his game-winner with 34 seconds left in game eight of the 1972 Summit Series. Who wouldn't want to grow up to be Paul Henderson? Every elite player dreams of scoring the biggest goal in the history of hockey, and he did it.

As the 2002 Winter Olympics approached, it had been fifty years since Canada had won a gold medal in hockey. And it was *our* game. So where was the next opportunity to be the next big hero? In Salt Lake City. And who wanted to be that guy? Me. That is why you play the game—to have a chance to be on a fuckin' postage stamp. That's what it's about.

My parents were there to cheer me on. My mom, who wouldn't watch me play when we lived five minutes from the rink in Russell, had discovered airplanes. She loved the first-class treatment and jetting all over and being treated like a VIP. My dad loved living the dream. He had been an elite athlete, so he knew what it was all about. I loved that my parents were there. The members of the team did not have to worry about our guests. Wayne Gretzky knows how to win and he knows how to take care of people. Buses and tours were arranged, and they had their own twenty-four-hour-a-day liaison with them. Everybody—parents, brothers, sisters, aunts, uncles, kids—felt a part of that whole experience. Gretz is as classy as it gets.

I had played in the previous Olympics in Nagano, so I knew the drill, you check into the village and they give you your room key. Our building housed all the Canadian athletes. I remember being asked over and over again, "Where are you guys staying?" At the village. "What village?" The *Olympic* village. And people would be shocked— "Really? You guys are staying with the regular athletes?"

"Yes," I would say. "We *are* regular athletes." I actually think that the others were more special than we were because we were making big money—all we had to do was take a two-week break out of our schedules. The athletes in all the other sports spent their entire lives getting to the Olympics, without recognition and without getting paid.

It was exciting to watch the other athletes prepare for their events. We all bonded when we watched the events in the lounge together. Canada's greatest winter athletes were all in one place, all cheering for each other, supporting each other. I really liked the figure skaters. They were cute. And I got along really well with the women on the Olympic hockey team, especially Vicky Sunohara and Jayna Hefford. I thought they were super people.

I didn't go to any events, because of all the security. It was just after 9/11, and in order to get on the bus to leave the village, you had to go through two checkpoints where you passed through metal detectors and then were wanded. And then, before the bus left the village, it was completely checked from top to bottom. When we practised, we had to go through the same process to leave, then get to the practice rink and go through the same level of security to get into the rink. After practice, on the way out of the rink, they checked us again, twice, and then the whole rigmarole again to get back into the village. It was a joke.

The campus provided food and a place to sleep. All the athletes from every country ate at one big place where there was food for every nationality, even a McDonald's. My Rangers linemate, Mike

York, was there as a member of the U.S. men's team. We would bump into each other and have a chat—"How are the games goin'?" Stuff like that. But we knew we were on a collision course, so we didn't care for each other.

Our first game of the seeding round was on February 15, 2002, against Sweden. We took a 5-2 beating, but I discovered I'd regained the feeling for hockey that I had lost years before. The wall of shit that had been built around me disappeared. I felt pure joy on the ice. Late in the third period, I was just so happy to be out there that I did not let up. I played as hard as I could every shift. I hadn't had a drink in months, but I was okay. The energy of the Olympics served as my drug. I was riding on adrenalin, so I was able to focus and keep on track.

We made it past Germany, 3-2, then we played the Czechs. I was on the fourth line again, with Joe Nieuwendyk and Brendan Shanahan. The first line consisted of Joe Sakic, Simon Gagné and Jarome Iginla, then there was Mario Lemieux, Paul Kariya and Steve Yzerman, and then Eric Lindros, Owen Nolan and Ryan Smyth.

My line hadn't played much—at most, we got maybe three shifts a period. But whenever we needed a big play or a big something, I was able to come through. In the third period against the Czechs, we just had a really good shift, running around in their zone, and the puck came to me behind the net. I threw a nice pass to Newie, and he one-timed it in and we ended up tying the score, 3-3.

Hašek never liked me at all, because I was the guy who got into his face. If he made a save and I was going to the net, I would give him a little tap here, a little tap there, and that stuff drove him insane because he thought it was his God-given right that nobody fuckin' touch him. Well, sorry, bud. I knew that in order for us to win we were going to have to get Hašek off his game, because he was the type of goalie who could win by himself. We saw that in Nagano.

There were a lot of opportunities, and we almost scored again. Roman Hamrlík—who I think is a gutless puke, who knew that in international hockey I couldn't pound the piss out of him afterward—gave me a vicious cross-check in front of the net.

I wasn't prepared for it, and my head snapped back. If the roles had been reversed, if I'd done that to him, there is no doubt in my mind that I would have been suspended. I would have been kicked out of the tournament. But I knew that the Rangers played the Islanders when we got back, and I remember saying to Hamrlík, "If I'm on the ice March 25, and you're going back to the puck, you'd better bring a fuckin' bodyguard because I'm going to run you from behind and break your fuckin' neck." And he was all, "C'mon, Teo, why, why you do thet? C'mon . . ." And I said, "Hey, man, an elephant never forgets."

Gretz, who is the ultimate sportsman, was really pissed. The refs were not calling penalties against the Czechs, so they got dirtier and dirtier until in the final seconds, when Hamrlík took me out. And there was no penalty. The referee, fuckin' Bill McCreary, just stood there.

So Gretz stepped up and spoke to the press. He said that if a Canadian guy had done the same thing to a European, it would be handled in a completely different way. It really got us going, the same way that Phil Esposito's emotional speech turned the Summit Series around in 1972 in Moscow. After Gretz spoke, we were fired up.

We beat Finland in the quarter-finals and outshot Belarus 51–14 to win 7–1 in the semis, which took us to the gold-medal game against the U.S. A silver medal would not be acceptable. We would win gold or we would lose, it was that simple.

In 1991, we had beaten the Americans in the final of the Canada Cup, and the rivalry had been building since then. The Soviet Union fell apart around the same time, so the U.S. stepped in to fill the void. They returned the favour, defeating us in the 1996 World Cup. They had cocky guys like Keith Tkachuk, Jeremy Roenick and Tony Amonte who acted like they were winners, but they weren't. It was just talk.

We were the two most talented teams, but Canada's advantage was experience. My line had 1,500 career NHL goals among the three of us, along with five Stanley Cup rings, and we were the *fourth* line. We were maybe the best team ever assembled. People may say the 1976 Canada Cup team was the best, but I say it's the 2002 Olympic team.

I remember skating out of the tunnel for the gold-medal game and looking up and feeling like I was in the twilight zone because everything slowed down. There were American and Canadian flags waving back and forth everywhere. It was like some kind of crazy scene in a movie. Two teams from North America were playing in the finals, and yet the world watched. It was the most-watched television show in Canadian history up to that point, with 10.6 million viewers. In the U.S., 10.7 per cent of homes watched—that's 38 million people.

At 8:49 of the first period, they scored the first goal when Amonte ripped one past Brodeur on a two-on-one break. I started to get anxious—"What if they score again? What if they win?" I had to block those thoughts out, but it was a roller-coaster ride for three hours.

About ten minutes in, Bill McCreary gave me a cross-checking minor for brushing past Chelios in front of the net. I had kept a lid on it the whole series, but I did mention to McCreary that it was a fuckin' joke call. At 14:54, Paul Kariya tied the game by picking up a cross-ice pass from Pronger. Then Iggy scored off a pass from Sakic at 18:33, shooting as he was flying in on the right wing, and it was 2–1 for us. Brian Rafalski tied the game at two, but Joe Sakic shot from the point and deflected it in off Brian Leetch. Late in the third period, Iggy scored an insurance goal and Sakic added one more after that. We won 5–2. The gold was ours. I can tell you in one word why we won: Sakic. He put out the greatest individual effort I have ever seen in a game of hockey.

Winning that game was the ultimate. After we won and were standing in that line, I was right at the very front, and it was emotional, very emotional. Especially after the disappointment in Nagano.

I scanned the stands for my parents. When I spotted them, I could see my dad going absolutely berserk. Here was a guy who had barely acknowledged my existence when I was growing up, and now he looked like he was in Rome, cheering for the gladiators. And I realized that *I* was that gladiator. *I* was the hero he was screaming for. He looked right at me, and I saw admiration. It blew me away. It was the greatest feeling ever.

I remember standing there during the anthem, thinking, "I probably won't ever play for Team Canada again. This is the pinnacle, in terms of hockey, for me. I'm so glad to have been part of it, but there's nothing more that I can accomplish in the game."

We celebrated at a restaurant in Salt Lake City, a bunch of us in the back, and *Calgary Sun* writer Eric Francis was there. He later told me that he saw me walk in with the gold around my neck. He said, "Hey, man, you stepped up and repaid Gretzky with a gold medal." I agreed it was controversial for Gretz to pick me for the team. But there was a reason why I was on that team, and Wayne knew it. Despite everything that was going on, there was no other guy who sensed what the team needed the way I did, and I always gave it to them, no matter what. Whether it was a play to score a goal, or to stir things up out there.

With that medal around my neck, I could not stop smiling. There was a peace in my life that I hadn't felt in a long time. All was perfect in my world, and for me that was a problem. Because I had built my life on being the underdog. Being the one who said, "I'll show you." Put the odds against me, and I loved it. I loved challenges. I think some of the problems I had been having were due to the fact I had met those challenges and got to the top. But all I knew how to do was manage the fight—once I'd won it, once I was at the top, I didn't have a clue.

So I got back from the Olympics after winning the gold medal, and then life kind of went to hell.

32

THE GAMBLER

VERONICA HAD MOVED back to New York at the beginning of my last year with the Rangers and we tried to get it together one more time. Things were good for a while, but even though I had faced my problems, I still had no tools to really deal with life. So what did I start doing? I traded one addiction for another. I started gambling. My very first paycheque in hockey came to forty dollars and I ended up handing it over to one of my teammates after he took me in a card game. At that time, I thought, "That ain't going to happen again." It was a foreshadowing of what was to come.

I got smart real quick. I learned how to cheat by miscounting or fix the game by using hand signals. For me, it was about winning, no matter what. My favourite game was blackjack. In junior, I would take twenty bucks, half my paycheque, and turn it into three hundred. I learned how to sense a run of cards. When you first start out, you get some sort of beginner's luck—that's what pulls you in. "Oh, this is easy!"

I would go down to the Moose Jaw Casino once a week. There were days when I would come out with rabbit ears, but gambling was like everything else—an escape from painful reality. I didn't gamble much in Calgary, because I was more into drinking and partying, and then the first year and a half in New York it was strip clubs and partying, but once I stopped the substances and my head was clear for betting, you could not keep me out of the casinos.

As I said, I think the Rangers were checking up on me. In the NHL Substance Abuse Program, gambling was a no-no and I didn't want to get suspended again, so I was sneaky. There was a casino an hour and a half from my house called the Mohegan Sun, and I started going there at least three times a week. I talked to the head of the casino and said, "I spend a lot of money here. If you want me to continue using your establishment, we have to change my name so nobody knows I am here." Total alcoholic thinking. So he renamed me Teddy Mohegan. When I walked into the casino, everybody would say, "Hey, Mr. Mohegan, how are you? Hey, Mr. Mohegan, can I get you something?" It was fucking crazy.

Just before Christmas, Travis came to visit us. Veronica and I were back in our old patterns. I wanted to go gambling with Trav, so I started an argument. I came downstairs and told Trav, "Hey, man, I have to blow off some steam. We're going to the casino." We called my Russian limo driver, Vlad, and he came right away. On the way, we decided we would play craps that night. I had ten thousand dollars and I slipped Trav a grand so he could come with me to the big-money table. Guys were dropping four or five grand per bet. I started putting down all this money, when this little old man in a walker kind of step-chucked his way over to the table and grabbed the dice. The game of craps revolves around the throwing of the dice. At least one of them has to bank off the felt at the end of the table. It is quite complicated, but you win or lose based on the numbers that show up on the dice. Anyway, this old guy was the first shooter, and he was so feeble that when he threw the dice, they barely made it to the wall. But all of a sudden he started hitting numbers. Trav was cheering because he was up to five thousand bucks in minutes. So the roll went around and came back to the old guy. He went hot, shooting number after number. There was a crowd of people six or seven deep behind us. He rolled for an hour and a half straight, and every time he rolled everyone would cheer and jump up and down. Even the stickman was smiling. I must have given the guy at least twenty grand in tips. Every time he rolled a number, I'd just fire a thousand-dollar chip across the table to him. It was insane. When he finally rolled a seven—which in craps means you lose and the house takes what is on the table—I was maxed out and Trav had nine grand in bets on the table. I thought he was going to have a heart attack, but then he looked at his chips and said, "Oh." Trav had fifty thousand dollars left and I had five times that.

We went up to the cashier's cage and she said, "Can I cut you a cheque, Mr. Mohegan?" And I said, "No, I want it all in cash." "You want $250,000 in cash?" "Yep." She called a boxman, who took us to this little room in the back. It was full of people in suits wearing cotton gloves. Three of them counted out the money, all in fifties and hundreds. They put it in a brown paper bag, followed us out to the limo, and we took off. It was 5:30 in the morning and I had practice in three hours, so I decided I'd better get something to eat. We got our limo driver to go to the McDonald's drive-thru and we all had Bacon-and-Egg McMuffins. That was the funniest part. We couldn't stop laughing. We had three hundred grand in cash and we were eating at McDonald's!

I started a habit of having the limo take me straight from the rink to the Mohegan Sun. One time, Chuck came down and I spent $150,000 that night. I maxed out every card I had and then took his. We didn't have enough money to buy a fuckin' sandwich on the way home. It was 7 a.m. by the time we left, and practice was in two hours. We had to go straight to the Playland Rink. Chuck was sitting across from me in the back of the limo and he said, "Bones, look at you. Look in the friggin' mirror, man. You are not happy with what you are doing. You are going to have to change your behaviour, not because you are an addict, not because of the league, but because you are not happy." He was right. I hung my head, and although I knew I wasn't going to do anything about it, I said, "I know."

If I knew we had an off-day coming up, I would call this really cool "host" who always hooked me up. I met him through Sandy McCarthy. This guy took care of me wherever I went. I had markers across North America. If I felt like Atlantic City, he would arrange for me to stay at the Trump Plaza. He'd call the casino and tell them I needed the helicopter sent to the heliport near Madison Square Garden. When I got there, I would stay up for two days playing blackjack and craps while I was booked into Donald Trump's penthouse suite. I would order lobster and steaks and gamble away a quarter-million. Then I'd hop on the helicopter and fly from Atlantic City to the helipad near the practice rink in Rye.

I couldn't drink or indulge in cocaine because I would get kicked out of the NHL, but boy, could I gamble. I was a gambling fiend.

I guess my disregard for money came from my upbringing. I did not give a fuck. I'd been poor when I was a kid, so I figured I did not need money. And that was a good thing, because I was bleeding it. I had a money manager, Dave Stinton, who did the right things for a hockey player. I didn't need to grow my money, I needed to protect it. Dave got me into mutual funds and bonds and all kinds of stuffy, boring crap. If I had left it alone, I would be sitting on twenty-five million bucks today. And as an agent, Don Baizley gave me nothing but the best advice. He was great for me—a father figure—but at the end of the day, he told Chuck that I signed his paycheque, he didn't sign mine, so there was not much he could do but watch it disappear.

33

I HATE HOCKEY

IN ORDER TO be a part of the Olympics I'd hung in there, but after that my play went downhill. So did the team's. After the Olympic break, we won only three of our first eleven games, and on March 18 the Rangers traded defencemen Igor Ulanov and Filip Novák, along with their first- and second-round picks in 2002 and their fourth-rounder in 2003, for winger Pavel Bure. After that, my ice time diminished. It got to me. I felt that I had carried the team for half a year and suddenly, when Bure came in, he was the greatest thing since sliced bread. I had not had a drink in fourteen months, and I admit I was on edge when Ronny Low and I had a big blowout about Bure in Toronto on April 4.

At the very end of the morning skate we usually did power-play drills. So when Ronny called out the names for the first unit—Bure, Lindros, Messier, Leetch and Malakhov—I couldn't believe it. All of a sudden Yorkie, Lindros and I were a bunch of scrubs? Had Bure ever won a Stanley Cup? Had Bure ever won a gold medal? And Messier? What the fuck was he doing on the first line? He had done nothing all year except give the press a few good sound bites. So make him your marketing guy, don't put him on your first-line power play.

Next, Ronny called the second unit—Yorkie, me and Adam Graves. I ignored him. It was a matter of principle. He chased down the ice toward me. "What the fuck is wrong with you?" he demanded to know. And I answered, "What the fuck is wrong with *you*?" Ronny said, "You ain't fucking playing tonight." "That's fine," I said. "You are the fuckin' coach, you can do whatever you want."

I walked off, and as soon as I got into the dressing room I got the call from Slats. "Get up to my room. Right. Fucking. *Now.*"

Maybe I wasn't playing as well as I should have been playing, I knew that, but I was pissed. So when he said, "What is fucking wrong with you?" I said, "What is wrong with *me*? What is wrong with fuckin' Ronny? I think I have done my part here. Fuckin' got my shit straightened around, and you bring in fuckin' Bure who has won nothing in his career. I beat him in junior. In fact, I have beaten him just about every time I have played him. And fuckin' Messier has done nothing all year." We both knew that Mark Messier had six Stanley Cups, but I'd accomplished a lot in the game too.

It was the first time I had ever spoken up to management like that. I was pissed. A little bit hurt too. "And," I said, "you know what? I deserve some fuckin' respect. I know that I fucked you over last year 'cause of what I went through. But still, whenever I had the opportunity to win, I was there for you, man. In the World Cup in '96, I came up to you when were losing the second game with ten minutes left, and I said, 'Slats, do you want me to go out there and start World War III?'" That was what we needed to win when we were tanking, but he had said no. Nevertheless we both remembered the offer.

What I really wanted to say to him that day was, "You know what? You fucked me over in the '96 World Cup. I was the best player you had, and I sat on the bench and I didn't say a word, even though I saw what was going on. Your fuckin' boys were dying out there—Mess and Gretz—and you were going to live or die with those boys and I didn't fuckin' say a word."

Whenever Slats and I had a conversation, it was always civil. He truly cared about me. I still call him every once in a while out of the blue to see how it's going with him. He respected me as a player, but I was so tired of all the bullshit. I was tired of the game. I had gone through a lot in three years in New York, and then after winning the Olympic gold medal, I didn't think I could accomplish any more.

Slats just said, "Be a team player," and I said, "Fine."

I went and spoke to Ronny. I said, "I know you think that Pavel Bure is better than me, but I don't think so. When I have played against him I have won the majority of times. So if you think you can win with Pavel Bure rather than me, that is your decision. Your ass is on the line. I understand that."

He said, "I am going with this decision." We ended up missing the playoffs and he was fired when the regular season ended less than two weeks later.

THE PLAYERS HELD an end-of-the-year party at the Russian Tea Room on West 57th Street in New York. The whole place was ours. The cost didn't matter—with our payroll, twenty grand for a get-together was chump change. We were sitting around, having a few laughs, and there was a bottle of vodka sitting directly in front of my right hand. I stared at that thing for two hours. The whole time, I was talking myself into a drink, then talking myself out of a drink, then talking myself back into it. "You deserve it. You earned a gold medal, for fuck sakes." Followed by, "You know that if you have a drink, you're going back to rehab. You know the pee tester will be there tomorrow morning." That is the epitome of alcoholism. Finally, I grabbed the bottle and poured myself a twelve-ouncer, shot it back, and done. Euphoria. Think of a cancer patient in a lot of pain and finally the doctor says, "Okay, you have suffered long enough, you can have morphine." The boys were looking at me, going, "Are you okay?" "Yeah," I nodded, "I've been wanting to do this for a long time."

I disappeared for three weeks. Vlad, my Russian limo driver, drove me and got me coke and some really pretty girls to hang out with. I stayed at the W Hotel near Times Square for the first week. Some nights I went out to the Mohegan Sun casino, other nights I would just stay in and party. I had no problem finding people to hang out with. I would be at a bar and some guy would recognize me. "Hey, Theo Fleury! You play for the Rangers!" "Yep, come on and party. I got a limo and broads—cocaine on the table in the hotel room, help yourself." Nobody could keep up with me, of course. They'd drop out after a couple of days. When I wore out my welcome, I would find a new hotel. There was a boutique in every high-end hotel, so I would go down and pick out clothes. I could hold it together long enough to do that. I didn't eat much, but it didn't upset my Crohn's disease. Turns out vodka and cocaine is the cure. Vlad was getting me pure coke, not stuff that has been cut. It was right off the boat, right off the brick, right up my nose.

A three-week, continuous, two-hundred-thousand-dollar party. I figured my career was over. "Thank you very much. It has been a slice. I hate hockey."

34

TWEAKING AND GEEKING

MY YOUNGER BROTHER Teddy and my dad had plans to visit me down in Santa Fe and play golf for a week after the 2001–02 season, so I knew I had to end my three-week cokefest. I flew out to my place, and while I waited for them I spent a lot of time at a ripper joint in Albuquerque called TD's Showclub. TD's has three different clubs that are affiliated—in Denver, Phoenix and Albuquerque—and the girls move from one to the other. They would start in lingerie and peel to a g-string. The usual titty-bar act.

When Stephanie came on stage, I thought she was really cute—very tiny with these huge knockers, and she had a long vine with small flowers tattooed across the top of them. I asked the waitress to bring her over. Steph did a lap dance for me and I gave her a couple hundred bucks. She sat down and we talked for a while, and we clicked. We exchanged phone numbers, and as I was driving back to Santa Fe that night, she called me. She said she and a few of her friends were going to a party in Albuquerque and did I want to come along?

My dad and Teddy were due the next day, so Steph and I made a date for later that week. The guys came and we spent the next couple of days at Sunset, the golf course my house backed onto, playing thirty-six holes a day. On the third day, after golf, I said, "I am out of here, I have a date. I'll see you guys tomorrow."

I picked Steph up at the airport. I was driving my blue Porsche 911 Cabriolet convertible—turbo, with the old body style. A 1995, the first year they introduced them. What a car. Supremely fast. I bought it off of Rangers defenceman Bryan Berard. One day he said, "I am getting rid of this car." I had won fifty grand at the Mohegan the night before, so I reached into my pocket and handed him a stack of cash and said, "Here. Done deal."

I could tell Steph liked the car, but she seemed antsy. We checked into the Hyatt Regency Tamaya Resort & Spa between Santa Fe and Albuquerque. It was incredibly beautiful and upscale, but that was not the first thing on her mind. As soon as we got into our room, she said, "Let's go get some blow."

I thought Steph was a really cool chick. Young, about 24 or so, fun and ready to party. We went hard for two days, drinking, doing coke, talking and hanging out at the casino, where we won a shitload of money. Finally, I said, "I gotta go. My dad and brother are waiting and I am in a charity golf tournament tomorrow."

At five the next morning, my eyeballs were sticking out about an inch and I hadn't slept for days. I dropped my dad and Teddy off at the airport and headed for the championship golf course, Inn of the Mountain Gods.

It was an absolutely gorgeous course with pine trees, a view of the mountains and an island fairway. But I did not want to be there. I was tweaking and geeking from my last three days of fun. I stood on the first tee, teed my ball up the usual three inches, and swung through. And got a hole in one—my first ever.

I WAS BACK in Santa Fe in transition. I had no contract, and both Dr. Shaw and Dr. Lewis were phoning me, saying, "If you don't get to treatment, you're done." Well, I'd had it. So I said to Dr. Lewis, "Fuck you, Lewis, I am gonna fuckin' come down and beat the shit out of you." I really hated the guy, another fuckin' authority figure, right?

But I had to stand up and say I had a problem, otherwise I risked getting caught and getting fired. If you're a hockey player, you want to play. That's why I went into the program.

However, I wasn't sincere. If you read the twelve steps, you have to admit you have a problem and that there's a God who is willing and capable of helping because you can't help yourself. There are all kinds of conditions you have to satisfy in dealing with your problem. You have to take stock of your situation and be honest if you expect to really recover.

I gave Dr. Shaw credit for having some integrity. He represented the players' association and was all about doing things to the help and benefit of the players. But at the time I thought Dr. Dave Lewis, with his military regime, was all about getting the player fixed so he could play. I mean, obviously the New York Rangers weren't paying some asshole to sit in a treatment centre in L.A. I felt they wanted to get me healthy enough to keep putting asses in the seats. The bigger the player, the bigger the problem. Because if you are a fourth-liner, you just go play in the AHL and dwindle away to a $150,000-a-year hockey player, and before you know it your career is over. I felt it was a massive conflict of interest.

Of course, you have to qualify all this by saying the guy who snorted the coke had a choice. You cannot take away personal responsibility. And I have learned since that Dr. Lewis wanted me to surrender and they were using the old good-cop bad-cop routine. I was just too bullheaded and angry for it to work.

I still felt badly about my behaviour because I knew I had let Slats and the team down. My fourth-year option had to be picked up that July, so in late May I called Don Baizley and said, "You know what? I owe the Rangers. Let's renegotiate something at a super-discounted price."

Baiz let Slats know that I realized I'd made a mess of the last season and I was willing to cut my price, to give him a deal. And you know what Slats said? "I can't afford to have Theo play, even for nothing."

That is a harsh comment. He couldn't even afford to have me play for free. But I understood. Part of the problem was that the Rangers had these fuckin' rookies who had been collecting Theo Fleury hockey cards for fifteen years, and they looked up to me. If I wanted to go out to a strip joint on the road, they were going too. They didn't give a shit who said what, they were going. And, not only did Glen have a mess of a superstar on his hands, but a couple of the kids who came with me hadn't tied their skates for two weeks, either. So the team declined to pick up my option.

I was devastated. I had never been rejected in hockey, and to feel that unwanted by a team, that really hurt.

Baiz said to me, "Man, we only have a short time and you're still drinking, still partying. There's no way you'll get a contract with anybody unless you go to treatment." The last place I wanted to be was locked up again. I knew I could get sober, but did I *want* to be sober? No.

Imagine if you had money and fame and girls and parties every night and someone said to you, "Hey, would you like to go to prison?" What would you do? I chose door number one. I went back to New York, because the house in Greenwich had been sold and Veronica told me to come and get my stuff. I walked through it and it was totally empty.

I was torn between Drea, the New York stripper I had been seeing at the end of my marriage, and Steph, the stripper in Albuquerque. I had to decide whether I was going to ask Drea to move with me to Santa Fe or keep seeing Steph. I had tons of Player's Club card points at the Mohegan Sun and they had just built a hotel, so Drea and I checked in there. But it wasn't like it had been with Steph at the Hyatt Regency. Drea had been going to Al-Anon and learning how to support me in sobriety, and that was freaking me out. So I started gambling like a fiend. A guy beside me at the craps table struck up a conversation and said, "Hey, can I get you some shit?" I said, "You certainly can," and tossed him a thousand-dollar chip. "How about four 8-balls?" I said. That would work out to about five hundred bucks, so I was offering him a five-hundred-dollar tip. An 8-ball is an eighth of an ounce of cocaine—in metric, 3.5 grams. The guy came through and so, for the rest of the night, I would go into a bathroom cubicle and dip my car key into my pocket. It was quick, easy and discreet. I won eighty thousand dollars and cashed in my chips. Then I wandered into the Mohegan's shopping mall and threw my Player's Club card on the counter to buy Steph a ten-thousand-dollar tennis bracelet. I had a quarter-million points, and each point is worth a dollar.

I told Drea I had to get back to Santa Fe so I could figure out what I was going to do—whether to go back to treatment so I could play or what. She took it pretty well. She was a good kid.

I showed up at the airport completely fucked and annihilated, with two and a half little cellophane packages still in my pocket. I checked in and threw the coke into a garbage can, and debated what to do with the diamond bracelet and a duffle bag full of cash. I figured going through security with it might raise some red flags, so I checked the bag. I got to Albuquerque, and guess what? My bag never showed up. Eighty grand gone. Whatever.

I went to see Steph and told her I didn't know what I should do, and she said, "You fuckin' stupid asshole. Go to treatment. You love to play hockey, and the only way you can play is by getting clean."

She was right. She left for work at TD's and I made a few calls, then took her little girl Aleca to the mall. We went to Tiffany's and bought Steph a thirty-thousand-dollar promise ring.

I got home that night and said, "Okay, here is the deal. I talked to the doctors. I have to go to Los Angeles for thirty days. And after thirty days, when I come out, they will allow me to negotiate a contract with whoever. Would you and Aleca be willing to come with me?"

She was speechless.

So I was back in treatment again, and she visited me every weekend. When I completed the program, I called Baiz and said, "All right, man, let's get 'er going." He asked me where I wanted to play. I said either Phoenix or Chicago, because Wayne Gretzky was in Phoenix and Brian Sutter was in Chicago.

Steph and I went to her mom's in San Diego and dropped off Aleca, then flew to Calgary to meet with Brian Sutter and play in the golf tournament I hosted each year for Crohn's disease and colitis.

It was quite a prestigious tournament. Some of the Flames owners and a lot of influential businessmen always turned out. So I pranced Steph in there—this tiny little thing in her Daisy Dukes with these absolutely huge breasts showing above and below her little pop top and the big tattoo across her chest. I introduced her to all these proper gentlemen as my fiancée.

It was interesting watching my two worlds collide. People always give strippers a rough ride, but I don't think they have anything to be ashamed of. I think people have a right to be anywhere with anybody at any time. I was giving a part of myself to her, showing her she had the right to be part of that world too. Besides, I knew those old oil and business guys pretty well. They were no different than me or anybody else. Where do you think a lot of them go when they are in Texas on business? A gentleman's club. Meanwhile, I knew the minute I turned around everyone was saying, "Oh my God, have you seen who Theo is with?"

Chuck was not a fan of Stephanie's. He said, "Bones, what are you doing? She has breasts on her the size of watermelons and she's completely used up—not just a young, innocent stripper. She is on the downward slide. Although she is kind of pretty, she has the brains of a snow pea." He was the only person who actually told me what he thought, and that is why I trusted him so much. But that didn't mean

I *listened* to him. I was a bit of a train wreck at that time, but I still think she was a good kid.

I met with Sutter and he said, "I'd like you to come play for us. We had a great year last year, and you would be the missing piece to the puzzle. With you, we could win a Stanley Cup."

It sounded so good, but oh God, it turned out to be a nightmare. Just a fucking nightmare.

35

CHICAGO

FROM MY GOLF TOURNAMENT, we drove to Russell for my hockey school. While there, I introduced Steph to my family and the Peltzes. They loved me unconditionally, so no one judged us.

Next, I met with the Phoenix guys, Mike Barnett and Gretz and Bobby Francis, the coach. Bobby had been my coach for the last half-season that I played in Salt Lake. Anyway, it turned out they didn't have a fuckin' clue. They did not get it. They didn't seem to realize I could not have even one drink. They were saying, "Aw, this is a great place to play! We have our own plane loaded with buckets of beer." I was in stage two of the substance abuse program. If I drank or took drugs, I could be suspended without pay. A flying bar was *not* what I needed.

They said the Coyotes were going places. They had drafted a whole bunch of young guys and wanted to keep things informal. For instance, I would be able to go to the rink in shorts and flip-flops. I was thinking, "Hmm, sounds like fun ... *too much* fun."

We continued to talk with both teams. Chicago had an edge because it was a real sports town. Besides, I wasn't sure it would be good to live in Phoenix, where all Steph's friends lived. She would be partying all the time. I had to stay totally clean, because wherever we went, we were met by a pee guy. And Steph gave it a good go. She went to counselling with me, and the doctors in the program even tried to get me to promise to dump her if she wouldn't quit partying, but she couldn't do it.

There were rumours that I might return to the Flames. But I didn't take Calgary too seriously because I knew the owners squeezed out pennies. Also, the Flames had Jarome Iginla, whose contract had expired at the end of 2001–02, and they wanted to keep him. At 25, he led the NHL in goals (52) and points (96). He also won the Lester B. Pearson Award, the MVP as voted by the players. As much as I would have loved to play with him again, there was no way the Flames' owners would shell out for both of us, even if it meant a Stanley Cup. I figured if the Cup had meant that much to them, they would never have traded away the team so soon after we won it.

I knew Iggy was a quality guy when I met him and saw how he treated his family. I respected how nice and caring he was with his parents. And I was pissed off at the way he looked in the press.

But Iggy had a right to be paid. Our last season together, 1998–99, Iggy made $850,000. He went in and asked for a raise and Al Coates said, "Forget it." If Iggy had moved south, he would have cleaned up. He sat out training camp and ended up with a three-year deal that paid him $1.7 million per. He was still the best bargain in hockey. And when he got off to a slow start, the headlines in the paper said things like "Iggy Flop." I could not believe it. Were they fuckin' kidding? He was making millions less than guys with less talent, and that is how they treated him?

Anyway, once the Flames were in serious negotiations with Iggy, I never heard from them. If I had, I think I would have finished my career in Calgary—and for less money, maybe even five or six million. Josh, Beaux and Tatym all lived there. It would've been pretty tough to turn that down.

In early July, Jay Feaster, the general manager of the Tampa Bay Lightning, told Baiz they were interested. But in my mind, Tampa was not an ideal situation for me. They had a very young team, and in their ten years in the league they had missed the playoffs nine times. I knew Vincent Lacavalier was a comer—he ended the 2002–03 season with 78 points—and Marty St-Louis had talent. When he was in Calgary with me in 1998–99, he shuttled up and down in our farm system and played 13 games with Calgary. He was a college kid from the University of Vermont who went undrafted because he was small—five foot nine, 180. Sound familiar? During his four years with the Catamounts he put up 267 points in 139 games, or 1.92 points a game. During my four years with the Moose Jaw Warriors, I put up 479 in 274 games, an average of 1.72. When Craig Button was GM of the Flames, he let St-Louis go. Tampa signed him as a free agent. Going into the boards in a game against the Pens in January 2002, he broke his fibula just above the right ankle. He missed 26 games but came back in 2003–04 to lead the league with 94 points, then beat Calgary in the Stanley Cup final. If I had said yes to Tampa, I would have ended up with another ring.

The next team I heard from was Toronto. Bill Watters and Baizley were on the phone a lot. But I knew if I played in Toronto, every move I made would be under a microscope. It is a tough town for athletes. The fans are great, but the media is fuckin' impossible. You cannot do anything right as far as those guys are concerned. If they criticize you for not passing enough and you start passing, do they acknowledge that? No, they complain you aren't shooting enough. The Toronto media try to scoop each other, so they are always working on rumours. Lots of times, they must just make it up. Next time you are in Toronto, pick up a sports section—they've got four papers there—and look at the headlines. They are all bullshit.

The guys on the Leafs would have been phenomenal, though. It would have been unbelievable playing on a line with Mats Sundin, who averaged 80 points a season. Tomas Kaberle was good on the point and Nikolai Antropov was a 21-year-old Russian with size, speed and a lot of talent. I had played six years on the Flames with Robert Reichel, so we were buds, and Gary Roberts and I were on the 1989 Stanley Cup team together. Tie Domi was a guy I'd rather play with than fight against. But after my experience in New York, I told Baiz to forget it. It would be like diving into the biggest fishbowl in hockey. Anyway, they hadn't won a Cup in thirty-five years.

So it was down to the Hawks and the Coyotes. Gretz and Sutter. I owed Gretz. If it weren't for him I wouldn't have a gold medal, but I was worried that if I played for Gretz I would disappoint him. I knew I was a full-blown alcoholic drug addict.

Then there was the money. Chicago offered four million a year for two years, while Phoenix offered two million with a chance to make four if I behaved myself. And Chicago had Sutter. He had stepped up for me in the press during the whole Graham James thing, and I think I felt he could save me, because I was dying.

So I called Baiz and said, "Let's go to Chicago."

Before I signed, I went to meet with Mike Smith, the GM, and said, "Mike, I am in the worst shape anybody could possibly be in. But you know what? As soon as I get my house winterized and ready in Santa Fe, I promise you I will come back and train." He said, "No problem. Just be ready by the time the season starts."

I MOVED TO CHICAGO and trained with their trainer for the last two weeks of August. Then some of the guys got together and we decided to get a head start on the season. Craig Anderson, Jocelyn Thibault and Michael Leighton were in goal, the defencemen included Jon Klemm, Lyle Odelein, Steve McCarthy and Steve Poapst, and for forwards we had Éric Dazé, Sergei Berezin, Michael Nylander and Alex Zhamnov. For two weeks, up until September 6, these guys and I all met at the Edge Ice Arena in Bensenville for informal practice. It was a good way to put together my cardio. I was still about 180, but I knew what to do. In order to help me stay sober, they hired my Santa Fe AA sponsor, JJ, to come and live in Chicago and babysit. They

paid him $200,000 and put him up in one of Mr. Wirtz's fully fur-
nished apartments. Bill Wirtz was the Blackhawks' owner. Not a very
popular guy. He blacked out Hawks games in the city because he said
that showing them on television was unfair to season-ticket holders.
I thought that was small thinking. Anyway, this apartment building
even had an elevator operator. JJ was in heaven.

Training camp started and things were going well. For our first exhibition game, at home against the Dallas Stars on September 21, Sutter
put me on a line with Nylander. I always liked playing with Mikey. He
had great timing and skill. I assisted on his first goal off a pass from Éric
Dazé. (Three days later, Dazé had surgery for a herniated disc, which
was too bad because the three of us had chemistry and Dazé had led the
team in scoring the previous season with 38 goals and 32 assists.) We
outshot them, but lost 3–2 in OT. Sutter had me on the ice for twenty-
four minutes. Considering the shape I was in, I played really well. I was
working really hard with Phil Walker, their trainer, and I figured that
by the time the season started, I would be there. Then Brian called
me into the office one day and just started losin' it on me—"You are in
fuckin' horrible shape. You can barely move out there. What the fuck,
Theo? We're paying you fuckin' millions and you're skating like shit."

I said, "I told Mike Smith before I even signed with you guys that
I was not in good shape. But I will make every effort to get myself in
shape, and I promise you that on October 10, when the season starts
and we face the Blue Jackets, I will be ready."

But they would not let up. Every day it was the same old shit, and
I had had enough. I was thinking, "You guys haven't won a Stanley
Cup since 1961, okay? What's wrong with this picture?"

I kept saying the same thing—"When October 10 hits, I will be
ready. That is when we start getting paid, and that is when it matters.
Not playing fuckin' Detroit in September."

I was still having terrible anxiety attacks on and off the ice. They
were worse than ever. My chest would close up and I couldn't catch

my breath. So one morning I went to a walk-in clinic and told the doctor about them. He said, "No problem, try this," and wrote me a prescription for a shitload of Paxil. Paxil is an antidepressant, like Prozac. The normal first dose is 20 milligrams a day. This doctor doubled that. The Paxil had a bizarre side effect on me—body shocks. No matter where I was—on the bench, at home, wherever—it was like sticking my finger in a light plug.

I was being drug-tested all the time. Three times a week, there was a knock at my door at 6 a.m. and my NHL pee tester would be standing there with a little bottle. In Chicago he would follow me into the bathroom to watch me fill it up.

I had moved in with Stephanie and Aleca, her 5-year-old. We lived in a beautiful apartment on Belmont Harbor, overlooking Lake Michigan. The rent was $10,000 a month. It was on the top level of this cool, old building downtown and it was like living in a movie. We had an elevator operator, a nanny, a maid and a chef. Life was good, but that didn't matter—we fought all the time anyway. She was as messed up as I was.

On October 1, after another one of Sutter's "you better fuckin' be ready" speeches, I was at my apartment and Steph and I got into a big, horrible argument. She stormed out of the living room and locked herself in the bedroom. And something just snapped. I said to myself, "I am going out. I am fuckin' going out." I grabbed my jacket and left. I hopped into a cab and told him to take me to the nearest liquor store. He waited for me, and I came out chugging Grey Goose. "I need some blow, man," I said and pulled out a roll. We headed down toward the projects. I got out and handed him a hundred bucks. He took off fast. It was dangerous down there.

I remember the overflowing garbage cans, torn green plastic bags and wet, ripped-up boxes piled against the walls of every building. The broken wrought-iron fences were all rusty and the gates were hanging off their hinges. There was wall-to-wall graffiti and the ground was covered in greasy wrappers. Nobody knew me, and nobody cared that I was going to get high that night. Perfect.

A black guy dressed hip-hop style was walking past. I said, "Hey, man, I'm looking for some blow." He stopped in front of me and gave me a really intense stare. But I felt absolutely no fear. I honestly did not care whether I lived or died—I just wanted to get high. A few seconds later, he said, "C'mon." He led me down the street and through a couple of alleys to a five-storey red-brick building. The windows were all boarded up. We stepped through a steel-caged door. The building smelled like shit and pee and maybe a dead body. I followed him up to the fourth floor, breathing through my mouth.

Most of the rooms just had mattresses with broken chairs and dressers. There was crap everywhere. The hallways were filled with dirty glass jars and butts and needles. Nice. We came to a closed door and knocked. It was opened by a Semenko-sized black guy with dreads. There were two dealers in the room. Everybody else was sleeping against the walls or passed out on the floor.

The first guy said, "You one crazy motherfucker, you know that? What you coming down here for? This ain't no place for you. You crazy motherfucker."

I shrugged. "I just want to get high, man." He shook his head and disappeared into the kitchen, then came back with an 8-ball. "Two hundred," he said.

I pulled out the roll from my front pocket and gave it to him. "Fuckin' A."

We all sat down around a dirty TV tray. I pulled the tinfoil off my Marlboro Lights, smoothed it down, chopped up the coke, rolled a bill and snorted the first line. It was top quality. Suddenly I didn't feel so anxious anymore. We partied together for a few more hours, the boys laughing and shaking their heads and calling me a crazy mother–fucker every five minutes.

Later that night, I checked into the Drake Hotel, five minutes from my apartment, under my own name. I had missed practice that morning, so Sutter was convinced I was kidnapped or dead. He knew me—there was no way I would miss a practice before the first game of the year. Cops and private security were looking for me. JJ was losin' it because they were paying him all this money to look after me and the first chance I get—gone. Steph was really upset too, because she thought she was the reason I'd left.

I didn't go anywhere for the next twenty-four hours. I just stayed in that room and let my brain go swimming in Paxil, coke, two six-packs and a twenty-sixer of Grey Goose. The next morning, October 3, the booze and blow were gone. I stared out the window at the Chicago skyline. I was near Belmont Harbor Dog Beach and could hear them yapping. My head really fuckin' hurt, and I had another panic attack. I wanted to die.

I pulled myself out of bed, lit a smoke and backed into the shower, letting the water pour over me. I managed to keep my cigarette going the whole time, and my lungs filled with steam and tobacco. My brain started to fire, and I began working on a bullshit excuse to explain why I had fallen off the face of the earth for two days.

I came strolling back into my apartment. When I walked through the door, Stephanie looked at me as if she were seeing a ghost. Baiz was there. So was Sutter. They were more worried and scared than mad. Sutter didn't say much. It was a bad fuckin' scene. There was a lot of sadness in his eyes.

Brian told me the substance abuse program was suspending me until December, and I said, "You know what, man? I just want to be left alone. I just want to play hockey. I don't want to go through your two-hour practices. I don't want you on me all the time. I think I deserve that. I have put up my numbers. I am tired. I don't need any more tough love, I just need some respect."

I was suspended for twenty-five days without pay. That two-day holiday ended up costing me $1,219,512.19.

I was ordered into therapy again and started seeing a new psychologist, Jonna Mogab. She was awesome. We were getting some really good work done. She helped me get through a lot of anger. We did this thing where she put out a whole bunch of cards, and each card had an emotion printed on it—anger, sadness, happiness, fear. There was a big stack of anger cards, a big stack of sadness cards and so on. We would talk and she would stop me every once in a while and ask, "So how did that make you feel?" I would pick up a big stack of anger cards and throw them in a pile.

After a while, she said, "You know, that sadness pile is pretty high." "I know," I said. I did not go near it. The anger cards kept piling up. Finally, she said, "I'm going to tell you something. You have used anger your entire life. It has helped you tell people to leave you alone and be intimidating, but that is not who you are. You are sweet, you are innocent. What happened was not your fault."

I just broke down.

"Underneath anger is this right here," she continued and patted the sadness pile. "You have never been able to get to that sadness because you've needed anger to protect you, but I'm telling you right now to look at your life. This innocent little boy in Russell was sad. His dad was never there for him, his mom was missing, some guy abused him. It's time to get some sanity into your life."

She hit the nail right on the head, and maybe it was because I was ready to hear it. I saw her every day for two months.

I started making changes. Jim contacted all my favourite gambling places—Mandalay Bay in Las Vegas, the Trump Marina, Trump Plaza, Harrah's in Joliet, the MGM Grand in Detroit and the Mohegan Sun. He sent each of them a letter, dated November 1, 2002, that said, "Dear Sir: As per our phone conversation, this will confirm that Theoren W. Fleury wants to have any and all lines of credit closed until further notice. Please feel free to contact me if you have any questions. Sincerely, James R. Jenkins."

THINGS WERE GOING OKAY with Stephanie and me. I was happy when my divorce from Veronica was finalized—it was a weight off my back. Veronica got five million dollars of my worth, we split the Greenwich house, she got the Sicamous house, boat and car, plus ongoing child support. Not a bad paycheque for seven years of marriage.

I was cleared to practise on November 25, and I was back in the lineup December 6 against the Ducks. As soon as I stepped on the ice, the crowed cheered. I opened the scoring on my fourth shift at 10:15 and the crowd went nuts, chanting, "Theo! Theo! Theo!" My teammates were all over me. This is why guys love to play in Chicago.

In the next game, I was standing against the boards, just across the blue line, and I one-timed a tiebreaker over Nikolai Khabibulin's right shoulder with 4:57 left in the third to beat the Lightning 3-1. I remember reading an article in the *Chicago Sun-Times* by a guy named Elliot Harris. He said, "Blackhawks winger Theo Fleury's goal-scoring ability is simply intoxicating. In the non-alcohol-related sense." I thought that was pretty funny.

We went on a three-game road trip, starting at Nassau Coliseum against the Isles. The fans were their usual classy selves, booing and yelling "Crackhead" whenever I touched the puck. This time, I didn't let them get to me. In fact, I felt pretty good. During the warmup, a couple of kids were waiting in Fleury sweaters. They had a sign that said, "We Are Glad You're Back." I got an assist that night. And we beat the Rangers the next night, starting with my shot from the top of the right circle, giving us a 1-0 lead at 13:36.

We lost against the Stars, then won or tied the next eight games. I was starting to think I had made the right decision in coming back. That is, until New Year's Eve in St. Louis.

JJ and I went to this bar with the guys. I convinced him I was cool to go. He said, "C'mon, man. Let's stay in." It wasn't his fault. It wouldn't have mattered who was in the hotel room with me. I am an alcoholic, I was feeling uncomfortable and I was going to go get some medicine.

The night started off fine. JJ was beside me and I was drinking Coke. I was getting antsy. There were girls around, and I had no game when I was sober. I couldn't approach a girl without something in my system. I went around to the other side of the bar, where no one could see me, and ordered a rum and Coke, but I told the bartender to put it in the same kind of tall glass as my Coke. I greased him a couple hundred and said, "Keep 'em coming. Doubles." Nobody had a clue. The night went on and finally JJ came up to me and said, "You little fucking bastard! You have been drinking all night." I was hammered and said, "You can't take a sandwich to a banquet."

He poured me into a cab and the night was swept under the rug because it was only alcohol and I wasn't tested the next day.

A few days later, on January 5, we played Detroit. I had a goal and an assist, but it was all I could do not to beat fuckin' Sean Avery with my stick. Every time I'd skate by him, he'd hold his thumb to the side of his nose and sniff. Avery uses personal defects against people on the ice. He's the new mouthpiece in the NHL. In 2008 he approached the press just before a Flames–Stars game in Calgary and referred to his ex-girlfriend—actress Elisha Cuthbert, who was dating Flames defenceman Dion Phaneuf—as his "sloppy seconds." He was suspended for six games, and when he served his sentence, Dallas told him to go pound sand. He had just signed a four-year, $15.5 million deal. The Rangers took him back in March 2009. In eight years in the NHL, he's changed teams four times—from Detroit, to L.A., to the Rangers, then Dallas and back to the Rangers. That's because he's a clown—about as popular in the dressing room as a case of the crabs.

The beginning of the end, as far as my career was concerned, came a couple of weeks after that Detroit game. On January 18, a Saturday night, we lost 4–2 in St. Louis, then we flew to Columbus for a game on Monday and when we landed I said to JJ, "I want go out with the guys. I am all good. I learned my lesson after New Year's." He said, "Are you sure, man?" "Absolutely." I was drinking Cokes at a bar with the guys and then started slipping the bartender money. And the next thing you know, we were at a strip club, and all I remember after that is waking up because somebody was banging on my hotel room door.

It was our travelling secretary. He was yelling that I was late for a team meeting with Brian Sutter in his suite. When I opened the door, he had this horrified look on his face. I said, "What is wrong?" He told me to go look in the mirror. I had a big cut over my eye, and my shirt looked like something out of a *Friday the 13th* movie. There was blood everywhere. I turned and looked at the bed. It was covered with blood too. And my ribs were really sore, as if I'd had the shit kicked out of me.

I had a quick shower, and by the time I got up to the suite all hell had broken loose with the coaching staff. They were coming down on the guys who had been with me, basically saying, "What the fuck are you guys doing letting Theo drink?" It wasn't their fault. The truth was, I should not have gone to the bar.

It got into the papers because a reporter had been tipped. After the game against the Blue Jackets he came up to me and said, "I heard about the altercation at a strip club last night." I said, "What're you talking about?" He said, "Well, where did you get the black eye?" I was caught totally off guard. I said, "I don't remember," and he proceeded to tell me.

The story that was reported was that Tyler Arnason, Phil Housley and I went to the Pure Platinum strip club, and I was so pissed that we were asked to leave. According to what I read, we got to the door and I punched the manager in the face. The bouncers came at me, and Houser and Arnie stepped up to stop me from being killed. The cops were called at 4 a.m., and the rest is history.

Once it came out in the media, there was a big meeting between the doctors from the substance abuse program, Mr. Wirtz and the coaches. I was still in stage two of the program, and Mr. Wirtz wanted to get rid of me. But for some reason, both doctors actually stood up for me and said it wasn't really my fault. I felt they had hung me out to dry in New York, but now in Chicago they were on my side. Maybe I was too valuable to the team at the time, or maybe they didn't like Bill Wirtz. He was an old asshole.

A month after the incident, the Hawks sent JJ was home. They decided "the effectiveness of his role had come to an end." I thought it was a stupid idea from the beginning, but he was a friend. We went on a nine-game slide and the Hawks put me on waivers without even telling me, then benched me for a couple of games. I mean, it was a handy excuse, right? We are losing, so it must be Fleury. It didn't have anything to do with the fact that we had no depth and Dazé spent the season injured, that our goalie, Jocelyn Thibault, sat out the final nine games to recover from post-concussion syndrome, that our captain, Alex Zhamnov, was arrested for drunk driving, or that Sutter and the GM, Mike Smith, hated each other so much they weren't speaking. No, it was just that Fleury got in a fight at a strip club so now we can't win. I hung in there, and even managed to get my shit together at the end of the season with three goals and 11 assists in the last 17 games. But in the third-last game of the season, I fucked the dog.

We were in St. Louis, and scheduled for back-to-back games. I was rooming with Chris Simon. I got up to my room after dinner, and everybody was gone. I said, "Fuck this," and ended up at Larry Flynt's Penthouse strip joint across the river, right where Kevin Stevens got picked up. I walked in, sat down, had a couple of drinks and some girls came over. I said, "Take a seat and I'll buy you girls drinks." One thing led to another, and I did a whole bunch of blow. And the riverboat was there, so I cruised over to the casino and did a bit of gambling. The next thing I knew, it was six in the morning.

Meanwhile, Steph checked the bank account and figured I had been at the casinos, which meant drinking and blow, so she called the doctors. At 4 p.m. on April 3, the pee guy was banging on my hotel room door. I was just about to leave for the rink, but I sat there and waited him out.

I had gotten a couple of hours' sleep that afternoon, but when the pee guy finally went away and I made it to practice, I was still fuckin' annihilated. I don't have a clue how the team didn't know that I was squished. I went out to play and had one of my best games of the year. Got three assists and I was first star of the game.

The next night was the last game I ever played in the NHL.

36

I THINK I'M GONNA KILL MYSELF

ON APRIL 4, 2003, in Chicago, I was still hung over from the night before and my reflexes were slow. I was standing in front of the net and a slapshot came high around the boards. I held up my glove to stop it, and it pinged off the glass, deflecting onto my right cheekbone. I played two more shifts and then went to the dressing room to see the doctor at the end of the period. My cheek did not hurt, so they put a visor on my helmet and I went back out. My eye was swelling and my ear was ringing big time, but I finished the game. After I showered, I looked in the mirror and saw a gargoyle looking back at me. I needed an X-ray, so I called Steph at home. I said, "You gotta come get me to go to the hospital. I think something is seriously wrong with my face." The X-ray showed my cheekbone was cracked from just underneath my eye to the side of my mouth. I went on an emergency waiting list for surgery. Meanwhile, I was given Vicodin, a highly addictive painkiller. I took a couple because my cheek was starting to kill me, and Steph hijacked the rest. She was a pill-popper. In fact, I got her two or three prescriptions out of it.

They operated on my cheek in Chicago—went in through my right eye socket, reconstructed my cheek and put a metal plate and a screw in my orbital bone just under my eye. I could not fly due to the pressure on my sinuses, so we drove from Chicago to Santa Fe, which is 1,300 miles—giving us more than twenty hours to talk. I just kept saying, "I don't wanna play hockey anymore. I really don't wanna play hockey." Steph said, "What are we going to do?" I said, "Well, we can move back to Santa Fe and put Aleca in school." There was lots of money left in the bank, about six million. I figured I could play golf every day and we could party a little, and basically retire.

We got there and were all set up, my cheek healed, although if you didn't know I was a hockey player you would have thought I'd been thrown through a plate-glass window or something. We got Aleca all settled in, and on April 19, 2003, I took Steph out for a celebratory dinner. I got completely annihilated, and when we got home I told her I was going out to find some blow. So I drove from bar to bar, and for the first time ever, I couldn't find any. I looked all night.

Material things had never meant much to me. Yeah, I liked my cool cars and nice suits, but I was never all about the stuff. But when I had a decorator put together my house in Santa Fe, she helped me commission a beautiful, one-of-a-kind, original desert scene that hung over the mantle in the living room. I just loved that painting. When I looked at it, I got the same restful feeling I had when I first came out to Las Campanas. I got home early that morning, and my painting was on the front step, cut into a million pieces.

Steph and I had been through hell that year. I had been suspended, then there was the Columbus incident and the broken cheekbone—it was a mess, and she'd stood by me. Yet when I didn't come home that night, she demolished my special painting. What did that say to me? Maybe that painting represented me and my career, a one-of-a-kind thing, and I was blaming her for destroying it, I don't know, but I absolutely snapped. I went into the house and tore it completely apart. Everything. I ripped the curtains down, kicked every door off the hinges, pulled plates and bowls and shit off the counters and threw them on the tile floor. I was insane.

Steph thought I was going to kill her, so she ran and locked herself in Aleca's room. I came after her and kicked the door down. Aleca was there, and she was frightened. I will always feel badly about that.

Steph had her cell phone and tried to call 911, but I grabbed it and broke it in half. She ran to the kitchen and picked up the phone and a big butcher knife and called the cops. I smashed the toaster and blender and whatever else was on the counter. Then I tore the phone off the wall, and she ran into the office. When I heard the sirens in the distance, I jumped into my Beemer and drove straight into the desert.

I drove for about ten minutes, so I was a couple of miles from the house. But the land was so flat out there, I could see the lights of the police cars reflecting off the open black sky. I knew they'd catch up to me eventually. I started walking back, and when I got there, they handcuffed me and took me to jail.

I was thrown into the drunk tank, where I passed out. When I woke up and looked around, there were about ten tough-looking Mexican guys staring back. I dropped my head in my hands and thought, "What just happened? What the fuck am I doing here?" I was fingerprinted and had a mug shot taken, then was put back into the cell with my Mexican buddies. By then, it was Friday night. I phoned my golfing buddy Claudie and said, "Claude, man, you gotta bail me out of here. I am going to lose it if I have to stay in here all weekend."

He said, "Don't worry, man, Steph is feeling really badly and she has already been over here and we are coming to get you."

Claude managed to pull some strings to get me out of there. He picked me up and Steph was in the back of the car. I got in still pissed off. Claudie said, "You're fucking throwing everything away here. What are you doing?" And then Steph piped up. "I'm sorry, I didn't mean to cut up your picture. I'm so sorry." And she started to cry. She looked so pathetic and vulnerable. I felt terrible. "How is Aleca?" I asked. Steph said she was okay. "I'm a fuckin' asshole," I said.

"You got that right," Claudie said.

So we kissed and made up and went back to the house and cleaned it up and had things fixed. I drank a few more times and we partied together, but I never lost my temper like that again.

I had one year left on my contract, but on May 1, Gary Bettman, the commissioner of the National Hockey League, agreed to put me in stage three of the program, which meant that as of May 6 I was suspended for six months, and in order to play again I had to enter treatment.

I decided I wanted to play the last year of my contract, so I got everything back on track. The doctors were calling me again, and I was going to meetings and getting ready to go back into treatment. Then one day I was watching myself in the mirror as I was running on the treadmill at the gym and I just stopped. I said, "This fucking sucks."

I went back home and told Steph I was finally done for good. She said, "What are you going to do?" And I said, "Just live in Santa Fe. We got a nice house, you are taking classes online. I am tired." So we planned a wedding for October. I never phoned the Blackhawks, didn't phone Don Baizley to tell him I wasn't coming back. Nothing.

The media called, but I didn't owe anybody anything, so I wasn't talking, and according to the *Chicago Tribune* all Sutter would say is, "I'm disappointed, but I'm not surprised. This is something that is going to be with Theo forever."

I think the whole league reacted to my leaving the way you would feel after having a big, happy dump. There were a lot of guys like me in the game, but they didn't want anyone to know that. My presence kept the bad news on the front of the sports pages. Hockey wants to be known as the school's good-looking, clean-cut jock, and I was really fucking with that image.

HAVING DECIDED I was done with hockey, and with nothing but time on my hands, I found a new level of messed up. During the day, I would lie on the couch and eat or sleep, then spend most nights in

Albuquerque because that is where my dealer was. Finally, I came home one day and Steph and Aleca were gone. I had bought her a brand-new Cadillac Escalade. She'd taken that along with a little money. I didn't care. She deserved it.

People who loved me tried to contact me. I remember my mom calling, freaking out on the phone—"What are you doing, killing yourself?" and I said, "I'm fine. Don't believe anything you hear or read. I am living healthy, golfing every day . . ." I didn't want anybody to come see me.

But eventually Claudie called Chuck and said, "You better get down here. Your buddy is fucked up bad." Chuck came down, and the place was a mess. He tried to talk me into straightening out and offered to help. He said, "I guess maybe I should be thankful that I am not a part of this whole chaotic mess. Your career is in total disarray . . . you have lost control of yourself. The drugs are becoming exponential in their pull on you. You're doing tons of it and wasting your money on the new hangers-on you find at the strip clubs. What about the kids—Beaux and Tay and Josh?"

I said, "Chuck, I am happy just partying. I don't want them to see me like this. Do you think I would be good for them right now?" Chuck said, "Bones, you just come and go out of people's lives, and it hurts them. You're a special guy. You have the ability to make the person you are with feel like the most important person in the world." And he talked to me about how, when we used to hang out, I would crank up the music and look at him and sing, and how it used to fucking queer him out. He'd say, "What are you doing? Look out the other window, you friggin' weirdo." And he reminded me of the time he went with me to an Alcoholics Anonymous meeting on Rodeo Drive in Beverly Hills and how it was full of freaks and famous people. Some bigwig producer had spoken that night and said that when he first figured out he needed help he asked a friend to take him to a place where the people had the same status that he did. The next day, his friend drove him to the grungiest, filthiest area of L.A. and they attended a meeting in a real dive. Then Chuck talked about how we loved each other like brothers and how much it meant to him that night in Colorado when we had prayed together. And then he said, "Come on, Bones, let's go home."

But I knew I couldn't. I had too much shit piled up that I had no idea how to even begin to get rid of it. I would lie down at night thinking about all the bad things that had happened to me and all the bad things I had done to others. I would flash back to lying in bed and snorting coke with a naked stripper and spending all kinds of money while Veronica and the kids were sleeping at home. And that fuckin' guilt and shame would grab my heart and squeeze it like a stress ball.

I told Chuck to leave without me.

I WENT HARD at it for three months. Just mounds of coke and lemon Stoli and strangers who followed me home from strip clubs. I basically stopped eating and sleeping. I wanted to die, but my body was too resilient. Finally, I bought a gun from a pawnshop and decided to blow my brains out. I was 36 years old.

I sat there on the couch, swigging frozen lemon Stoli, staring at the gun and a single bullet on the glass coffee table. What did I have to live for? More nights of pure hell? Life was only livable when I was obliterated. I was a worthless piece of shit and I knew it. No good to my kids—fuck, I could barely even remember their faces. Couldn't keep a relationship together—Shannon, Veronica and Steph all basically hated me. My parents were fuckin' disappointed in me, my brothers said they didn't want to watch me die. Chuck, my buddy Chuck, was gone. Hockey was over, fuckin' *over,* man. Nobody really cared about me—Crispy, Sutter, Slats, all I was to them was a piece of fuckin' meat.

You know that feeling when you have to do something that you really don't want to do and you are mentally preparing yourself? Like taking some really fuckin' nasty medicine or sitting outside the principal's office at school or staring down at the water from a really high diving board? Each breath is sticking to your lungs and it is hard to swallow because your heart is taking up all the room in your throat. Then you finally hit the point where you say, "Okay, fuck it, here I go." Well, that is where I was at two o'clock that morning. I was ready to jump.

I grabbed the bullet, loaded the gun and jammed it in my mouth. I don't know—maybe if I'd had it ready and didn't have to take the time to put the bullet in the chamber, I might have gone through with it. But once the barrel was rattling off my teeth and my finger was on the trigger, I'd cooled off just enough to hesitate.

It's not as if I'd felt this sudden urge to live. I still felt like shit and wished I were dead. I think that's why, after I ran outside and chucked the gun into the desert, I was screaming at the universe like a madman. But it was the easy way out, and I had never taken the easy way out. Besides, killing myself was just too fuckin' scary.

In weird twist of fate, my 16-year-old son Josh called and gave me reason to go on for the time being. I hadn't heard from him in months. When I picked up the phone he said, "Hey, how's it going?" I said, "Good, you?" He said, "What are you doing?" I said, "You know what I'm doing."

There was silence, and then Josh said, "Well, what do you think about moving to Calgary? We'll get a place together 'cause I can't live with mom anymore."

Shannon had married, and she was a good mom, but Josh had grown up without his father for too long. I had to go back to Calgary. He and Beaux and Tatym needed me.

I put the Santa Fe house up for sale, but for the longest time it didn't sell. I finally took a fuckin' bath on it.

IT WAS JULY, and I will never forget that fucking road trip. I stopped in Albuquerque to see my dealer, because Calgary has shit cocaine. I bought five 8-balls and stuffed them all around the engine. I also had a little vial in my front pocket. I timed it perfectly—it was twenty-two hours to Calgary, so I had to leave at 3 a.m. to get there in time for last call.

I did a lot of blow in the car on the way, which made me hyper-vigilant. Every tree, every sign, every electrical pole was vivid, and I was zoned right into the road. By the time I got to the border, I was just fuckin' tweaking and shitting my pants. I drove up to the window and looked at the border guard's face. I was paranoid and thought, "Holy fuck, what if he knows about the shit in the engine? What if he can tell?" The guard pointed his finger at my chest, and I thought I was going to pass out. "Hey!" he said, "you're Theo Fleury!"

I smiled and said, "Awesome! How's it goin?" It was just like the McLovin' scene from that movie *Superbad.* We shot the shit for a couple of minutes, and he told me to drive on through. As soon as I left the border I drove straight to Lethbridge, Alberta, picked up a twelve-pack and chugged three beers before my hands stopped shaking. I'd finished the case by the time I saw the lights of Calgary, and then I had to pull over for a minute because I was having a major anxiety attack. "Am I really doing this? Oh God, should I be here? What the fuck am I doing? Is it too late to turn around?"

Sure enough, man, at 1:45 a.m. I pulled up to the Melrose Café on 17th Avenue, where all my friends were waiting for me. I walked in, picked up my drink, held it high up in the air in a toast and said, "Hi! I made it."

37

A REALLY DARK PLACE

WHEN I CAME BACK to Calgary I partied hard. Over the next three years I did about fifteen pounds of coke. That's a two-thousand-dollar-a-week habit.

Josh and I were renting an executive suite downtown, two blocks from Eau Claire. I tried to monitor Josh at the beginning, but the way I was leading my life, who was I to tell him what to do? Joshy was kind of a loner. We started working on our relationship, and I'm proud of where he's at today, but for a while there, he was pretty sad. I felt guilty, but there wasn't really much I could say to him. I just had to show up and be an example. At first, I failed to do that. Shannon told me it was like watching a beautiful sweater she had lovingly knit by hand start to unravel. Hanging out with me meant unlimited money, Pam Anderson lookalikes and restaurants every night. Living with his mom and eating broccoli for dinner didn't quite have the same appeal.

My night would begin at a bar, then I would end up back at my apartment for two or three days of continuous partying. I was in a really dark place. Josh saw it all. It was a bad scene.

WHILE I WAS PARTYING, I ran into a hockey player named Steve Parsons. He had been a tough guy in the minors for years. Fight-

ing was a big, big part of his game—he'd been in more than three hundred fights in his career. A huge guy from Vancouver—six foot four, 255
pounds—he wasn't that talented, but he said that he learned at a young
age that if you have a thick neck and a heavy hand teams will always
have room for you. He was real sweet, nice person—off the ice.

Steve had been off for a couple of years with a wrist injury, and two
senior men's league teams were after him to play—Lloydminster and
a rez team from up north called the Horse Lake Thunder. He was
trying to decide who to play for, like a free agent. Horse Lake had
left me a couple of messages, but I hadn't bothered returning their
calls. I was done with hockey. Why would I play in some northern
bush league when I'd just walked away from the NHL? I was sick of
fuckin' trainin' and refs and all that bullshit. Besides, playing on the
rez was taking your life in your hands. My brothers Teddy and Trav
had played a lot of rez hockey for both white and Native teams. There
are rules, but there are no rules. Things start out normally, and then
stuff will start to happen. Say one team starts blowing away the other
team—Natives get very angry, very fast.

Trav tells a funny story about a rez game one night. His and Teddy's team—a white team—were invited to play in a game on the
Ebb and Flow Reserve. Naturally, half the team came down with
the Ebb and Flow flu. Trav and Teddy could only scrounge up six
other guys, including the goalie. Teddy ended up playing fifty-five
minutes—the only time he came off was for a penalty. The game was
so rough, Teddy was slammed to the ice and broke his nose. One of
Teddy and Trav's big defencemen was jumped, and when he tried
to defend himself, he was kicked out of the game. On his way to the
dressing room, the only thing between him and the crowd was a rope.
He was surrounded by a mob and they were closing in, so he had his
stick up swinging and yelling, "C'mon, who's coming close?"

Teddy and Trav's team won, but the ref was assaulted, thrown
down to the ice a couple of times, and when the Native team was

skating off the goalie spit in his face. Finally, they had to walk out of the rink in a pack, because it was too be dangerous to go one at a time. As they were loading their stuff into their Suburban, this little kid— around 4 years old—was standing near the car and he turned his face up to Trav with kind of a blank look and said, "You fuckin' cheaters."

Anyway, Steve had decided that he liked what Horse Lake had to offer, so just after Christmas 2004 he gave me a call. He said he'd heard that Horse Lake wanted me to play up on the rez as well. I said, "No way, not at chance. I'm done. Besides, I'll get scalped up there." Steve said, "Theo, you will be the safest man in hockey. We've got five enforcers at the NHL level." I thought about it a minute, then said, "I don't think so." Steve wasn't giving up that easily, "Theo, you're a hockey player. It's what you do, it's what you know, it's what you are good at. You've been in hockey for thirty-five years. I don't know if you can just turn the page on it. If you play, Theo, believe me, you will be safe."

"Not interested," I said and hung up. I called my brother Trav, and he said, "Well, it might be a good thing." Trav was worried about me. Every day he saw me zoned out, lying on the couch, flipping channels—my weight was up to at least 220. I was just a butterball, five by five. Hockey without any pressure sounded good. I thought I would feel better if I could love the game again. I had won a Stanley Cup, a Canada Cup, the World Junior Championship and an Olympic gold medal, but I hadn't won the Allan Cup, the championship of Senior AAA men's hockey. The Allan Cup has been around since 1908, so there's a lot of history there. It means a lot to hockey. Besides, it's not as if I had anything else to do except party at Cowboys bar, and that gets kind of old after a while. What can you say to the exact same people every single night? So I called Steve back. "Let's do it."

Chief Dion Horseman met me in Calgary, and he was a really cool guy. He was 32 years old—the youngest chief in Canada. A really different cat—ambitious, fun, a visionary. He wanted to have the best team in the senior hockey. Why? He felt it would inspire the younger kids in his community to play hockey instead of getting into trouble, and at the same time give the people in Horse Lake some pride. So the chief and I went out and just got fuckin' legless, the two of us.

I asked him, "How is this all going to work? What does it look like?" He said, "Well, I'll fly you up every weekend, or whenever you want. Your mom and dad can come and watch you play, if you want. You can buy new equipment, whatever you want, I'll take care of it." My cousin Todd Holt, who was five years younger than me, was playing up there. I really liked the kid. Holty was one of the most gifted players ever. Unbelievable talent. A pure scorer—get it to him when he's open and it's in. He was only five foot seven, 160 pounds, but the San Jose Sharks drafted him. He played for the Swift Current Broncos from 1989 to 1994, so Graham James was his coach for six years. Toddy started drinking and ended up in rough shape up in Horse Lake, but no matter how much he partied, he still had this unbelievable touch around the net.

Horse Lake First Nation is near Beaverlodge, Alberta, which is six hours northwest of Edmonton. It makes the middle of nowhere seem somewhere. Once you get to Beaverlodge, you hit a dirt road with no lights, then go seven kilometres and suddenly it opens up to one of the most beautiful rinks I have ever played in outside of the NHL. It's almost like a church. It was brand new and cost more than $9 million. There was a substantial amount of money on the rez, because they had a really nice royalty deal from an oil and gas company.

Most the other guys on the team were Native or part Native. There was Brent Dodginghorse, a six-foot, 195-pound treaty Indian from the Tsuu T'ina reserve near Calgary. He played left wing for the Hitmen for two years, got into eighteen fights and won most of them. He's into rodeo now. Gino Odjick, at six-three and 215, is an Algonquin and one of the heavyweight champs of the NHL in his time. There is tough like Ronnie Stern and Paul Kruse, and then there are those who are in a whole other league of tough—Dave Brown, Marty McSorley, Sandy McCarthy, Bob Probert and Odjick were guys who could kill you with one punch. They split hockey helmets with their fists—I have seen it happen. One night in Calgary, when I was still with the Flames, we were playing the Flyers and I watched Dave Brown cave in Stu Grimson's face. Stu had a screw sticking out of his eye for six weeks to hold his orbital bone in place. Gino was an enforcer with the Canucks, Flyers, Isles and Canadiens. He took on everybody in the NHL—184 fights altogether. I saw him fight a ton of times when we played the Canucks. Back in the fall of 1996, he really got into it with Jamie Huscroft, who was about his size. The gloves came off and they were just pounding each other, like dinosaurs. A couple of months later, he and Todd Simpson were boxing, and referee Kerry Fraser tried to break it up and Gino almost took his head off. Since retiring, Gino works with kids, warning them against substance abuse.

My first time at the rink, we walked in and opened the door to the
Within a week of my agreeing to play, they chartered a plane and flew Steve Parsons, Brent Dodginghorse and me up to Grand Prairie. The chief picked us up and took us to a sporting goods store. He had an account there and said, "Anything you want, it's yours." We were like kids—"I'll have ten of these and ten of those sticks and . . ." The three of us spent ten grand on sticks and new gear. I said, "Are you sure?" and the chief said, "Yeah, whatever." I had my own patterned sticks from Easton that were flown to Horse Lake. I was pumped.

My first time at the rink, we walked in and opened the door to the dressing room and saw twenty empty equipment bags on the floor and hockey gear dumped all over the place. At first, I figured they'd been robbed or something. When you play hockey, you pack up your stuff in your bag, take it home and air it out. I turned to the chief and said, "What the fuck?" But it was equipment the chief had provided for the community. The Native kids would come in, grab a left skate and a right skate—sometimes they'd fit and sometimes they wouldn't—a pair of gloves, any brand, any size, and they'd go out on the ice with a stick they found in the pile. Incredibly, they had nothing but talent. We would watch them come out and hit crossbars, ping the puck off the goalposts, make beautiful passes, knock pucks out of the air. I watched guys pick up the puck and carry it down the ice like a lacrosse ball. Their motor skills were just phenomenal. These kids were 9 and 10 years old and totally independent—coming to the rink on their own, getting dressed, hanging out. A pretty self-sufficient young group, for sure. They ended up spending a lot of time around us, so we would make sure we gave them sticks and extra stuff we had, or teach them how to tape their stick or tie their skates properly. I have to admit, I really got off on that. I loved dealing with the kids.

I WAS ALL SET to start in my first game with the Thunder, in Grande Prairie against the Athletics, and found out I couldn't play. It was all over TSN, the CBC, CTV, all over the newspapers—Hockey Alberta had ruled I was ineligible. Four thousand people had shown up and ended up watching a men's beer-league game.

Some fuckin' dickhead from the NHL office had called and said, "You have a contract for last year." Meaning 2003–04. And I said, "I *did* have a contract, but I don't have any cheque stubs from Chicago because I was not reinstated." The chief hired a lawyer, and we went to court. We argued that my contract was void, and Bob Pulford, the Blackhawks' senior vice-president, was behind us. After all, if the court had found that my contract was still in effect, it would mean I had a right to come back and play in Chicago as long as I went to treatment. Or the Blackhawks would have to write me a cheque for $4.5 million. Pulford was probably having chest pains. The only reason this made headlines was because of the NHL lockout. Sports reporters had to write *something* about hockey.

It didn't seem to matter what I did or where I went, everything I did was always controversial, But I never backed down from a fight, ever, and as I told reporters, when the guys who were trying to stop me from playing dropped the gloves, I was prepared to take it as far as we needed to go.

My appeal was granted, and the next day, Saturday, January 22, 2005, I played my first game in Horse Lake. We had about two thousand fans—they usually got a hundred. I scored a goal and two assists against the Spirit River Rangers and we won, 6–5. I was officially in the bush leagues.

We went to Fairview the next weekend, but we had been partying and both Steve and I were pretty hung over—still half in the bag, to be honest. I got tied up with a guy on the ice, and he got me down on their blue line. I knew it was make-or-break time. If I was going to let guys come at me so that they could make a name for themselves or tell their buddies, "Fleury's a pussy, in fact I took care of him tonight," I would be dead. I had to be nasty, hard to play against. So I got up and was trying to kick the guy's skate out from under him while cross-checking him in the head at the same time. Steve saw the whole thing developing, but he was by our blue line, about fifty feet away. He came flying down the ice like a fuckin' semi and clotheslined the guy from behind. It was a dirty tactic, but it worked. He pretty much incapacitated the guy. I took my stick and started sticking my attacker in his neck and chest. There would be no question after this that I was there to play for real, and God help any fucker who did not take me seriously. We got on the bus after the game and I looked at Steve and said, "You know what? In all my years I have never seen anybody stick up for me like that." We established a brotherhood right then, right off the hop.

Playing in the North Peace Hockey League was just a gong show, a fuckin' gong show. It was insane. We were the toughest team in the history of hockey. Nobody came within five feet of me. There were Parsons and Odjick, and then Sasha Lakovic, who I had played with on the Flames, joined us along with his brother Greg. They were both mental. And Dody Wood was there. He would fight anybody. In fact, when he played for the Sharks he had gone up against Gino, who was with Vancouver at the time. He'd also danced with Darren McCarty when he was the enforcer for Detroit, and Tie Domi from the Leafs. We had another kid, Jason Beauchamp, who'd played in the minors and was insane-tough. If you really wanted to fight when you played us, there was no one to pick off our bench unless you had your tombstone ready. We were a cocky, bullyish bunch, and I was the ringleader.

The Thunder's rink was a super-intimidating place to play, let me tell you. During the warmup the Native people played fuckin' drums and did that chanting-singing, "Ai ai aia aia aia aia." Powwow music. Oh, it was fuckin' scary, man. I mean, we were the home team, so we were comfortable, but Steve would be chirping at the visiting teams on the red line during warmups and stretching—"How was the bus ride into the rez tonight?" You could see the look of terror in their eyes, they were just so nervous—sucking their thumbs, going, "I don't want to go out there!" And of course we had the rain dance going and I'd be out there telling them all how we were going to score five goals and spear someone in the nuts, and Steve would back me up, saying that if they touched me he would clothesline them and take their fuckin' heads off. You could see teams coming in just shaking. And of course, it was a big family event for the people on the rez. Everything from babies in brightly coloured snowsuits—some with shoes or boots, some in bare feet—to elders, 70 or 80 years old. It was such a family environment.

You have probably heard of "Indian time." Well, it is no joke. They would schedule a game for seven o'clock, but we wouldn't get underway until at least eight. The ice wouldn't be ready, the concession wouldn't be open, the lights wouldn't be on until somebody bothered to get there—and you could never be sure when *that* would be.

We gave the rez the exposure they wanted, and they wanted us to play a certain way, so that is how we did it. The chief was like the captain of our ship. He had an obsession for game-worn jerseys. If you know anything about game-worn jerseys, they are not cheap—collectors pay top dollar. My jerseys start at about two thousand dollars. Well, the chief would wear game-worn jerseys seven days a week. And I never saw him wear the same one twice, ever. He had sweaters worn by Gretzky, Messier, me, and other big-name NHLers. I bet he had fifty thousand dollars' worth of them. Here was a guy running a multimillion-dollar reserve (all the money goes to the chief, and he allocates it), and he's 32 years old with five kids, wearing track pants and a vintage hockey jersey.

The chief's appetite for beer, scraps and controversy set the tone for everyone else. When your leader acts a certain way, everybody else kind of assumes the same identity. And that is exactly what happened to us as a team. We were a bad-ass crew who played by our own set of rules. And we had the chief on our side. We used to go to this bar called Champs in Grand Prairie after games. It had become a Mecca for our fans. Sometimes, we'd have five or six hundred people all kind of gathering around us. One night, we'd won the provincials and Champs had prepared a big spread for us—pizza and chicken fingers, lasagna and salads. The chief had arranged it for the players and our families, and of course there was an open bar. Steve and I were both drinking pretty heavily at the time, so it would be nothing for us to order twenty-five vodka and waters, twenty-five Coors Lights and twenty-five rum and Cokes just for me and Steve and whoever stopped by. We also asked the waitress for fifty shooters while she was at it. I remember the bill came and it was nine thousand dollars. That included the flats of beer out the back door for our after-party, which was always a gong show. I watched the chief walk out to his truck and come back and peel off ten grand and hand it to the owner like it was nothing, just the cost of doing business.

That's just how the chief was, extravagant. Even in the NHL, you have a roommate, but not the Horse Lake Thunder. One time, he flew everyone into Edmonton for four days and we practised—twice—at the Northlands Coliseum. The ice cost $500 an hour compared to $140 at a city rink, and he invited everyone to bring their girlfriends, wives, parents, kids, and we all got our own rooms. If you needed another room for a family member, he would pick up the tab for that too. We had the best buses, the best hotels, the best facilities, the best equipment, the best jerseys, team jackets, track suits, everything we needed and more. This guy treated us like we were in the NHL. It was really phenomenal.

Our record that year was 79–3–1. We killed every team. My brother Travis was not happy about our play. Trav had kept me at arm's length because it hurt him too much to see me partying the way I was. He put it to me this way: "If you wanna go for supper and come back to the normal life and hang out with me, I am there." He came to one of our games in Innisfail and left pissed off. He had played a lot of Native hockey and didn't like our intimidation factor. He said Innisfail was a one-sided game and that we were basically just bullies. "The Thunder is just nasty. You got Lakovic suspended from every league he played in. He's a skilled player, he doesn't need to run guys and intentionally try to hurt them and fight and stuff. This is senior hockey—these guys gotta work the next day. All those guys, they have normal lives, they have normal jobs. And your buddy Parsons, there is no mercy with him. He could really hurt somebody and he plays that card. And crippling somebody is just for bragging rights for the chief. C'mon, man."

I understand how it looked to Trav, but there was shit going down that he and the people in the stands were not aware of. What had happened was that an Innisfail player was being overly lippy, calling me everything in the book—a drunk and a crackhead—and calling Parsons a fat fuck and a drunk and a traitor. The guy just wouldn't shut up. When the score was still 0–0, Parsons was lined up for the faceoff beside him and said, "I'll tell you what, I am gonna let everything you are saying slide, but as soon as we go up by five goals I am gonna jump you and beat the shit out of you."

This guy was beyond cocky. He said, "Sure, sure, you guys ain't gonna get a five-goal lead." Parsons stayed calm and kind of smiled and said, "We will, and when it happens you're getting it."

And as soon as he finished the sentence, we got the puck and *bam!* it was 1–0. A couple of shifts later it was 2–0, then 3–0. Parsons skated by their bench and said, "Three zero, Billy—two more." A while later, it was 4–0. Then 4–1. The Innisfail player came back and laughed in Steve's face. In the next period it was 5–1, and within a shift and a half it was 6–1.

Both benches knew what Steve was gonna do. The cocky guy came out for the faceoff, and so did Steve. The puck dropped, the play was underway and Steve went to find him. The Innisfail player saw Steve coming and tried to go for a line change, but it was too late. Steve fuckin' grabbed him and bullied it up a little, but he'd called his shot and couldn't back off of it. He kicked the crap out of this kid until the linesman managed to get him off. If a bee stings you, burn down the hive.

We were pretty ruthless—it was us against the world. We didn't have any allies, except within the walls of our locker room. The games were like wars. We wouldn't go out there looking for trouble, but guys would get frustrated when they couldn't score, so we'd say, "Well, okay, we can go that way too if you want."

When I played for Horse Lake, I was shocked at the racism we faced. I know people stepped it up against us because we were tough and ugly, and I was cool with that, but some just hated Aboriginal people. When we played off the rez, we heard everything from "fucking featherheads" and "wagon burners" to names even worse. I could not believe the prejudice that existed in my country, a country I'd represented at the

Olympics—twice. It was absolutely embarrassing. When I was a kid, I was hassled sometimes about being part Native, but until I played for Horse Lake I had no idea what Native people go through.

The TV sports networks, TSN and Sportsnet, followed us on the road, so the games were sold out. Senior men's hockey usually pulled in around 500 to 600 fans, but the rinks were filled to capacity from 2,500 to 6,000 to watch us play. Lots of people from Horse Lake followed us everywhere because they were proud of us. We were on the road as a community, not as a bunch of individuals. Sometimes when we went into a visiting team's building, suddenly there wouldn't be enough tickets for our fans from the rez. Other times, our fans were shuffled off to the cheap seats up in the rafters. That was so wrong. The Horse Lake Thunder was the reason the small-town rinks were filling up. People came to see stars, not the usual teams. We made a lot of money for those teams we played. Every single one of those buildings was sold out.

We were on the road to the Allan Cup in the 2005 playoff run. We won our first series against Stony Plain, and then on February 25 we began a series against the Bentley Generals. Bentley's little rink held only eight hundred people, so we ended up playing at the Centrium in Red Deer, Alberta, instead. That's where the Rebels, a junior team in the Western Hockey League, play. Twelve thousand people came to watch us. We sold out the building, both nights. The Rebels have trouble doing that.

I didn't know it until he told me recently, but my buddy and old roomie Pete Montana was working in Red Deer. He said that when he first heard I was coming he was pissed, not because the Allan Cup isn't a prestigious trophy, but because he thought I should be in the NHL, not in the bush leagues. He told me that he said to himself, "Theo is going be a Hall of Famer . . . What the hell is he doing playing for Horse Lake in the Allan Cup playoffs?" He thought it was wrong, but he decided to go see the game anyway.

Pete said he was sitting with the play-by-play guys in the press box, and prior to the game he decided he'd come down to the bench and talk to me. And when Pete talks about this part of the story, he still gets pretty emotional. He said he went down underneath the stands where the dressing rooms were, and I was standing outside about twenty yards away. He said I had a lit cigarette hanging from my bottom lip and I was concentrating hard, squinting through the haze as I worked on my stick. Pete said he stopped cold. He couldn't do it. He could not come over. Pete said to me later, "It just broke my heart. Here was this superstar, this kid who I'd seen battle his way against all kinds of odds to finally make it with this huge deal with the Rangers. How does your life not get better? I mean, you had just done what no one in your family could ever do. Create this wonderful legacy and you just fucked it all away. So I went back upstairs and I walked into the press box."

When the guys asked Pete if he had talked to me, he told them no. And from that day on, whenever the topic of our friendship came up, he shut his mouth and said, "I don't know him anymore."

38

TIGHT JEANS AND LONG BLONDE HAIR

WE WON THE FIRST GAME of the Alberta semifinals, 2–0, and went back to the hotel. It had this little lounge, and we were having a couple of beers when in walked this girl. She was wearing tight jeans and a red satin shirt and she had long blonde hair—the kind that swings around like in a shampoo commercial. Everyone turned and looked. She was just gorgeous. I had seen a hundred thousand beautiful chicks in bars, but this one had a million-watt smile, a waist you could wrap two hands around, and she was with a friend of mine who came up to the game. I wasn't dating anybody at the time. I was sick of strippers, and anyway, who are you going to find at the bar? A bunch of fuckin' bar stars.

Everyone came back to party in my room because I had a big suite at the Red Deer Lodge. The entire bar loaded onto the team bus. I was in the back, carving up some lines, and there was a joint as big as a cigar being passed around.

My room was wall-to-wall people. Jenn and I started a conversation, but we couldn't hear each other, so we headed into the bathroom to talk. It turned out she was from Bredenbury, Saskatchewan—about an hour from Russell. We hit it off and ended up spending two days together. She was a hard worker, a dental assistant, and we discovered that because we were from similar backgrounds, we had the same outlook on life. We kissed and fooled around and got along really well in that department. She got up the next morning to leave for Calgary, and I said, "I am going to be in town this afternoon when the game is over. I'll come pick you up." When she flashed me that smile, I could feel my heart pounding.

We were all so fuckin' loaded after partying for two days and barely getting any sleep that we did not win the second game. We lost 4–2. But we took the next two games easily, 8–3 and 6–2, and advanced to the finals against Innisfail. We swept them three straight, then swept Powell River to qualify for the Allan Cup.

But I had found a girl who could party with me, who was cool and was from around my hometown—and when I was with her I didn't hurt. We both had a lot of baggage. She had a really hard time trusting, and because I'd had a lot of therapy, I could see where she was at. I knew I could help her. She moved in with me right away. Early in our relationship, she was jealous because I got a lot of attention, so when we had fights, she would pack up all her stuff and try to walk out. But I would stand by the door and say, "What are you running from? You don't need to run anymore. I'm not going anywhere. I'm not going to leave you."

We battled hard for the first two weeks. And then we went out for Chinese one night and she said, "I can't be with you anymore." And I said, "Excuse me? I don't try out."

She was so pretty that she wasn't used to hearing that. I said, "I didn't spend every fuckin' day with you for two weeks so you could pull the plug whenever you felt like it." She answered, "Well, what kind of a woman would I be if I were with a man who did not want to be a part of his children's lives? Good people take care of their kids, and I want to be a good person."

I was slowly repairing my relationship with Beaux and Tatym. I would go and see them every couple of weeks, but I didn't want them to know me in partying mode. Tatym was absolutely terrified of me— she wouldn't come near me. Jennifer encouraged me to get some kind of custody with the kids, some kind of official visitation rights. She was right, of course. And I was lonely and I wanted her, so I had to start working harder to pull it together. I convinced her to give us a try. She came with me to the Allan Cup in Lloydminster, Saskatchewan. My parents met us there.

Six teams took part in the Allan Cup: the champions of B.C./Alberta (us), Manitoba/Saskatchewan (Mid West Islanders), Ontario (Thunder Bay Bombers), Quebec (Montmagny Sentinelles), the Maritimes (Can-Am Cobras) and the host team (Lloydminster Border Kings). Each team had their own dressing room. We were there with twenty-four guys, a coaching staff and a training staff—probably thirty of us in all, and we were the highest-profile team by a mile. But instead of giving us a room tucked away underneath the rink, like every other team had, our dressing room was right in the lobby of the arena. So between periods or after games, we had to wade through hundreds of people. It was one of the most insensitive things I have ever seen.

And these were not friendly people. I was walking around with a bull's-eye on my chest. One night, Parsons brought his dad and we were in the stands watching a game. Suddenly I hear, "Crackhead! Crackhead!" I looked back and there was some friggin' redneck in a Levi's Stormrider jacket and a freaking Ski-doo hat laughing his ass off. I stood up and challenged him. (Steve told me later that my eyes were bugging out.) Steve's dad got pissed off, climbed up the stands and asked this twerp if he had a problem. Our whole team started squaring off against thirty fans, so we had to leave the game. We couldn't stick around. The next day as we made our way through the lobby to warm up, there were people all around, poking at us and yelling shit like we were wrestlers or something.

In the round robin, we beat Lloydminster 9–2 and the Can-Am Cobras 7–2, earning a bye into the semifinals. There, we met the Thunder Bay Bombers, who had lost both their games in the round robin, but had shut out Lloydminster 5–0 in the quarter-finals. It looked like it was gonna be a cakewalk.

The way we approached the game was to come out on the ice and stick our middle fingers up at everyone in the building—not literally, of course, but that was our attitude. We made an enemy out of every fan—*and* every official—and usually the intimidation factor worked in our favour. But it was not in the cards in this game. Five times, Thunder Bay had a five-on-three power play. Typically, you get one of those a night. We also ran into a numbers game with our roster. Our number one goalie, Marc-André Leclerc, was really good, but the chief wanted more import skaters instead. So we had to dress an Alberta-carded goalie, Bryce Wandler. He had talent, but he froze up under the pressure. The chief's gamble didn't pay off. By the end of the first period, Thunder Bay was up 4–1, and we lost 7–5, despite outshooting the Bombers 39–26. Thunder Bay went on to win the Allan Cup.

As far as the reffing goes, we got hosed. There are two ways to look at it—we got hosed undeservedly or we got hosed deservedly. I believe the refs had made up their minds that they weren't going to let these tough guys from an Indian reserve win a national championship. And they made sure we spent enough time in the penalty box so that it didn't happen.

When we got back to our dressing room, we saw that someone had ripped our jerseys out of their garment bags and thrown them into a big dogpile. Gino's jersey and my jersey were gone, and the smell of urine was so strong that we had to put them in garbage bags and send them to the cleaners. The dressing room had been locked, so whoever broke in had key access. I felt badly for the chief. He'd made a big financial investment there, with all the meals, the hotels, the flights, the bar tabs and the gear. Winning was the only acceptable outcome. But I guess the hockey gods caught up to us.

LOSING THE ALLAN CUP triggered a major reaction in me, and Crown Royal brought it to the surface. I showered and was leaving the rink when I got a text message from Jenn. She said the refs were brutal, told me to keep my head up, that it was going to be okay. Stuff like that. I had never had a girl do that for me before. She understood what I was going through. I wanted to spend the rest of my life with her. We got back to the hotel, and I asked her to marry me. She said yes without any hesitation and I took that as a very good sign.

We went for dinner with my folks and celebrated. Then Jenn, Steve Parsons and I went out to the bar. She and I were slow-dancing on the floor when suddenly a table of preppy-looking jocks in their Abercrombie and Fitch T-shirts recognized me and started yelling, "You fuckin' loser. You crackhead." The usual.

Jenn freaked out. She broke away from me and went over to their table. "You freaking idiots! What have you ever done with your pathetic little lives?" She was pointing at me and screaming, "He has a Stanley Cup and gold medal that he won for his country. He has won one of everything. How dare you say those things to him? You aren't fit to lick his boots." Steve and I went over and stood behind her and Steve said, "Okay, Jenn, I think we better get going." And as we made our way to the door, Jenn picked up a barstool and just winged it at them. Steve said, "Oh shit," and the three of us started running. The jocks caught up with us in the parking lot and came at us, but instead of jumping us they began apologizing to me, trying to shake my hand, telling me how they had always been fans. Just a big bunch of assholes.

Back at Steve's hotel room, I started drinking Crown Royal. The Allan Cup loss was eating at me. Jenn suggested we play some poker to change the mood. We played a few hands while I got completely obliterated. I called Steve a bully and told him I didn't care how big he was, I wasn't afraid of him. He told me to cool it, but I kept at it, getting more and more aggressive until finally Jenn insisted we go back to our room.

When we were alone I started going off about my childhood, yelling at her, blaming her for stuff Veronica had done and arguing with other people from my past. Later, Jenn told me I was having screaming matches with ghosts.

At the time, Jenn attempted to make sense of what I was saying. She said, "Suck it up, Theoren. Everybody has a story. Everybody has had it hard. You need to get off your high horse and move on. You're 37 years old, for God's sake. Let it go!"

She tried to leave, but I wouldn't let her, so she locked herself in the bathroom, crying and thinking, "Omigod, this guy's insane."

We argued through the night until we had nothing left. About 7 a.m. I fell into bed and Jenn was standing at the door ready to leave when we heard a knock. It was my parents. They had come to take us for breakfast.

I told Jenn not to let them in, but she opened the door and slipped out into the hallway.

As soon as I saw their faces, I started in on them. I told them that they'd never given a shit about me until I made it to the NHL and then suddenly they were involved in my life and coming to my games, but it was too late. "As long as there was something in it for you, you were there. But I needed you. I needed you to pull yourselves together and be there for me when I was a kid," I said. "Let's face it, before I made it, I was just another mouth to feed." Then I moved on to the subject of Graham James. "How could you let that happen to me? How could you turn your own kid over to a pedophile?" I yelled at my mom for abandoning me and spending my entire childhood in her room and being too weak to come see me when I was alone and scared in the hospital when I was 13. I yelled at my dad for being a drunk the whole time I was growing up. All the anger that had been building for years came spewing out, and it was ugly. They sat at the end of my bed, and we were all crying. And then they apologized.

If you had a childhood like I had, it is really important that your parents say they are sorry. It helps you move on with your adult life. It takes away the resentment, because you don't feel like you have to continue with behaviour that lets them know how hurt you were by what they did. You finally have that confirmation—they know what they did to you and they know it was wrong.

Finally, they left and Jenn came back in the room. This time, *she* was the one who said she wasn't leaving. I had avoided dealing with what was going on in my life because my problems were just too overwhelming. Jenn said, "Let's just take this big pile of shit and chip away at it." So we would do one thing and realize, "Oh, that wasn't as bad as I thought it would be." And then we would tackle the next thing. We are still working on that pile.

Other things came up, and Jenn and I were still butting heads. We had a huge fight one night about how I let people take advantage of me. Jenn felt very protective, and she became furious when I would just write a cheque if a friend or family member asked for money. And she just could not handle the amount of booze and drugs I went through. I was a chemist, man. I could control my buzz just as if I was flying a plane. To get a little drunker, I would ease up on the cocaine and add a couple of shots of vodka. When I needed to sober up, I would do a line. But living with an addict is not fun. And Jenn was a recreational user, not in nearly as deep as I was.

At the end of this fight, Jenn went to bed and I was in the bathroom, sitting on the floor with my head in my hands in an incredible amount of hurt. I was dying a slow, painful, lonely death because alcohol doesn't take your life right away. It eats away at your soul and your spirit. I was done playing hockey and I didn't know what the rest of my life was going to look like. I knew I'd had a lot of great women in my life who had all loved me and cared for me, and I could see that this was another relationship I was going to fuck up if I didn't do something about my behaviour. Suddenly, I hit my knees and said, "God, please, please, please take this obsession away," and I sat there crying and praying for hours. I thought about being in cocaine-induced rages in the desert, talking to fuckin' cacti, yelling at God, "Fuck you! I have had enough!" And I could not stop, no matter what I tried to do. I had no will to stop. I needed some outside intervention. I needed God. My life was a disaster.

Finally, I went to bed and woke up the next morning feeling different. Really different. I went back into the bathroom and looked at myself in the big mirror and said, "Holy shit—it's gone!" Jenn was sleeping, and I stood over the bed and said, "I'm done." She rolled over and opened her eyes and said, "Done? With what? With our relationship?"

"No," I said. "I'm done drinking." It was my aha! moment. That was September 18, 2005, and since then I have not had any desire whatsoever to have a drink or use drugs or be with another woman.

I have tattoos of the birthdates of the kids—Tatym, Beaux, Josh and our new baby, Skylah. I have a chief on my left arm, my guardian angel. On my neck I have my astrological sign, Cancer, but each day I make it a point to meditate for a moment while looking at the Chinese symbol for "loyalty" that I have tatted on the inside of the top of my left forearm. I told Jenn I am never going to cheat again. I am going to be loyal, and I mean it.

39

BELFAST

I MET Jim Yaworski through my brother Travis. They coached a Junior B team together. Jim called me about investing in a computer company, which I did. Then he invited me to play in a golf tournament and asked, "Would you be interested in coming to Belfast and playing for the Belfast Giants?" He explained that hockey was fairly new in Northern Ireland. The team had been formed in 2000 and was now part of the Elite Ice Hockey League. I asked how much it would pay, and he said, "Well, we have a salary cap, so you won't make much—maybe just enough to cover your expenses—but we'll get you a car and an apartment."

Right before we teed off, I called Jenn at the dental office and said, "Hey, do you want to spend the winter in Belfast this year?" And she answered, "Where the hell is that?" In Ireland, I told her. "Yeah, let's go," she said. "Let's do it."

We moved to Belfast on October 13, 2005, and it was awesome. I was dry, and not long after, Jenn was dry too. At first, she wanted to keep drinking—she liked a glass of wine before dinner—but I was up front about wanting to be with someone who was sober too, and she understood.

When I went over there, I weighed 225 pounds—after I quit drinking, I just ate and ate and ate. But after playing for a while I dropped down to 190. I was on the ice and playing in my first game just hours after landing. I scored three goals and five assists and got into a fight with a guy named Freddie Oduya, who played for Edinburgh. He'd played with the Atlanta Thrashers' farm team, the Orlando Solar Bears, and was traded to the Calgary Flames in 1999 for Eric Landry, but he never saw ice in The Show, so I think he had something to prove. He stood six foot three and weighed 218, and his nickname was "Freddy Knuckles." Didn't matter—I knew if I didn't step up I would be killed. He kept going after me, kept taking me into the boards, and finally after a spear I took a swing, then dropped my gloves and went at it. My helmet flew off and I was just whaling away. I managed to knock him on his ass, and then the refs came in. In Belfast, you fought your own battles. It was a different mentality. Nobody protected the talent—not even the refs. You were on your own.

My job was to entertain the crowd, and I think I can say I did my part. They would yell at me, I would beak back, and they loved it. Sometimes I would throw the game puck to my biggest critic—my way of saying thanks for the show, buddy. The fans in Coventry were the worst. During one game in January, we had to call security to our bench a few times. They were calling me all kinds of names and refer-ring to my drug use. The PA announcer was egging them on. I finally just said, "Fuck it" and left the game. There is a real mob mentality among sports fans there. Hockey in Belfast isn't a joke—it's definitely bush, but it turned out that a lot of guys thought they could make a name for themselves by going after me. So it was like I had a bull's-eye on my chest sometimes.

We won the regular-season championship but lost in the playoffs because our goalie fell apart. A recurring theme. I was named the British Ice Hockey Writers Association's Elite League Player of the Year, which was a big honour.

Belfast was the best thing that could have happened to Jenn and me. We had an eighteen-month engagement to see if we could actually live together. We were able to travel and see a whole bunch of really cool stuff, like castles and Giant's Causeway, a strange rock formation caused by a volcano. The legend says it was built by a giant, Finn McCool, so he could walk to Scotland to fight his enemy. We went up there nine times. It was just a great place to go and hike and walk around, just absolutely beautiful. The area around it is the greenest place you can imagine.

And we had lots of visitors—my parents and hers, as well as friends, and Trav and his girlfriend, Amanda. We got to see the Braveheart monument, which is kind of like Scotland's Statue of Liberty. It was just phenomenal. And we went to Edinburgh and St. Andrews golf course and had our pictures taken on the bridge.

It was cool to see another part of the world because, for the first six to eight months of our relationship, we were locked up in a house partying. The idea that we could function so much better without drugs or alcohol was eye-opening. We never left each other's side. I explained to the team that I was sober and that if Jenn didn't come on the road trips with me, I wasn't going either. Occasionally, Jenn still wanted a glass of wine, but she stuck it out. Which was no easy task when we were living in the middle of a pub culture.

We had our moments—sometimes it was touch and go. But I finally found somebody who does not care whether I am rich or poor, somebody who embraces my successes and my failures and who loves me unconditionally.

Not all of the games while I played for the Giants went smoothly. I lost my temper if the crowd got too abusive, and I still had a problem with refs. Hey, I quit drinking, I didn't have a personality transplant! The Giants asked me to come back because I was putting the game on the map over there, but I had done what I'd come to Ireland to do.

40

JENN AND THE BUTTERFLIES

WE CAME HOME and had an incredible wedding in August 2006. It was fantastic. Three hundred and thirty people came to Russell, Manitoba. We were married overlooking a lake on the prairies. Water is always kind of calming for everyone, and it was just a beautiful day. Hot with a nice little prairie wind. Josh, Beaux and Tatym were there.

About forty-five minutes before the wedding, a whole cloud of colourful butterflies showed up. They circled through the crowd and swirled around our heads. During the ceremony, there was one black butterfly with white stripes on its wings that sat on the pole above us. Partway through, it fluttered over to my dad and landed on his leg. Then, as soon as Jenn and I said, "I do," it rode upward on the breeze and flew away.

EPILOGUE

RECENTLY, I was on a plane, rereading this whole book, and I said to Kirstie, my writing partner, "Fuck, was I selfish."

Today, I am in a whole new place. When I was done hockey, I was afraid. What was I gonna do for the rest of my life? I wasn't a hockey player anymore, so what was my identity? I obviously didn't leave the game on my terms. I was angry with the NHL and its substance abuse program. Dr. Lewis and Dr. Shaw sent me a stage-four letter in July 2006. It said, "Dear Mr. Fleury, Further to the recent review of you [sic] involvement with the Substance Abuse and Behavioral Health (SABH) program (July 8 2006 in Vancouver, BC), you are now placed in STAGE FOUR of the NHLPA/NHL Substance Abuse and Behavioral Health (SABH) program. This suspension begins July 8, 2006."

Then they laid out an eleven-point plan that included the usual promises—I will remain abstinent from all drugs and alcohol . . . I will not attend titty clubs or gamble and I will get regular pee tests . . . and if I don't do all this, I understand that I could be permanently suspended. At that time I was still fighting the demands of the NHL Substance Abuse Program. I thought they had too much control over me. They had the right to put all kinds of restrictions on my freedom so that I would get sober. I think I bucked it so hard because, bottom line, I had not taken responsibility. You know, I never worried about consequences for the things I did, and in the end that is the biggest thing I have learned. If you throw a lit match into a dry pile of leaves, it will catch fire.

I have been sober more than three years now. I didn't just quit drinking out of sheer willpower. All those treatment centres, all those wonderful alcoholics I talked to along the way, helped me get to this point. I get up every morning and pray. I say the Lord's Prayer and I say the Third Step Prayer from the Big Book of AA.

As far as Graham James goes, I don't think about him anymore. If I did, it would just put me back into victim mode and obviously that did not work for me. While writing this book, I had to talk about my experiences, but they didn't have the same bite—I don't get the same fight-or-flight response when these memories are triggered, and today I realize that what happened was not my fault. I think that is the most important thing. So don't feel sorry for me—I am not asking for sympathy. I am telling my story because it is important. As you read this book, you will have seen me go from not having a fuckin' clue of how to deal with anything to respecting myself. I am confident again, and that has opened a lot of doors in my personal and professional life.

Today, things are great. Life is way better, less pressure, less hassle. I'm part of the Calgary community as a businessman now—not as a hero, not as somebody they can ridicule and point fingers at. It's kind of neat to be on that end of it. I will do whatever it takes to be successful. And it helps that Jenn is there and keeps me grounded and focused, because sometimes I can get a little bit ahead of myself and get too many things on the go. She puts it all into perspective for me. On September 7, 2008, our baby girl, Skylah Mary Anne Fleury, was born. She is tiny and feisty, and because I realize what I gave up with Josh, Beaux and Tatym, I am treasuring this time with her.

I took another run at the Allan Cup in the spring of 2009 with the Steinbach North Stars, but we lost in the semis. I had seven points in four games and it was fun to compete again. I am not sure what is next for me in hockey, but I do know I love the game again.

Life is simple when you grow up on the prairies. People are honest and sincere and great hockey fans. You go to New York and your head is just spinning all the time. I went there and I lost who I was. I had money and money is power. Because I was abused I needed that power. I would walk into a strip club with five grand in my pocket and own the room. I really got off on that. Today I am back to being the guy I was when I played for the Russell Rams. I have found the values I learned growing up there; hardworking, simple, honest and accountable people taught me those values. And to put a guy who is already overstimulated right in the middle of New York City, it's just like, whoa! But you know what? I don't regret anything. I think that everything happens for a reason. I wouldn't change anything that happened to me, because I get into trouble when I start thinking about the what-ifs—poor me, poor me, pour me another drink. It is important to me to share my experiences in order to create strength and hope for others. No matter how far down you go, it is never too late to come back. I'm exactly where I'm supposed to be today, and that's all that matters. I've overcome a lot of things in my life because of that higher-power stuff that I never really understood until I was sober. But there was something out there looking out for me.

As far as my past relationships with women go, Stephanie's mother, who had also been a stripper, called me a while back. Steph got deep into the life and lost custody of Aleca. I felt sad hearing that. Veronica and I have spent more years in court than we spent married, but she and Jenn and the kids and I are in counselling, so at least we're talking. I am working hard at being a good dad. My relationships with my kids—that stuff is a process. It will take time for them to trust me again. I think what I want them to see is how hard I have worked for them so that when it comes time for them to go into the real world, they will have a strong work ethic, which is what it takes to be successful.

I decided it was time to mend fences with others too, so I am back on good terms with the Calgary Flames. I attend their alumni events, which raise money for good causes like the homeless. This past winter I volunteered my time to help with women's hockey. I worked with the Union College women's team in Schenectady, New York, and joined a pre-tournament practice to inspire a women's Midget

AAA team, the Calgary Flyers. I also lent my support to the Esso Cup, the first-ever national championship for women's midget hockey.

I play recreational hockey with Catriona Le May Doan's husband, Bart. Bart was assistant coach of the Olympic Oval X-Treme, so we would go out and give the girls some competition three to four times a year. They had some good, skilled players, one-third of the Olympic team, and it was always a good time.

We continue to run the Theoren Fleury M&M Meats Crohn's and Colitis Golf Tournament. It has been going for eighteen years and has raised more than a million dollars.

These days, I volunteer a lot of time at the Calgary Dream Centre. It is a place that helps people who have lost their way get back on track with skills training and sobriety. I tell these guys my story and it seems to help them. I know it helps me stay sober, one day at a time.

Physically, I am stronger than ever. I work out constantly and have a knowledgeable trainer named Mike Porter who is taking me to new heights. I benched 225 pounds after just three months of training—I had not lifted for six years. I take Pilates with Steph Davis, who has helped me immeasurably. Being in this kind of shape is good for my head as well as my body.

What happened to me psychologically happens to a lot of victims of sexual abuse—feeling like "I can't get rid of these memories, so I deserve to have bad things happen to me. In fact, I hate myself so much that I am going to live a life that ensures that bad things happen to me." Thankfully, people like Jonna Mogab in Chicago and Dr. Reesal helped unlink me from the event. They taught me that if you want your life back, you cannot hand it over to the memory and let the perpetrator steal your future.

So if you are a kid who is in the situation I was in, and somebody older is using you for sex, call for help. You can call the police or you can search for kids' help lines on the Internet. Seriously, you are not alone. Pick up the phone.

INDEX

Otto, Joel, 64
  during 1989 playoffs, 69, 72, 74, 81,
    84–85
  as a fighter, 77, 78
  first impression of Theoren, 49
  with Team USA, 137, 138
  as victim of pranks, 61
Ozolinsh, Sandis, 197

Pagé, Pierre, 105–6, 107
Parsons, Steve, 284–86, 290, 293–94,
    301–2
Patrick, James, 163
Patterson, Colin, 61, 64, 69, 72, 78, 86
Peca, Mike, 237
Pelawa, George, 45
Peltz, Ede, 19, 216
Peltz, Len, 19, 125
Peplinski, Jim, 61, 65, 70, 72, 73, 77, 97
Petit, Michel, 110
Petterson, Colin, 58
Petz, Jim, 9
Petz, Ted, 10, 15
Philadelphia Flyers, 46, 49
Phoenix Coyotes, 262, 265
Piestany, Slovakia, 37–44
Pilon, Rich, 205
Popovic, Peter, 199
Poulin, Patrick, 67
practical jokes, 60–62
prednisone, 115
Priestley, Jason, 200, 239
Probert, Bob, 100–101
Promises Westside Residential Treatment
    Center, 224–25
Pronger, Chris, 236
Pryakhin, Sergei, 64
psychologists, 70, 127, 148, 215–16, 270
Pulford, Bob, 289
"Punch-up in Piestany," 41–44
Pure Platinum strip club, 273–74
Purinton, Dale, 205

Quebec Nordiques, 66
Quinlan, Tom, 45
Quintal, Stéphane, 199, 205

racism, against Natives, 294–95, 300
Rafalski, Brian, 245
Ramage, Rob, 61, 75, 78, 96
Ramsay, Jim, 205
Ranheim, Paul, 97
Reesal, Robin, 127
Reese, Jeff, 110
referees, 40, 42, 78, 81, 82–83, 102, 162,
    222, 244, 300
Regehr, Robyn, 184
Regina Pats, fans' resentment of Theoren,
    45–46
Reierson, Dave, 54
Reinhart, Paul, 67–68
"rez hockey," 284–300
Richer, Stéphane, 79
Richter, Mike, 135, 137–39, 206, 234
Risebrough, Doug, 68, 203
  competitiveness, 65
  as Flames' coach, 97, 102, 106
  as Flames' general manager, 91
  trades Gilmour to Toronto, 108–11
Rittinger, John, 129
Roberts, Gary, 67, 69, 72, 75, 78, 141
Robinson, Larry, 80–81, 83
Roenick, Jeremy, 78, 163
Rønning, Hans, 41, 42
Roy, Patrick,
  during 1989 playoffs, 79, 80, 81,
    84–85, 86
  during 1999 playoffs, 196
  fight during 1997 playoffs, 194
  golfs with Theoren, 189–90
  salary, 197
  as team leader, 195
  Theoren's success playing against,
    210–11
Russell Rams, 9–10, 14, 19–21